C4D 9.5: Real-World 3D Animation Production

LARRY MITCHELL

CHARLES RIVER MEDIA

CHARLES RIVER MEDIA, INC.

Hingham, Massachusetts

Cover Design: Tyler Creative

CHARLES RIVER MEDIA, INC.
10 Downer Avenue
Hingham, Massachusetts 02043
781-740-0400
781-740-8816 (FAX)
info@charlesriver.com
www.charlesriver.com

This book is printed on acid-free paper.

Larry Mitchell. *C4D 9.5: Real-World 3D Animation Production*
ISBN: 1-58450-437-4

Library of Congress Cataloging-in-Publication Data

Mitchell, Larry, 1964-
  C4d 9.5:Real-World 3D animation production / Larry Mitchell.
      p. cm.
  Includes index.
  ISBN 1-58450-437-4 (pbk. with cd : alk. paper)
  1. Computer graphics. 2. Cinema 4D XL. 3. Three-dimensional display
systems. 4. Computer animation. I. Title.

T385.M577 2005
006.6'96—dc22
                        2005032718

ed in the United States of America
5 4 3 2 First Edition

ES RIVER MEDIA titles are available for site license or bulk purchase by institutions, user
orporations, etc. For additional information, please contact the Special Sales
nt at 781-740-0400.

r replacement of a defective DVD-ROM must be accompanied by the original disc, your
ess, telephone number, date of purchase, and purchase price. Please state
the problem, and send the information to CHARLES RIVER MEDIA, INC.,
enue, Hingham, Massachusetts 02043. CRM's sole obligation to the purchaser
disc, based on defective materials or faulty workmanship, but not on the
ctionality of the product.

C4D 9.5: Real-World 3D Animation Production

CD

WITHDRAWN

*This book is dedicated to providing the fuel of inspiration
for the creative soul, starting with my son, Larry Mitchell Jr.*

CONTENTS

INTRODUCTION AND ACKNOWLEDGMENTS

WHY I WROTE THIS BOOK

Besides my dear friend, Alan Lynch, telling me, "Larry, go write a book," I wrote this book and produced the tutorial videos for the purpose of empowering creative minds to visualize their thoughts for the rest of the world to see. What I mean by this is, recognizing that computer graphics is inherently complicated (ones and zeros making pixels), I wanted to provide a path to take the reader from curiosity to competence by following me as my apprentice.

So often I've heard the complaint that when someone picks up a 3D animation book to find the answer to a visualization problem, the answer is so long and complicated that they wonder if they can do it. They often start with hope and end with doubt.

This book will show simplified methods of accomplishing real-world 3D animation production goals. This means that the approaches shown here are a subset of many other approaches to solve the same production challenge. The difference in this book is that, rather than focusing on explaining the tools comprehensively, we will remain focused on the project goal.

NO SILVER BULLET

I remember the first time I recorded a 3D animation to tape frame-by-frame (1992). It was at a FOX Television station, and I was recording to a D2 tape machine for an Orlando ACM SIGGRAPH presentation later that evening. There was no recording to DV on my planet yet.

The process was painful, as one person handled pre-roll of the D2 deck, one handled loading the next frame, one handled output from a Newtek Video Toaster, and one person kept us all in check in case we missed a frame. After 4 hours recording all 300 frames of this animation through this makeshift assembly line process, we felt like we'd created fire. And all this came after integrating about 17 software applications to create the 3D rendered images to be recorded.

Fast-forward to today, and recording animation to tape has become almost as transparently effortless as printing a document. Still, there is no silver bullet 3D application. No one software program does it all. This is actually a good thing because highly focused software developers, who can apply much better focus to one aspect of 3D software, produce solutions for us that help bring our incredible visions to light and to life.

This does, however, make for an interesting situation when teaching how to produce 3D animation for real-world production. When clients walk in the door, they won't ask you to please produce an animation done entirely in that one great 3D program you're working in. They're more likely to say, "Give me something better than my competition," and they really won't care how you do it.

In writing this book, I hope to inspire you to value the goal (the visual image output) more than the process.

So, in this Cinema 4D® book, we will look at a software-integrated approach to 3D animation production in which Cinema 4D is the center of our focus and is used fluidly in concert with several other applications. This Cinema 4D–centric approach is intended to give you a good sense of how real-world 3D animation production challenges can be met, not only with a great tool, but with a great tool box.

NOT EXHAUSTIVE C4D

This is not an exhaustive look at C4D, but rather a real-world, hands-on approach to 3D animation production. Rather than being a Cinema 4D reference with intimate explanations of each menu function, this book takes the apprentice approach, founded on the principle that we learn best by doing.

I would strongly recommend that this book be part of your 3D animation library so that in a production crisis, through your ability to solve by cross-referencing between such books, a solution can be found.

CINEMA 4D 9.5

This book includes tutorials for both Cinema 4D 9.1 and 9.5. Because Cinema 4D 9.5 is basically enhancements, refinements, and a few of additions to the cool toolset found in Cinema 4D 9.1, there generally isn't any learning curve to go from Cinema 4D 9.1 to 9.5. Enhancements like the Browser being changed to a menu item (Content Browser: a fully developed and highly intuitive new area of Cinema 4D), the new full-blown atmospheric generator Sky plugin, enhanced object baking, and ambient occlusion are just some of the Cinema 4D 9.5–only features that you'll explore.

SOFTWARE COVERED IN THIS BOOK

Besides Cinema 4D, several other 3D software applications, content and plugins are covered. The extent to which they are covered is limited to what you need to know to complete the tutorial. Each of these other software applications could consume chapters or books to really explain their full functional operation.

Demo versions of most software applications covered in this book are also available from the DVD-ROM accompanying this book. Demo versions are of course limited in functionality. For those few applications without a demo version, the written and video tutorials are intended to educate you on the integrated production process, so that when you encounter such a 3D animation production challenge, you will already know what tools and what work flow are required to solve it immediately.

HARDWARE USED

ON THE DVD

I thought it would be of comparative value for you to know what kind of hardware was used to produce the tutorials in this book and DVD. Several times while rendering a test area of a project, you will hear and see the render times involved so that you can know approximately what is to be expected based on your system configuration and capabilities.

Here's the hardware used to produce the tutorials;

- CPU: 3.4 Ghz Pentium® 4 CPU
- Memory: 2 GB RAM
- OS: Windows® XP SP2
- Monitors: Dual 19-inch monitors
- Video Card: NVidia® Quadro® FX 3000 (256 MB)

HARDWARE RECOMMENDED

Though you can complete the tutorials in this book and DVD-ROM with less, here are the hardware recommendations based on each software application:

PUBLISHER	SOFTWARE	OS	RAM	CPU
MAXON	Cinema 4D 9.1/9.5	Mac OS X® 10.3/ Windows XP	1024 MB	2 GHz
efrontier	Poser® 6	Mac OS X 10.2/ Windows XP	512 MB	700 MHz
UZR	iModeller 3D 2.6	Mac OS X 10.2/ Windows XP	512 MB	1.5 GHz
Adobe®	Photoshop® CS2	Mac OS X 10.2.8– 10.3.8 / Windows XP	1024 MB	1.5 GHz
Adobe	After Effects® 6.5 Pro	Mac OS X 10.3.2/ Windows XP	512 MB	1.5 GHz
Right Hemisphere	Deep Creator™ 2.1	Windows XP	512 MB	2 GHz

In addition, I would recommend a video card such as the NVidia Quadro FX 3000 with 256 MB. Several of the software applications make extensive use of Open GL. In a work session with a client, the performance difference of using such a video card can make the difference between explaining to them that the motion playback really will be smooth, and simply showing them smooth motion.

Also, if possible, try to work with two monitors. Cinema 4D works amazingly well on two monitors and Version 9.5 has enhanced support for this. Let's roll!

ACKNOWLEDGEMENTS

First I'd like to thank my wife Teri for supporting me in this effort, while hardly seeing me, even though I worked entirely from home (disappearing into my Bat Cave) on this book.

I'd like to thank Alan Lynch for having the "but of course you should write a book" faith in me that I should do this.

To embark into the world of authoring my first book, and being blessed to have a publisher like Jenifer Niles, yeah, I'm the lucky one.

To my MAXON (Paul Babb and Diana Lee) and my software and hardware contributors (NVidia, Adobe, Right Hemisphere, UZR, 2d3, Cineform, Mocapdata, Marlin Studios, e-frontier, Archvision, Reiss Studio, Hemera Images, Serious Magic, Zygote, Code Gardeners, Buffalo Tech), you guys rock.

And I'd like to say thank you to my immediate support staff (Ami Ahlstedt, Kevin Gouvia and Julian Mitchell), thanks for catching my fumbles.

1

CINEMA 4D 9 OVERVIEW

In This Chapter

- Overview
- The Interface
- Multidocument Operations
- Project Settings
- Preferences

CINEMA 4D 9 INTERFACE MAP

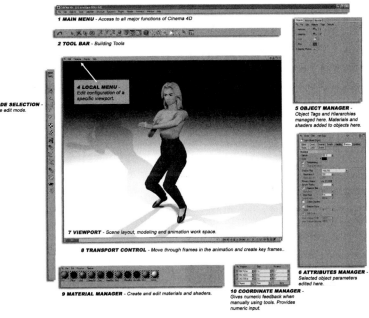

1 MAIN MENU - Access to all major functions of Cinema 4D

2 TOOL BAR - Building Tools

4 LOCAL MENU - Edit configuration of a specific viewport.

3 MODE SELECTION - Set the edit mode.

5 OBJECT MANAGER - Object Tags and Hierarchies managed here. Materials and shaders added to objects here.

7 VIEWPORT - Scene layout, modeling and animation work space.

8 TRANSPORT CONTROL - Move through frames in the animation and create key frames..

6 ATTRIBUTES MANAGER - Selected object parameters edited here.

9 MATERIAL MANAGER - Create and edit materials and shaders.

10 COORDINATE MANAGER - Gives numeric feedback when manually using tools. Provides numeric input.

11 STATUS BAR - Displays render time, render progress and tool tips.

1

This chapter is different from the other chapters in the book, as it is meant to provide a basis for performing the steps in future chapters and act as a reference for processes and functions used in the later tutorial-based chapters.

As with many productivity software applications, there are many intricacies and nuances within Cinema 4D. Neither this chapter nor this book will attempt to explore them all. This chapter will instead focus on providing the foundation for effectively performing and learning all the production projects presented in later tutorial chapters.

OVERVIEW

Cinema 4D provides an integrated environment for creating incredible worlds and everything that lives in them by modeling objects, applying texturing to them, positioning them and lighting them in a scene, then animating to life and rendering them for use in print, Web, video, film, physical product prototyping and video games. In short, Cinema 4D is the digital magician's workshop.

Because of Cinema 4D's consistent and seamless interface, a logical work flow, creativity, experimentation, and exploration are well supported with application features such as a user-configurable interface, a drag-and-drop object manager with hierarchical structure, visual selection hinting of object elements while modeling, a node-based visual expression editor, and a user-configurable number of undo buffers.

THE INTERFACE

Navigating Cinema 4D is made simple by the visual and clutter-free, icon-driven, user-configurable interface.

For those unfamiliar with Cinema 4D, taking the time to familiarize yourself with the following areas of the interface will allow you to focus on the core material of the tutorial chapters without spending much time searching through Cinema 4D (see Figure 1.1).

Main Menu

The main menu provides the standard software interface access by (starting from the left) grouping file and then edit functions as is customary in today's productivity software, then going on with menus specific to Cinema 4D.

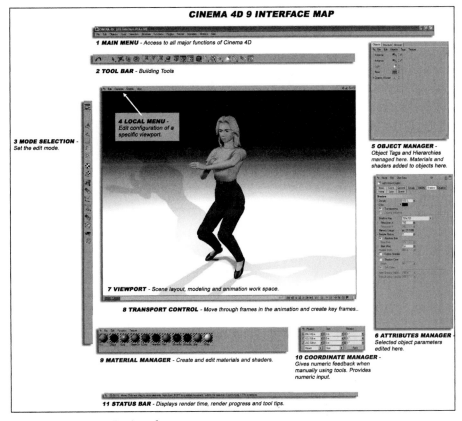

FIGURE 1.1   Cinema 4D 9 interface map.

Here's a brief rundown of the primary functions in the main menu:

File: Gets data into and out of Cinema 4D.

Edit: Provides standard productivity edit functions (cut, copy, paste) as well as project and program settings.

Objects: Objects can be added to the scene from here.

Tools: Menu access to functions from both the tool bar and the mode selection can be made here.

Selection: Selection of modeling and scene elements can be controlled here.

Structure: Modeling functions at the detail level can be selected here. Items from the structure menu can also be accessed by right-clicking (Windows®) or command-clicking (Macintosh®) in the viewport.

Functions: Modeling functions that convert parametric objects to polygon objects as well as functions that affect multiple selected objects are here.

Plug-ins: These are additional program modules that can add specific functionality to Cinema 4D.

Render: Settings related to image and animation are primarily here.

Animation: Settings relating to what to animate and how to playback are here.

Window: Layout selection and manager windows are accessed here.

Help: This is used to enter serial numbers or to access help documents.

Tool Bar

Undo/redo: (Figure 1.2) Provides icon access to multiple levels of undo and redo. By going to the edit menu and selecting Preferences, then selecting Document, the number of undo buffers can be set using Undo Depth.

Selection tool types: (Figure 1.3) Live Selection allows the selection of object elements (points, polygons, edges, objects) by dragging the mouse with the left button held down. Rectangle Selection allows selection by dragging a rectangle with the left mouse button held down. Freehand Selection allows selection by drawing a boundary around the elements to be selected. Polygon Selection allows selection by clicking a polygonal boundary around the elements to be selected.

FIGURE 1.2   Undo/redo icon.   **FIGURE 1.3**   Live Selection tool icon.

Once a selection is made and the left mouse button is released, you can add to the selection by holding the shift key and selecting additional elements.

Once a selection is made and the left mouse button is released, you can remove elements from the selection by holding the control key (Windows)/command key (Mac) and selecting the elements to be removed from the current selection.

Additional selection types can be found in the selection menu. Loop Selection and Ring Selection can be used to easily and intuitively select a series of polygons, points, or edges in organic modeling (such as modeling a human head). Without these selection methods, such modeling tasks would be daunting.

Object translation (move, scale, rotate):   (Figure 1.4) Selecting the translation icon of move, scale, or rotate activates that tool until another tool is selected. The object or object element can then be freely transformed. While a translation tool is selected, holding the shift key down will temporarily constrain translation to one axis, thereby increasing the ease of user manipulation control.

 Hitting the spacebar on the keyboard toggles between the selection tool and the last selected translation tool. This makes fine tuning during modeling much easier.

Axis locks: (Figure 1.5) Restrict object translation in the selected axis.

FIGURE 1.4   Move, scale, rotate.

FIGURE 1.5   Axis locks.

Consider an animation sequence in which you want to have text fly across the screen from right to left with a brief pause in the center of the screen. Once the text objects are placed at the appropriate Y position (height), the only movement to be done will be in the X axis (traveling right to left). By locking the Y (traveling top to bottom) and Z (traveling front to back) axes, you can only move the text in the X axis, thereby preventing any error in placement of the text objects in the Y axis. This can dramatically speed up work flow for certain project setups.

 It is possible to achieve this same result with various other methods. Choose the appropriate method depending on the project details.

The Object/World Coordinate System (Figure 1.6) translates the selected object by either its axis or the world axis. In an animation sequence where a straw (rotated 15 degrees in both the pitch and bank axis) must be moved into a glass of soda, locking the X and Z axis allows the straw to be moved up and down. Using the World Coordinate System allows the straw to be moved straight up and down parallel with the glass, but using the Object Coordinate System allows the straw to be moved as though it is being inserted at a 15 degree angle in the pitch and bank for a more realistic animation.

The Render icons (shown in Figure 1.7) are: preview render, final render, and render settings. These are used to preview and produce the final output images.

The icons shown in Figure 1.8 contain the tools that are the basis for objects added to the project.

FIGURE 1.6   Object Coordinate System.

FIGURE 1.7   Render icons.

FIGURE 1.8   Primitive, curves, NURBS, modeling, scene, and deformation icons.

The Selection Filter for Editor Display (shown in Figure 1.9; first icon) lets you choose which object types are selectable in the viewport. This is particularly handy if, for example, you have a dense city scene and do not want to accidentally select the lights. The Display Filter (shown in Figure 1.9; second icon) similarly lets you choose which objects are visible in the editor. This is handy, for example, in a dense city scene when you wish to view only the lights to more easily arrange them.

Mode Selection

The Layout Selector (shown in Figure 1.10) is used to instantly configure Cinema 4D for work in specific aspects of 3D design such as modeling, 3D painting, and character animation.

FIGURE 1.9   Selection Filter for Editor Display and Display Filter icons.

FIGURE 1.10   Mode selection icon.

The Make Editable tool (shown in Figure 1.11) is used to convert objects to polygon objects. In order to use the polygon, edge, or point tools, parametric primitives must first be converted into polygon objects by selecting the object and then selecting the Make Editable icon or by using the keyboard shortcut "c." Once converted, all polygon editing tools can be used to manipulate the object.

The Use Model tool (shown in Figure 1.12) is used to transform objects without transforming their axis. This tool is used during the modeling process. When you are scaling an object while the Use Model tool is selected, the object's visible shape and size are changed but the object's axes'

FIGURE 1.11   Make Editable icon.

FIGURE 1.12   Use Model icon.

scale is not changed. This subtle detail can dramatically affect object behavior in dynamic simulations.

The Use Object Axis tool (shown in Figure 1.13) is used to transform an object's axis. In Cinema 4D, move, scale, and rotate are applied to an object's axis. Using the Use Object Axis tool allows the object's axis to be manipulated. After modeling an organic shape, you may find that your object doesn't rotate around its visible center. With the Use Object Axis tool selected and using the Move tool, you can place the object's axis in the object's visible center to allow more natural rotation.

The Use Point tool (shown in Figure 1.14) is used to edit object points. This tool allows for editing objects at the lowest level of detail. For example, when modeling a spoon, this mode allows for detailed manipulation to create all shaping and contours.

FIGURE 1.13   Use Object Axis icon.

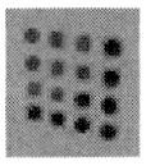

FIGURE 1.14   Use Point icon.

The Use Edge tool (shown in Figure 1.15) is used to edit object edges. With a five-sided box with an open top, this tool allows selection of an edge of the open top and then extrusion of this edge to create a top lid that could then be animated to show the box opening and closing.

The Use Polygon tool (shown in Figure 1.16) is used to edit object polygons. This tool allows the manipulation of the surfaces of an object to not only change their shape, but to add or subtract from the object geometry to create objects significantly different from the starting primitive object. Imagine starting with a cube object and manipulating the polygons into a spaceship, for example.

FIGURE 1.15   Use Edge icon.

FIGURE 1.16   Use Polygon icon.

The Use Texture tool (shown in Figure 1.17) is used to transform object textures. While Cinema 4D provides excellent automatic placement of textures on objects, this tool allows for a visible and interactive process for fine-tuning the placement of textures on objects.

The Use Texture Axis tool (shown in Figure 1.18) is used to transform object texture axis. In some cases, this tool is used to change the orientation of textures on objects.

FIGURE 1.17   Use Texture icon.   **FIGURE 1.18**   Use Texture Axis icon.

The Use Object tool (shown in Figure 1.19) is used to transform an object during animation. Objects in animation are translated in this object mode.

The Use Animation tool (shown in Figure 1.20) is used to transform and edit an object's key-framed motion path. If you animate a logo moving around the screen over time, using this tool allows you to visibly edit the motion path of the logo by selecting the points along the logo's motion path and using the move, scale, or rotate tool.

FIGURE 1.19   Use Object icon.   **FIGURE 1.20**   Use Animation icon.

The Use Inverse Kinematics tool (shown in Figure 1.21) is used to move hierarchical objects interactively. This tool is particularly helpful in posing characters (i.e., sitting, standing, fighting, etc.) for character animation.

The Default, Auto Switch, and Tweak modes (shown in Figure 1.22) are used to change the behavior of basic editing tools such as Move during the modeling process. In the Default mode, object editing is done in the selected mode (polygon, edge, or points). In the Auto Switch mode, while selecting the elements of an object, points, edges, and polygons are highlighted as you move the cursor over them. Selecting an element (point, edge, or polygon) results in switching to that editing mode. Tweak mode allows editing in point, edge, and polygon mode simultaneously. It's like playing with clay.

FIGURE 1.21   Use Inverse Kinematics icon.   **FIGURE 1.22**   Default, Auto Switch, and Tweak icons.

The following tools are useful when testing aspects of a complex scene:

- Turn On/Off Animation (shown in Figure 1.23) is used to test behavior of a scene without its timeline-based animation. As expressions operate independently of the timeline, expression-based animation will be unaffected by this function.
- Turn On/Off Deformers (shown in Figure 1.24) is used to view all objects in their original undeformed state. For example, this would turn off all twists, bends, tapers, and explosions in a scene.

FIGURE 1.23 Turn Off Animation icon.

FIGURE 1.24 Turn Off Deformers icon.

- Turn On/Off Expressions (shown in Figure 1.25) is used to test behavior of a scene without its expression-based animation. If, for example, you have a logo animated by key frames to move across the screen, for which expressions are used to have spot lights stay targeted on the logo, this icon can be used to test just the movement of the logo without the expression-controlled spotlights.
- Turn On/Off Generators (shown in Figure 1.26) is used to disable all (particle) generators in a scene. If you've animated smoke rising from a cup of coffee using particles, this icon turns off the smoke.

FIGURE 1.25 Turn Off Expressions icon.

FIGURE 1.26 Turn Off Generators icon.

The local menu in each viewport is used to configure that particular viewport's settings. Settings that control how objects in the viewport are seen while editing, which elements of the HUD (heads up display) are seen in the viewport, filtering to select what kind of objects can be seen in the viewport, selection of the viewport projection type, and loading and manipulating reference images for the viewport can be done in each viewport Local menu.

The Object Manager is used to provide hierarchical object management (parent–child relationships) as well as associating various tags and tag types with objects. (More on tags later in the modeling and animation chapters.)

The two gray dots to the right of each object in the Object Manager are the Visibility Switches. The top switch controls the visibility of the object in the editor, and the bottom switch controls the visibility in the renderer.

Selecting the visibility switches changes the state from gray to red to green. Both switches have the three visibility modes shown in Table 1.1.

TABLE 1.1   Visibility Modes

Gray (default)	Visible
Red	Not visible
Green	Always visible

If a sphere is grouped to be a child of a cube object, and the cube object's Editor Display Switch is red, then the sphere will not be seen in the editor. However, if the sphere's Editor Display Switch is green, then the sphere will be seen even though its parent's Editor Display Switch is set to red.

Directly below the Object Manager is the Attributes Manager, where the selected object's parameters can be adjusted and key framed to be animated. Property groups for the selected object are accessed from tabs within the Attributes Manager. By pressing the shift key and selecting additional tabs, several tabs can be opened together. For example, if we were to add a light to a living room scene, the light's icon would be added to the Object Manager and its settings could be adjusted in the Attributes Manager.

Depending on the object (type) added, various tabs appear in the Attributes Manager. A cube and a light have different tabs, as a cube's settings relate to its dimensions and segments, whereas a light's settings relate to its illumination characteristics. It's also possible to set each object's wire frame color in the Attributes Manager to visually differentiate between many objects in a complex scene.

The viewport is where all visual feedback is seen and where manual object transformation and editing are done. The viewport is where you would, for example, actually see and visually edit all objects in your living room scene.

In the Material Manager, materials (textures) and shaders are created and edited. As we will see in later chapters, materials can act as the paint on the surface of our objects (as in a material defining a pattern on a wall) or define the substance from which an object appears to be made (as in a drinking glass).

The Coordinate Manager provides numeric feedback while manually transforming objects (and object elements) in the viewport and provides numeric input for precise control. Sometimes it's quicker and easier to type in "90 degrees" rather than dragging the mouse carefully. This is where the Coordinate Manager is very helpful. Additionally, the Coordinate Manager provides a quick method for checking the difference between the size and scale of objects.

The status bar provides live tool tips as you mouse over tools. It provides tool tips for the selected tool and rendering status and shows the most recent render time.

MULTIDOCUMENT OPERATIONS

In Cinema 4D, each project is a document. Much like working in a word processor, multiple documents may be opened at the same time. This provides a few very powerful advantages.

Imagine that you are modeling a living room set. You have modeled and placed a sofa, a chair, and the floor and now want to model the center table. Depending on the placement of your furniture so far, and depending on the complexity of the design of the center table, the existing elements (sofa, chair, and floor) may obstruct your view of the center table as you model it. This is particularly obvious in solid views.

You can simply go to the File menu and select New to create a new project document and model the center table there, without the visual obstruction of the sofa, chair, and floor. Then, in the Object Manager, select the center table icon and copy it, and use the Window menu to select the original project document. Then paste the center table into the scene to have the sofa, chair, center table, and floor all together. Any materials you assigned the center table while modeling it in its separate project are also pasted into the Materials Manager.

Additionally, the multidocument feature of Cinema 4D allows you to take selected objects from one scene and add them to another scene. If, for example, you have a scene of a man standing outside, next to a car, and want to add the man to the living room scene, with the living room scene loaded, open the scene of the man and the car. It will open as a separate project. You would select the parent object (the man) and copy it, then select the living room scene from the bottom of the Window menu and paste the man into the living room. Although this brings all materials used by the man object, it may be wise to check those materials (for the man object) in the living room scene to ensure that any external images used are loaded.

PROJECT SETTINGS

While you are animating, some settings must generally be set for each project, such as how long the animation is, on what frame it starts and ends, and how many frames of animation are to be rendered for each second the animation is seen. When the project is saved, this information is saved with the project and has no effect on other projects.

PREFERENCES

Although the default settings you initially find in Cinema 4D for the operation of the software are basically well thought out and selected, you may find it useful to make some adjustments for aesthetics (button and interface styles, colors of interface elements, etc.) or functionality (levels of undo, backup documents, open GL versus software shading, etc.).

When you are editing in points mode, if the colors of objects in the scene make it difficult to see the object points you are trying to select, select Edit/Preferences then Viewport/Colors and adjust the color of active points and/or inactive points to colors more easily seen so that your work flow is improved.

SUMMARY

In this chapter we've had a look at:

- A broad overview of Cinema 4D 9
- The areas and purpose of the interface
- The unique multidocument functionality
- The simplicity of making project settings
- Some areas of the interface that the user can configure

From this brief tour of Cinema 4D 9, we will now launch into the fun of building our projects.

2

BASIC MODELING

In This Chapter

- Tutorial 1: The Coffee Cup
- Tutorial 2: The Microphone

Software used: Cinema 4D 9

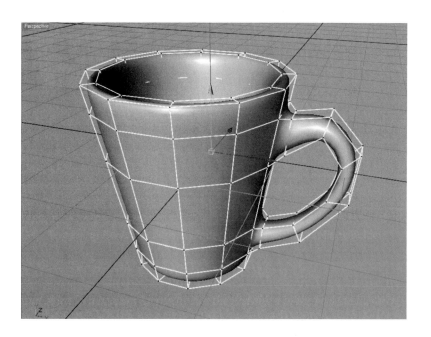

In this chapter, we'll look at issues that affect your work flow when modeling for photorealism in Cinema 4D 9. When you model objects from the real world, being flexible in your approach is valuable, just as building a real-world object requires you be open to (and skilled at) using various tools. Before modeling for photorealism, considering the following issues is helpful:

Advanced users may wish to skip to a more challenging chapter.

Ease of object modification: While there are many ways to model an object, it is important to make backup copies of the original, unmodified source objects before making destructive (permanent one-way) modeling changes to complex source objects. Additionally, when deforming an object, use modifier objects rather than dragging points (when possible) for greater flexibility to make changes you want or upon client review.

Choice of materials that integrate well with each other: Careful thought should be given to materials that must overlap or layer with each other so that differences in internal algorithms (such as between materials and shaders) do not lead to visible surface artifacts. For example, when creating a brick wall with graffiti on it that will be seen partially through the windshield of a car, the brick wall could be one material layer and the graffiti could be another. The algorithm (method) of setting the transparency for the graffiti to be placed on the wall may appear OK until seen through the windshield of the car. Since there are various ways of achieving a desired outcome, care should be taken to choose the method most effective for the specific project you are working on.

The true level of detail needed for final delivery: This issue goes both ways. Just because you may be modeling a football stadium for photorealism doesn't mean that you would model the details of the hotdog stand in the bleachers if the shot is the full stadium and the delivery medium is NTSC video. On the other hand, if the shot is of 100 square feet around the hotdog stand and the medium is a 20' × 40' wall ad in the LAX airport concourse, you might want to detail all of those objects. Be very clear on the intended and potential delivery media for the project, or you may find yourself reverse engineering your own work and working harder rather than smarter.

Will the chosen modeling detail choices survive large print delivery?   This issue can be sneaky when an image looks perfect on your computer screen and then shows tell-tale signs of digital limits when printed large. An example would be a chrome logo that when printed at 6' × 4' may show tell-tale signs in the polygon faceting and the reflection map blurring and aliasing. So, the larger the print will be, the more you may want to consider subdivision of curved sections and higher-resolution image maps. An 8½" × 11" render at 300 DPI (dots per inch) would be 2550 × 3300 pixels and would require much more RAM and time to render than an 800 × 600 pixel test render.

Choice of perspective or orthogonal reference images: Perspective images are taken at angles that allow you to see more than one side at a time. Orthogonal views show a single side at a time. Orthogonal and perspective images are both valuable as reference images, but in different ways. Orthogonal images make great references as backdrops in the orthogonal modeling windows. They function as literal modeling trace references as well as guides for polygon selection to identify surfaces that receive image maps from the real-world object. This is mainly because orthogonal reference images isolate the sides of the object to be modeled. Perspective reference images can be used from Cinema 4D's browser to get a sense of the spatial relationship between sides of an object. So, if you were to model an alarm clock, you might take photos of the front, side, and top for use in Cinema 4D's orthogonal views. A photo of the alarm clock at a perspective angle, viewed in Cinema 4D's browser can help you verify the spatial relationship between modeling in the orthogonal views.

Does the object require specific lighting support for realism? If portions of the real object are dark and contain much detail, it is necessary to light these dark detailed areas well. If the object has transparent or reflective areas, it is important to be aware of how much light reflects from these areas. If detailed areas (such as text labels) must be used as image maps, it is also important to ensure that they are very well lit to prevent a loss of detail that may then require you to digitally reconstruct this detail and thereby unnecessarily slow down your work flow.

Now let's look at the issues involved in modeling two real-world objects. We will go through the steps to model a coffee cup and a microphone and stand using the polygon modeling tools in Cinema 4D 9. These tutorials are also on the accompanying DVD-ROM as video tutorials, along with the tutorial project files.

ON THE DVD

Remember, as you make progress in each tutorial, save your Cinema 4D projects.

TUTORIAL 1 **THE COFFEE CUP**

FIGURE 2.1 The coffee cup that will be built in this tutorial.

Covered in this tutorial:

- Parametric primitives: Cylinder, Tube
- Modeling with reference images
- Polygon modeling: Extrude, Bridge, Knife, Connect, Optimize
- HyperNURBS
- Creating materials

ON THE DVD

In this tutorial, we will build a coffee cup polygon model based on a reference photo of a real coffee cup. All of the images used in this tutorial are located in "Tutorials/ProjectFiles/Chapter 02/Tutorial-01" on the Projects DVD-ROM.

1. To model our coffee cup, we start by opening the reference image **CupFront-01.jpg** and map it on a primitive plane object (Figure 2.2). The first step is to add a new material and set the color channel texture to the reference image and uncheck the **Specular** channel before closing the material requester. Next we add a **Plane** primitive and set its **Orientation** to Z (in its Attributes Manager, **Object** Properties). To apply the reference image to the plane, drag the material from the Materials Manager and drop it onto the Plane icon in the Objects Manager and set the plane's width to 500 to match the aspect ratio of the reference image.

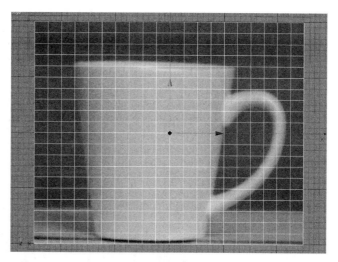

FIGURE 2.2   Plane mapped with the coffee cup reference photo.

2. Working only in the front view, change the display to **Gouraud Shading**. Add a primitive **Cylinder** and check its **X-Ray** option. Center the cylinder on the reference image of the coffee cup. Use the cylinder's parameter handles to shape its width to match the width of the bottom of the coffee cup. In the Attributes Manager, in the **Object** tab, set the **Height Segments** to 1 and **Rotation Segments** to 12 and in the **Caps** tab, set the **Caps Segments** to 2. Now select the **Make Editable** icon to convert this parametric primitive to a polygon mesh object. Your front view should now look like Figure 2.3.

FIGURE 2.3   A primitive cylinder is shaped and positioned against the reference image.

The Cylinder's icon in the Objects Manager has now changed to a Polygon icon, indicating that parametric adjustments are no longer available for this object.

3. In the top view, switch to the **Point** mode and select the **Live Selection** tool (**Only Select Visible Elements** checked). This will ensure that selecting points in the top view will only allow those points visible from the top to be selected. Now select the inner row of points and use the scale tool to change their scale to form the thickness of the inner wall of the coffee cup (as shown in Figure 2.4).

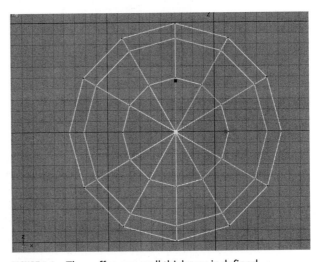

FIGURE 2.4   The coffee cup wall thickness is defined.

4. Still in the top view, switch to the **Polygon** mode and use the **Live Selection** tool to select the inner top polygons. Then switch to the front view, right-click to select the **Extrude** tool, and with the left mouse button held down, drag the mouse to the left to bring the selected polygons down and create the empty space within the coffee cup that holds liquid (shown in Figure 2.5). Orbit the cup in the perspective view to see the result so far.

5. In the front view, switch to **Point** mode and the **Live Selection** tool and uncheck **Only Select Visible Elements** and use the mouse to select all points at the top of the cup. Select the **Scale** tool and select anywhere in the viewport (but not on the cup polygons) and move to the right to scale the width of the top of the cup to match the reference image. Now, from the perspective view, you will see the cup start to look more like our reference photo (shown in Figure 2.6).

FIGURE 2.5   Top polygons are selected and extruded down.

FIGURE 2.6   Top points scaled out to match the reference photo.

6. To create your cup handle, add a primitive **Tube** object and in the Attributes Manager, set its **Orientation** to –Z and check the **X-Ray** option. Move the tube so that it's centered on the right edge of the cup in the reference photo (shown in Figure 2.7), between the upper and lower ends of the cup handle. Using either the parameter handles (little orange balls on the tube object) or the parameters in the **Object** tab of

the Attributes Manager, you can adjust the tube's **Inner Radius** to match the distance between the inner edges of the reference photo cup handle ends (shown in Figure 2.8). Adjust the **Outer Radius** to match the general thickness of the coffee cup handle as seen in the reference image (shown in Figure 2.8). Then, using the tube's **Slice** tab (found in the Attributes Manager), adjust the **From** and **To** parameters to set the start and end of the tube object to be next to the cup and set the **Rotation Segments** to 5 and **Height** to 35 in the **Objects** tab (shown in Figure 2.8).

FIGURE 2.7   Initial placement of the tube.

FIGURE 2.8   The tube more closely matches the coffee cup handle now.

Be sure to leave enough space between the tube object and the cup to be able to se-lect the polygons at the end of the tube later.

7. Convert the tube object to a polygon object by clicking the **Make Ed-itable** icon. Switch to **Point** mode and choose the **Live Selection** tool (**Only Select Visible Elements** unchecked). In the front view, then select the points in the tube object and move them to roughly match the shape of the cup handle in the reference image (shown in Figure 2.9).

FIGURE 2.9   The tube's points are moved to more closely match the coffee cup handle in the reference photo.

 To quickly switch between Live Selection and Move tools, press the keyboard space bar.

8. In the Objects Manager, select both cylinder and tube objects. From the **Functions** menu, select **Connect** to merge the cylinder and the tube into a new polygon object (which appears at the top of the Ob-jects Manager hierarchy and is named "Cylinder.1"). Delete the orig-inal objects (cylinder and tube).

9. Now switch to **Polygon** mode and deselect all polygons by choosing the **Live Selection** tool and clicking in the front viewport (but not on the polygons). Right-click and select the **Knife** tool. In the Attri-butes Manager, uncheck **Restrict To Selection**, **Visible Only**, and **Create N-gons**. Place the mouse slightly above the top outer corner of the reference image coffee cup handle and hold the **Shift** key down and drag across (to the left) to just outside the cup to make the first cut. Make similar cuts just below the top end of the reference

image coffee cup handle, just above the bottom end of the reference image coffee cup handle, and just below the bottom end of the reference image coffee cup handle. At this point your cup should look like Figure 2.10.

FIGURE 2.10   Four knife cuts applied to the cup.

In Cinema 4D, knife cuts are made to add geometry detail to objects.

10. At this point you should hold the **Live Selection** tool icon down and choose the **Polygon Selection** tool (**Only Select Visible Elements** unchecked). Make left-button mouse clicks around the cup to form a polygon selection (excluding the handle polygons). The cup polygons should all be red now. Choose the **Rotate** tool. In the top view, this displays the three rotation bands (red: X axis, blue: Z axis, and black: Y axis). Using the thin gray rotation band, rotate the cup polygons (around the Y axis) to be parallel with the cup handle polygons (shown in Figure 2.11). In the Objects Manager, double-click the "**Cylinder.1**" text and rename it "**Coffee Cup.**" Set both display switches of the reference image (Plane) to red so that the reference image will not be seen in the viewport and will not be seen when the image is rendered. Uncheck the coffee cup **X-Ray**. Choose the **Live Selection** tool. Working in the perspective view, zoom in closely and select the two triangular polygons at the end of the top of the handle (shown in Figure 2.12) and right-click to choose **Untriangulate** and then **OK** to convert the two triangular polygons into one quadrangle (four-sided polygon Figure 2.13). Do the same for the two triangular polygons at

the bottom end of the handle. Hold the **Shift** key down and select the polygon on the cup directly across from (and parallel to) the currently selected polygon on the bottom end of the handle.

 At this point, only one polygon, the bottom end of the handle facing the cup, and the corresponding polygon on the cup should be selected.

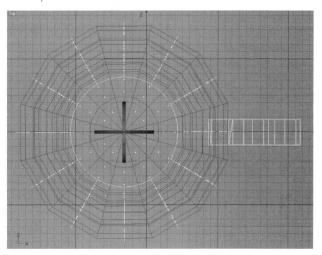

FIGURE 2.11   The cup polygons are rotated so that a side is parallel to the handle polygons.

FIGURE 2.12   Two polygons (at the top of the handle) facing the cup are selected.

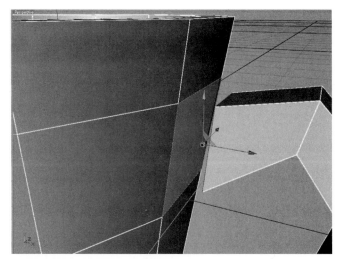

FIGURE 2.13   A polygon at the top of the handle and the polygon directly across on the cup are selected in preparation for use of the Bridge tool.

 It may be necessary to zoom and rotate the view to select these polygons.

11. Next right-click and select the **Bridge** tool and drag a line across corresponding corners of the two selected polygons to build the polygons that connect the bottom of the handle to the cup. Repeat this process on the top of the handle (shown in Figure 2.14).

 Be very careful to only bridge to corresponding corners. Not following this rule will result in distorted models.

12. Switch to display all four viewports and press **Alt-O** to frame the coffee cup within all four viewports. With the coffee cup selected in the Objects Manager, holding the **Alt** key down and adding a **Hyper-NURBS** object makes the HyperNURBS object the parent of the coffee cup. The HyperNURBS make the coffee cup object appear smooth and no longer faceted. Working in the perspective view, deselect the coffee cup to observe the defective connection between the cup and handle.

13. Switch to **Points** mode and select the coffee cup in the Objects Manager. Using the **Live Selection** tool, deselect all points and right-click to choose **Optimize**, then **OK**. The connection between the cup and handle is now repaired. Your coffee cup should now look like Figure 2.15.

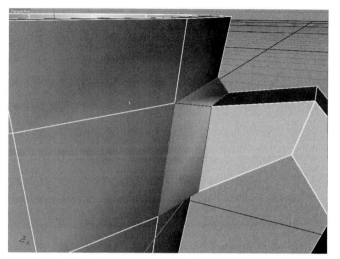

FIGURE 2.14   The polygon on the top of the handle is bridged to the polygon on the cup.

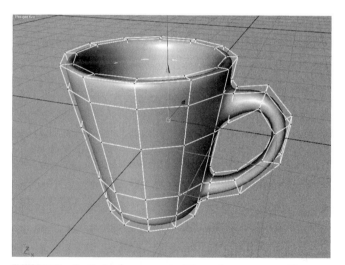

FIGURE 2.15   Optimize has corrected the polygons created by bridging the handle with the cup.

14. In the Materials Manager, create a new material, and double-click the material sample ball. In the **Color** channel set the **Color** to 255, 207, 86 and in the **Specular** channel set the **Width** to 68% and the **Height** to 38%; then close the material requester. To apply this material to the coffee cup, from the Materials Manager, drag the new material onto the coffee cup icon in the Objects Manager. Render the perspective view to see the finished coffee cup (shown in Figure 2.16).

FIGURE 2.16   Finished coffee cup model.

Summary

In this tutorial, you learned how to model a simple object with a single surface material from a photograph. While modeling without a photo reference can be very useful, developing the skills to faithfully produce 3D models from real-world objects increases the probability that you can deliver on target when in production.

| **TUTORIAL 2** | **THE MICROPHONE** |

FIGURE 2.17   The reference microphone photo and the microphone that will be built in this tutorial.

Covered in this tutorial:

- Boolean object
- Modeling with reference images
- Multimaterial objects
- Displacement mapping
- Material projection methods
- Polygon modeling: loop selection, edge modeling

In this tutorial, you will build a model of a microphone mounted on a tabletop microphone holder and stand. You will work from a reference photo of a microphone and will also look at how reference photos are at times imprecise guides for modeling because of the inherent perspective distortion in photography.

This tutorial will be broken into four sections: (1) base and neck of microphone stand, (2) microphone, (3) microphone holder, and (4) all materials created and applied. Finished project files for each section of this tutorial are included on the accompanying DVD-ROM in the tutorials folder. All of the images used in this tutorial are located in "Tutorials/ProjectFiles/Chapter 02/Tutorial-02" on the Projects DVD-ROM.

ON THE DVD

Base and Neck of Microphone Stand

1. Start by adding a **Plane** primitive and set its **Orientation** to –Z axis. Set the **Height** to 500 to match the aspect ratio of the reference image. In the Materials Manager, create a new material and set the **Color** channel's **Texture** to "Mic-1.png."

This image of the microphone was prepared in Adobe Photoshop. The microphone (without the background) was placed in a new layer and was saved as a PNG file with transparency. So this file has an alpha channel.

While it is possible to place a reference image as a background in the viewport, in this tutorial, you will place the reference image (with an alpha channel) on an object. This allows you to build a 3D model around the reference image and even orbit in the perspective view to visually compare how the 3D model matches the reference image. This is a very simple, yet very powerful, process to master.

Check the material's **Alpha** channel and set its **Texture** to "**Mic-1.png**" and close the material requester. In the Materials Manager, drag the new material onto the plane icon in the Objects Manager. In the Objects Manager, deselect the plane. The perspective view now shows the reference image mapped on the plane without the photo background (shown in Figure 2.18).

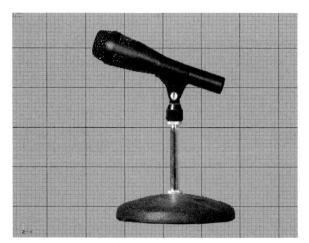

FIGURE 2.18   The reference image mapped onto a plane. The photo's background is removed to allow focus on only the microphone.

Working in the front view, use its local menu to set the Display to **Gouraud Shading**. From the front view, you can see that some curvature in the photograph won't align perfectly as we start to model in 3D.

2. To start modeling the microphone stand neck and base, add a primitive **Cylinder** object. Check cylinder's **X-Ray** option, set the **Height Segments** to 1, **Rotation Segments** to 24, and the **Caps** to 1. With the **Move** tool selected in **Object** mode, move the cylinder to center it on the neck and base of the microphone stand (shown in Figure 2.19).

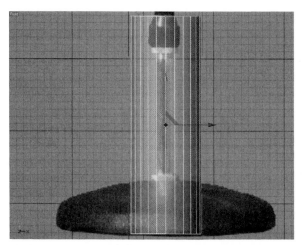

FIGURE 2.19   A cylinder is added to start modeling the neck of the microphone.

The "o" key allows you to frame a selected object to fill the current viewport.

3. Make the parametric cylinder editable and switch to **Point** mode. Using the **Live Selection** tool (**Only Select Visible Elements** unchecked), select all points at the bottom of the cylinder and use the **Scale** tool (dragging in an empty space in the viewport *and not on the cylinder*) to make them as wide as the black microphone base (shown in Figure 2.20). You can now see that the photo reference and the 3D model don't line up perfectly on the bottom of the base, so rather than a direct reference, the photo is more of a scale and position-relative reference for 3D modeling.

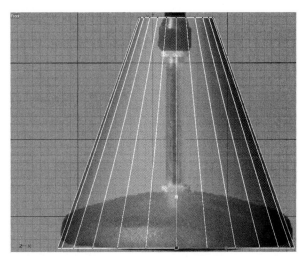

FIGURE 2.20   The bottom of the cylinder is now scaled to be as wide as the microphone base in the reference photo.

4. In **Polygon** mode, from the **Structure** menu, use the **Knife** tool (**Restrict To Selection**, **Visible Only**, and **Create N-gons** unchecked) with the **Shift** key held down to make a cut across the cylinder at the elevation of the first bend in the shape of the base of the microphone stand. Be sure to start and end outside the cylinder when you cut. Make another cut on the cylinder at the top of the base of the microphone stand (shown in Figure 2.21).

Rather than cutting off parts of a polygon object, using the Knife tool to cut adds detail to the object. Holding the Shift key while cutting with the Knife tool constrains the angle of the cut to 45-degree increments. This increment can be adjusted in the Knife tool's Attributes Manager, Options tab.

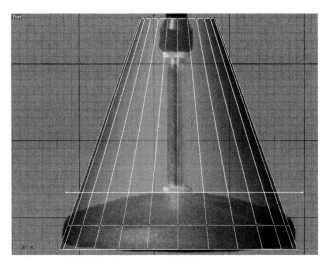

FIGURE 2.21   Knife tool at the end of the second cut.

5. In **Point** mode select only the second row of points (created by the first Knife tool cut) from the bottom and use the **Scale** tool to scale them to the same width as the first bend in the microphone stand base. Select the next higher row of points and scale them in to the width of the bottom of the first bright metal piece of the microphone stand neck. Use the **Knife** tool to make a cut between the previous two cuts (where the polygon appears to be much too narrow compared to the reference image). Select the new row of points made by the new cut. Use the **Scale** tool to fit them to the reference image. Your model should now look like Figure 2.22.

6. At the very top of the cylinder, select the top row of points and scale them in to match the top of the microphone stand neck. Use the **Knife** tool to make cuts to the cylinder along the microphone stand neck wherever there is a change in diameter. Your model should now look like Figure 2.23.

 Toggle (to red) the object's Editor Display Switch (upper gray dot) in the Objects Manager to get a clear view of the reference image when necessary.

7. In **Polygon** mode with the **Live Selection** tool (**Only Selected Visible Elements** unchecked), select the second row of polygons from the top (wide black plastic area). Turn on the **Y Axis Lock** and scale the polygons to match the reference image. Select the long polygons in the smooth chrome area of the microphone stand neck

FIGURE 2.22   The shape of the microphone base is roughed out.

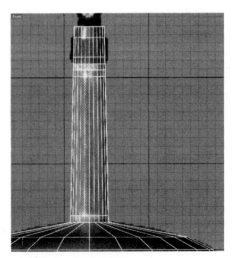

FIGURE 2.23   The shape of the microphone neck is roughed out.

and use the **Extrude** tool to extrude them in to match the reference image (shown in Figure 2.24).

8. In **Point** mode, working on the bottom of the polygons extruded at the end of step 7, select the top row of points. In the perspective view, zoom in to work on the selected points. With the **Ctrl** key held down, deselect the outer ring of points (shown in Figure 2.25). Orbit the

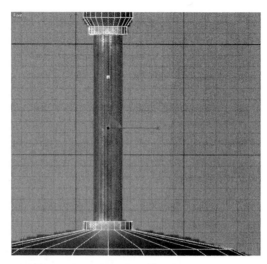

FIGURE 2.24   The object neck now matches the reference photo's shape.

FIGURE 2.25   Points at the bottom of the neck are selected and scaled to match the reference photo.

perspective view to see all the points. In the front view, scale the selected points in to match the reference image so that the bottom of the neck matches the reference photo. Repeat this process on the points at the top of the long polygons to better match the neck of the 3D model to the reference image.

9. In the Objects Manager, toggle the reference image render display to red. In the perspective view, with the cylinder selected, use the "**o**" key to frame the 3D model of the microphone stand and render the view. Your rendered view should look like Figure 2.26 now.

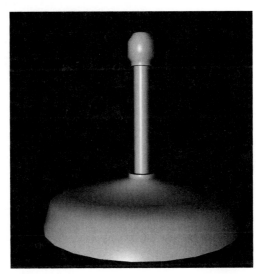

FIGURE 2.26   The microphone base is modeled.

Microphone

10. To build the microphone, first add a primitive **Cylinder** and check its **X-Ray** option. Set **Height Segments** to 1, **Caps** to 1, and **Rotation Segments** to 24. Be sure the reference image plane object's Editor Display Switch is gray. Center the cylinder on the microphone. In the Coordinates Manager, set **Rotation B** to −70 degrees. Use the parametric handles to shape the cylinder to the length of the microphone. Make the cylinder editable and switch to **Polygon** mode. Use the **Knife** tool to make cuts in the polygons where the reference image of the microphone changes in size. Since the Shift key constrains movement in 45-degree increments and since the microphone's angle is unknown at this time, don't use the Shift key with these cuts (shown in Figure 2.27).

11. Switch to **Point** mode, and from the small end of the microphone, select the first two rows of points with the **Live Selection** tool (**Only Select Visible Elements** unchecked). Turn off the **Y Axis Lock** and use the **Scale** tool to make the two rows of selected points match the width of the microphone's narrow section. Their position along the microphone will temporarily be incorrect (shown in Figure 2.28). Using

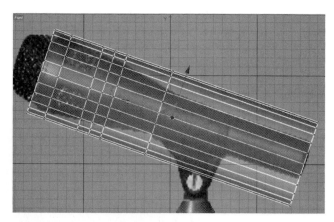

FIGURE 2.27   Early steps of the microphone model with five Knife tool cuts.

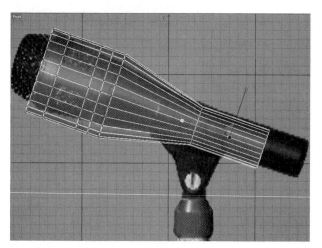

FIGURE 2.28   Rough microphone model.

the **Move** tool, drag the **Y** axis (green arrow) to the left to position the inner points where the shape of the microphone starts to grow. Then using the **Live Selection** tool (**Only Select Visible Elements** unchecked), select just the last row of points that are now out of place and use the **Move** tool to drag (**Y** axis) them back to the end of the microphone. **Scale** the second row of points to match the reference image. Using the **Live Selection** tool (**Only Select Visible Elements** unchecked), select all five rows of points in the microphone head and scale them so that the cylinder now forms the basic shape of the microphone. Select the last row of points in the microphone head and move them to match the reference image. Your front view should look like Figure 2.29 now.

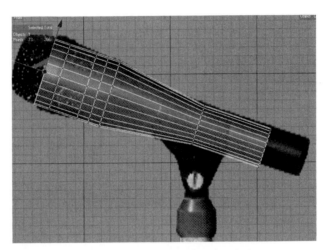

FIGURE 2.29   The object points moved and scaled to more closely match the reference photo.

ON THE DVD

12. For a closer view of the "**Mic-1.png**" image on the accompanying DVD-ROM, Chapter 02, Tutorial 02, in the Objects Manager, change the **Objects** tab to Browser and use the Browser menu **File/Import File** to browse for "**Tutorials/ProjectFiles/Chapter 02/Tutorial-02/Mic-1/tex/Mic-1.png**." If you double-click the thumbnail image, a full-size view will open. This full-size view has the standard Cinema 4D pan and zoom icons in the upper right corner.

*In Cinema 4D 9.5, you can do this from the main menu with Window/Content Browser and navigate to "**Tutorials/ProjectFiles/Chapter 02/Tutorial-02/Mic-1/tex/Mic-1.png**."*

The odd blocky white background around the reference photo (Figure 2.30) in this view occurs because the .PNG file has an alpha channel. This will not cause any modeling difficulty for use of the reference image to build the microphone.

13. To model the three cutouts at the head of the microphone, select the cylinder in the Objects Manager and uncheck the **X-Ray** option. In the perspective view, using the **Live Selection** tool (**Only Select Visible Elements** checked), working with the second row of polygons from the end of the microphone head, select the top six polygons

FIGURE 2.30   A view of the microphone reference photo in the Cinema 4D 9 Browser.

(shown in Figure 2.31). Orbiting the perspective view to see around the polygon object, skip the next two polygons in the row and select the next six polygons. Again orbiting the perspective view to see around the polygon object, skip the next two polygons in the row and select the next six polygons. Of the 24 polygons in this row, you should now have 18 selected and 6 unselected. Use the **Extrude** tool to pull the selected polygons in to match the depth of the microphone screen as seen in Mic-1.png (shown in Figure 2.32). From the **Selection** menu, use **Set Selection** to create a polygon selection. These polygons will be the microphone screen.

In Cinema 4D, when working in Polygon mode, selecting polygons and then using Set Selection creates a polygon selection tag in the Objects Manager that can be named and allows you to later apply a unique material to just that area of the object. A polygon object can have many selections set so that one object can easily have many materials. This is one method used to make amazing models in Cinema 4D.

FIGURE 2.31   The first set of polygons to be cut out are selected.

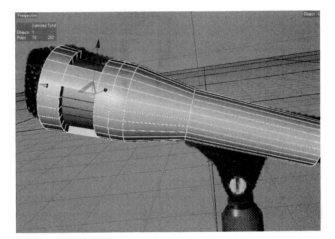

FIGURE 2.32   Three groups of polygons (six polygons in each group) are selected and extruded in to model the cutouts at the head of the microphone to match the reference photo.

14. Orbiting the perspective view, you will see the polygons at the end of the head of the microphone (they look like 24 slices of pie). Select them all with the **Live Selection** tool (**Only Select Visible Elements** checked). Right-click to choose the **Extrude Inner** tool and drag the selected polygon in slightly to form the difference between the end of the microphone metal casing and the microphone screen (shown in Figure 2.33). In the front view use the **Extrude** tool to extrude the polygons out to match the length of the microphone

screen. Use the **Scale** tool to taper the selected polygons to match the scale of the microphone screen as seen in the reference image. In the Objects Manager double-click the polygon selection on the cylinder object made earlier for the screen. In the front view, using the **Live Selection** tool (**Only Select Visible Elements** unchecked), select all polygons used to create the screen at the end of the microphone head and **Set Selection** again to add them to the screen polygon selection. Now, with all polygons deselected, double-clicking on the screen polygon selection selects all of the screen polygons. Your views should now look like Figure 2.34.

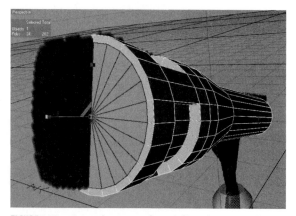

FIGURE 2.33   An early stage of modeling the microphone screen.

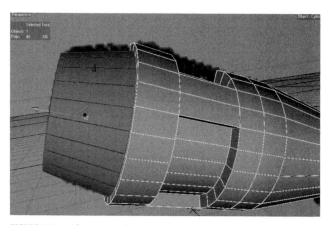

FIGURE 2.34   The microphone screen modeling is now completed.

15. Use the **Browser** to view the "**Tutorials/ProjectFiles/Chapter 02/ Tutorial-02/Mic-1/tex/Mic-1.png**" image and observe the small groove where the microphone neck meets the microphone head.

16. To model the groove in the microphone head, with the cylinder polygons visible and the **X-Ray** option checked, switch to **Edge** mode and the front view. From the **Selection** menu choose **Loop Selection** and select the loop of edges that join the microphone neck and the microphone head (see Figure 2.35).

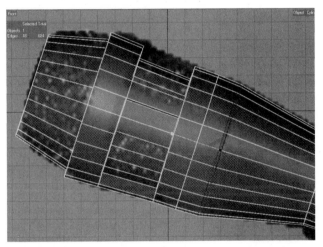

FIGURE 2.35   A Loop Selection is made to start modeling the microphone head's groove area.

 In Edge mode, Cinema 4D 9 indicates which edges will be selected with a mouse click by turning edges yellow as the mouse moves over them and turns selected edges red.

17. Now zoom in for a close view of the selected edges in the front view and right-click to choose **Bevel**. Drag to widen the groove until it is approximately as large as the groove in the image viewer reference image. With the Bevel tool still active, make another small bevel. This second bevel will help the groove maintain a sharp break. You then make a **Loop Selection** of the inner loop and use the **Scale** tool to scale this in enough to be visible as a groove (as seen in Figure 2.36).

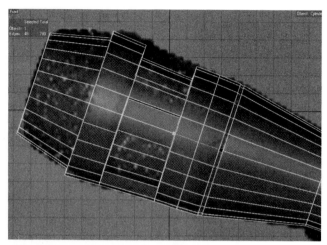

FIGURE 2.36   Modeling the groove is completed.

Microphone Holder

18. You can switch the Objects Manager to the **Browser** to view the "**Tutorials/ProjectFiles/Chapter 02/Tutorial-02/Mic-1/tex/Mic-1.png**" image and observe the design of the microphone holder and screw head.

19. In the Objects Manager, rename "cylinder.1" to "**Microphone**" and rename "cylinder" to "**base&neck**."

You can choose any names you wish. Just be sure that the names you choose have some functional value. This is very important when working in a production team and when returning to a modeling project after some time has passed.

20. The Microphone object has an edge that closely matches the position of the front of the microphone holder. In the front view in **Polygon** mode, use the **Knife** tool to make a cut on the microphone to match the back of the microphone holder as seen in the reference image. Use the **Live Selection** tool (**Only Select Visible Elements** unchecked) to select the polygons on the Microphone object (where the holder holds the microphone) between the two knife cuts. Then copy (**Ctrl-c**) and paste (**Ctrl-v**) them to create a new object in the Objects Manager ("Microphone.1"). Now, rename "Microphone.1" as "**Holder**." Toggle the Microphone's **Editor Display Switch** red so that only the holder object is seen in the viewport. From the **Selection** menu, choose **Invert** so that all polygons other than those for the holder are now selected and delete them. Switching to **Point** mode reveals that deleting

the polygons left behind orphaned and unattached points. Right-click and choose **Optimize**, then **OK** to delete the orphaned points (see Figure 2.37).

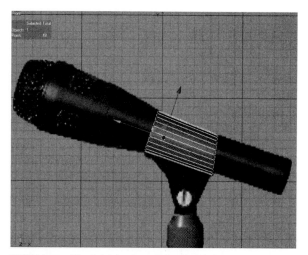

FIGURE 2.37   The initial microphone holder polygons.

21. In the perspective view, with the **Live Selection** tool (**Only Select Visible Elements** checked) select the top four polygons and delete them and right-click and choose **Optimize**, then **OK** to delete the orphaned points (see Figure 2.38).

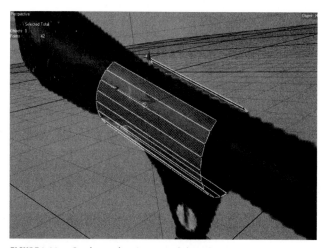

FIGURE 2.38   Orphaned points are deleted.

22. In the front view, frame the holder object ("**o**"). Working on only the left points for now, use the **Live Selection** tool (**Only Select Visible Elements** unchecked) and the **Move** tool to match the front of the holder 3D model to the front of the holder in the reference image. Right-click to choose the **Extrude** tool and check **Create Caps** in Options and drag to extrude the holder to be like 1/8"-thick metal (see Figure 2.39).

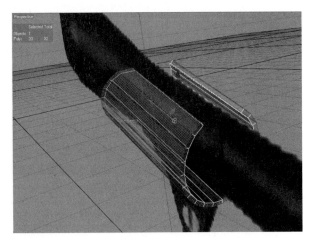

FIGURE 2.39   The microphone holder is extruded to have thickness.

 The Create Caps option causes the Extrude tool to make the extruded polygon form a closed volume.

23. Frame the holder. Orbit the perspective view to see the bottom of the holder. Use the **Live Selection** tool (**Only Select Visible Elements** checked) and select the two bottom center polygons. From the front view, use the **Knife** tool (**Restrict To Selection** checked) to cut perpendicular to the selected polygons at the point where the microphone holder's upright element ends (just before the left edge of the selected polygons). There are now four polygons on the bottom of the microphone holder (two short ones to the left and two long ones to the right). In the front view, with the **Live Selection** tool (**Only Select Visible Elements** unchecked), hold the control key down and deselect the short polygons to the left. **Extrude** the bottom polygons, stopping above the screw in the reference image. **Extrude** once more, stopping below the screw in the reference image. In the right view use the **Live Selection** and **Scale** tools to

straighten the points until they go straight down without flaring out. Your microphone holder should look like Figure 2.40 now.

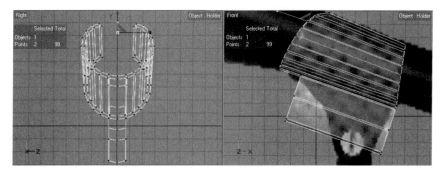

FIGURE 2.40   The bottom of the microphone holder is extruded.

 The space bar can be used to switch between the Scale tool and the Live Selection tool just like switching back and forth between the Move tool and the Live Selection tool.

24. In the front view, move the microphone holder points to match the reference image, stopping just above the bottom of the screw. **Extrude** the bottom two polygons to the end of the microphone holder element and position the points to match the reference image (shown in Figure 2.41). Check the right view for any necessary point clean up.

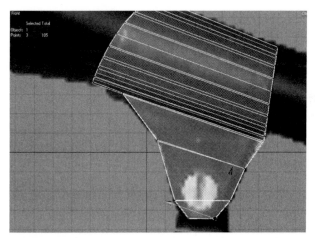

FIGURE 2.41   The microphone holder more closely matches the reference image now.

25. To model the microphone holder screw, add a primitive **Cylinder** and set the **Orientation** to –Z, **Radius** to 9, **Height** to 5, **Height Segments** to 1, **Caps** to 1, **X-Ray** checked. In the right view, in **Model** mode, use the **Move** tool to have a third of the cylinder in the side of (penetrating) the microphone holder element. In the front view, center the cylinder on the screw (shown in Figure 2.42). Add a primitive **Cube** object to create the shape of the slot in the screw. Using the parameters in the Attributes Manager (or the parameter handles), shape the cube to be as wide as indicated in the reference image. Make the cube twice as tall as the slotted space in the screw. In the right view, move the cube to intersect the screw without going all the way through the screw (shown in Figure 2.43).

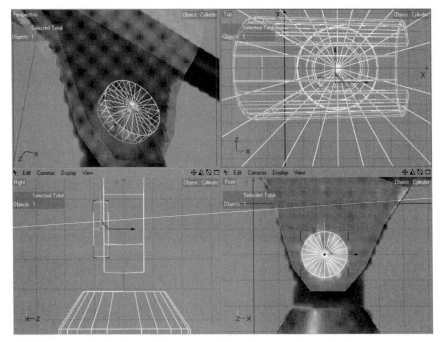

FIGURE 2.42   A cylinder is used to start modeling the microphone holder screw.

26. For the cube to cut a slot in the cylinder, use the **Objects** menu **Modeling/Boole** to add a boolean object. In the Objects Manager, drag the cube into the Boolean, then drag the cylinder into the Boolean. In the Objects Manager, select the boolean object and use the **Objects** menu **Modeling/Instance** to add an instance of the boolean object (creating an instance copy of the screw). In the Coordinates Manager, set the **Rotation H** (**Y** axis) of the screw instance to 180 degrees and place it

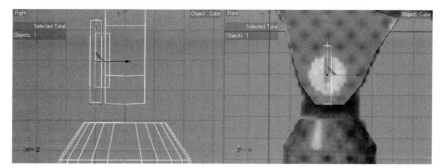

FIGURE 2.43   A cube is shaped and positioned to be used to cut a slot into the cylinder.

on the back side of the microphone holder element so that the original screw and the screw instance are parallel to each other. Use the right and top views to align the instance with the Boolean. Your viewports and Objects Manager should look like Figure 2.44 now.

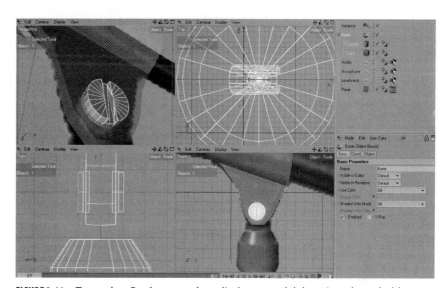

FIGURE 2.44   Two cubes Boolean-cut the cylinder to model the microphone holder screw.

The second object in a boolean hierarchy cuts the first object in the boolean hierarchy.

27. To organize your modeling hierarchy, in the Objects Manager, drag the "**Boole**" and the "**Instance**" into the holder object. Select the microphone, base&neck, and holder. Use the **Objects** menu **Group Objects** in the Objects Manager and name this new group "**Mic**."

28. Add a primitive **Cube** and adjust its parameters to be small enough to fit between the bottom of the microphone holder and the top of the base&neck. Check cube's **Fillet** option and further adjust the parameters to make the cube fit.

29. With all four views visible and with the mic object selected in the Objects Manager, press **Alt+o** to frame the microphone in all four viewports. Render the perspective view to see the model so far (shown in Figure 2.45).

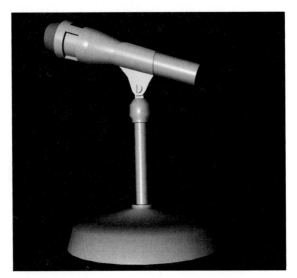

FIGURE 2.45   Microphone modeling completed.

Materials Created and Applied

30. In the Objects Manager, select the base&neck object. In the front view, switch to **Polygon** mode and use the **Live Selection** tool (**Only Select Visible Elements** unchecked) to select all polygons in the base of the stand. *In the reference image, the base is the wide, black bottom section and is wide and black.* Orbit the perspective view to verify that all polygons in the base are selected and use the **Selection** menu **Set Selection** to create a polygon selection. In the Objects Manager double-click the new polygon selection and change its name in **Basic Properties** to "**base**." Unselect the polygon selection by clicking in an unused area of the Objects Manager.

31. In the reference image, just above the base is a rough material. This material is also seen close to the top of the neck of the microphone stand. In the front view, zoom in to the area just above the base&neck

and select the polygons that correspond to the lower rough material as seen in the reference image. With the **Shift** key held down, select the top polygons that correspond to the top rough material area in the reference image and set a polygon selection (shown in Figure 2.46). Name this polygon selection "**rough**." Unselect the polygon selection.

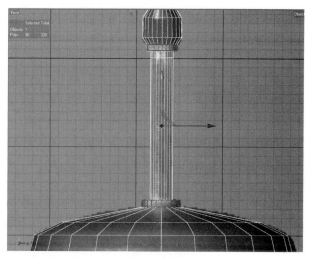

FIGURE 2.46   Rough polygons selected.

32. Now select the row of polygons that correspond to the threaded area of the neck (just below the top rough area). Set a polygon selection. Name this selection "**threaded**" and then unselect the same polygon selection.

33. Select the row of polygons that correspond to the area in the reference image that are black and corrugated to be easily turned by hand and set a polygon selection and name it "**hand turn**." Unselect the polygon selection.

34. Select the two remaining rows of polygons (one above and one below the hand turn polygons [shown in Figure 2.47]), set a selection, and name it "**black smooth**." Unselect the polygon selection. In the Objects Manager, in the holder hierarchy, rename the boolean object as "**Screw**."

35. In the perspective view, using the **Live Selection** tool (**Only Select Visible Elements** checked), select the row of polygons on the microphone object that correspond to the areas shown in Figure 2.48. Set a selection and name it "**Lines**."

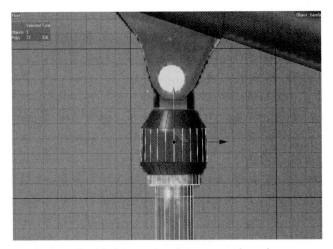

FIGURE 2.47 The black smooth polygons are selected.

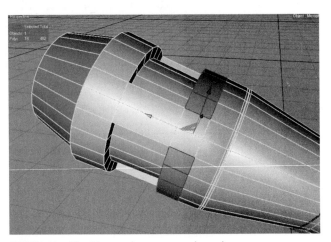

FIGURE 2.48 The Lines polygons are selected.

In the above selection process, select six polygons, then skip two. Continue this sequence along the row of polygons orbiting the perspective view to see all 24 polygons in the row.

36. In the Materials Manager, to create the "**base**" material, start by selecting **File/New Material** and double-click the material sample. Name the material "**base**." Right-click on the material preview and

change the size to **Huge**. In the **Color** channel, set the **Brightness** to 10. In the **Bump** channel, set the **Strength** to 20 and set **Texture** to Noise. Click the **Noise** texture and set the **Noise Type** to Electric and set **Global Scale** to 10. In the **Specular** channel, set the **Width** to 66%. Close the material requester.

37. Now drag the base material sample to the base&neck icon in the Objects Manager. Drag the first polygon selection on the base&neck object into the material's **Selection** field to restrict this material to just the base of the microphone stand (shown in Figure 2.49). Deselect everything to observe how the material has been applied.

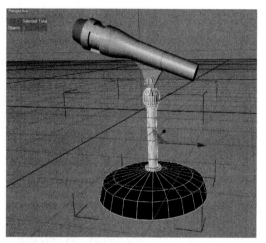

FIGURE 2.49   The base material applied to the microphone's base.

38. Create a new material and name it "**neck**." In the **Color** channel, set the **Brightness** to 21. Check the **Environment** channel and load the "**Tutorials/ProjectFiles/Chapter 02/Tutorial-02/Mic-1/tex/ Desert-1.jpg**" image from the DVD-ROM into the **Texture** and set the **Environment Brightness** to 60. Drag the neck material onto the base&neck icon in the Objects Manager. Since this was the second material added and there is no polygon selection to restrict this material, it covers the entire base&neck object. Drag the base material to the right of the neck material.

ON THE DVD

Because Cinema 4D stacks materials left-to-right, the base material is placed on top of the neck material and is therefore visible.

39. In the Materials Manager, copy (**Ctrl-c**) and paste (**Ctrl-v**) the neck material and name the new material "**rough.**" Check the **Bump** channel and set the **Strength** to 200 and set the **Texture** to Tiles. Click on **Tiles** and set the **Pattern** to Squares, **Grout Width** to 0, **Bevel Width** to 100, and **Global Scale** to 51 and close the material requester (shown in Figure 2.50). Drag the rough material to the base&neck icon in the Objects Manager and drag the rough polygon selection into the **Selection** field. In the perspective view, zoom in to take a close look at the upper polygons with the rough material at the top of the neck and render. The material looks much too large. Select the rough material in the Objects Manager and set the **Tile X** and **Tile Y** to 10 in the Attributes Manager. Render the perspective view again to see the rough area greatly improved.

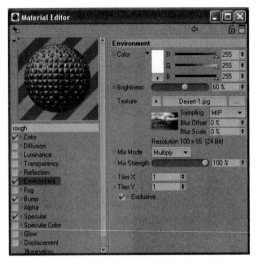

FIGURE 2.50   Rough material.

40. To create the threaded material, make a copy of the rough material and name it "**threaded.**" In the **Bump** channel **Texture**, click on **Tiles** and change the **Pattern** from Squares to **Lines 1** and close the material requester. Drag the threaded material to the base&neck icon in the Objects Manager, and drag the threaded polygon selection into the **Selection** field and set the **Tile X** and **Tile Y** to 20 in the Attributes Manager.

41. To make the material for the smooth black area of the neck, make a copy of the base material and name it "**smooth.**" Uncheck the **Bump** channel and set the **Specular** channel **Width** and **Height** to 50% and close the material requester. Drag the smooth material to

the base&neck icon in the Objects Manager and drag the black smooth polygon selection into the **Selection** field.

42. To make the material for the hand turn black area of the neck, make a copy of the smooth material and name it "**hand turn**" and set the material preview shape to **Cylinder**. Check the **Displacement** channel and set the **Texture** to Tiles and **Height** to 1 m. Click on **Tiles** and set the **Pattern** to Lines 1, **Tiles** Color 2 to white (**R** = 200, **G** = 255, **B** = 255), **Grout Width** to 5%, **Bevel Width** to 80%, and **Global Scale** to 10% and close the material requester. Drag the hand turn material to the base&neck icon in the Objects Manager and drag the hand turn polygon selection into the **Selection** field.

43. Rendering the perspective view shows only a slight bulge in the hand turn area of the neck. This is because there aren't enough polygons to be displaced by the applied material.

44. While in **Polygon** mode, double-click the hand turn polygon selection to select only the polygons in that selection. Use the **Knife** tool (**Restrict To Selection, Visible Only** unchecked) and hold the **Shift** key down to make a cut immediately above the selected polygons. Make a similar cut immediately below the selected polygons. See Figure 2.51.

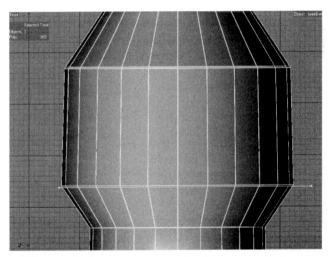

FIGURE 2.51   Knife cuts made immediately above and below the hand turn polygons.

These cuts create two thin rows of polygons to absorb the radical change in polygon geometry that we are about to create with heavy subdivision and strong displacement. Without these two thin rows of polygons, the smooth black areas of the neck would render faceted.

45. Now right-click and choose **Subdivide** and set **Subdivision** to 5. This converts the 24 polygons originally selected into 24,576 polygons. Render the perspective view to see the hand turn area corrected (shown in Figure 2.52).

In other tutorials, you will use Sub-Polygon Displacement to achieve similar results. In this case, however, use of Sub-Polygon Displacement would result in faceted polygons above and below the hand turn area.

FIGURE 2.52   Displacement-mapped material.

ON THE DVD

46. To make the material for the microphone holder, make a copy of the base material and name it "**holder.**" Check the **Environment** channel and set the **Texture** to use the image "**Tutorials/ProjectFiles/ Chapter 02/Tutorial-02/Mic-1/tex/Desert-1.jpg**" from the DVD-ROM and set the **Brightness** to 5. Check the **Bump** channel and set the **Texture** to Noise. Click **Noise** and set the **Noise type** to Electric, **Global Scale** to 10, and all three fields of **Relative Scale** to 10. Close the material requester and drag the holder material to the holder icon in the Objects Manager.

47. Drag the neck material to the Screw icon in the Objects Manager. Drag the holder material to the Microphone icon in the Objects Manager.

48. Make a copy of the holder material and name it "**lines.**" Check the **Bump** channel and set the **Strength** to 24 and **Texture** to Tile. Click **Tile** and set **Pattern** to Lines 1 and close the material requester. Drag the lines material to the Microphone icon in the Objects Manager and drag the lines polygon selection into the **Selection** field and set **Tiles X** and **Tiles Y** to 10.

49. Create a new material and name it "**screen.**" In the **Color** channel, set the **Texture** to "**Tutorials/ProjectFiles/Chapter 02/Tutorial-02/Mic-1/tex/Screen-1.jpg**" from the DVD-ROM, (a cropped photo of the real microphone screen). In the **Bump** channel, set the **Texture** to "**Tutorials/ProjectFiles/Chapter 02/Tutorial-02/Mic-1/tex/Screen-1.jpg**" from the DVD-ROM and **Strength** to 100. In the **Specular** channel, set the **Width** to 40 and **Height** to 65. In the **Specular Color** channel, set the **Texture** to "**Tutorials/ProjectFiles/Chapter 02/Tutorial-02/Mic-1/tex/Screen-1.jpg**" from the DVD-ROM and close the material requester. Drag the screen material to the Microphone icon in the Objects Manager and drag the screen polygon selection into the **Selection** field and change the **Projection** method from UVW Mapping to **Spherical**; set **Tiles X** to 10 and **Tiles Y** to 30.

ON THE DVD

50. Select the Mic object in the Objects Manager. In the perspective view, frame the selected object ("**o**") and render to see the completed microphone.

51. Place a **Floor** at the very bottom of the microphone stand. Add a **Light** and use the top and front views to position the light above and to the right of the microphone. Select the light in the Objects Manager and use the **Objects** menu to choose **Modeling/Instance** to create an instance copy of the light. In the top view, drag the light instance across to the left of the microphone so that it is positioned on the other side of the Z axis (thin blue line). In the Objects Manager, copy and paste the light instance to create a second instance. In the top view, position the second light instance to be behind the microphone such that the original light and the two light instances form an equidistant triangle. Select the original light and set the **Shadow** type and **Brightness** to 60% and render the perspective view for a final look at the modeled microphone (shown in Figure 2.53).

FIGURE 2.53   Finished tutorial.

Summary

Depending on the level of detail required for the finished image, a carefully created material can be more efficient than modeling lots of detailed geometry. Still, depending on the material you create, the memory and CPU resources required to render the final image can prove as challenging as detailed geometry. Planning which method of modeling and texturing each project requires becomes more crucial as the demand for higher-quality 3D images increases.

3

INTERMEDIATE MODELING

In This Chapter

- Tutorial 1: The Prototype Cell Phone
- Tutorial 2: Rotoscope—The Tourist
- Tutorial 3: The Metaball Particle Fountain
- Tutorial 4: iModeller 3D Pro 2.6 and the Doll Head

 Software used: Cinema 4D 9, Hemera PhotoObjects, iModeller 3D Pro 2.6

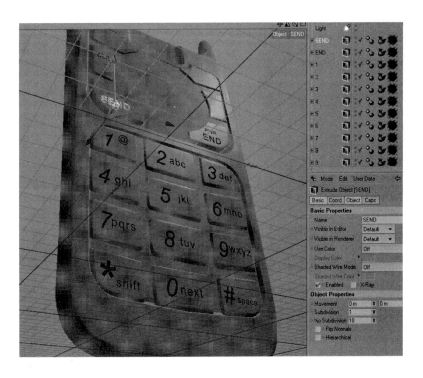

In this chapter, we'll look at four challenging aspects of 3D modeling in Cinema 4D 9. First you will build a complex 3D model of a prototype cell phone based on reference photos of a real cell phone. Then, using a rotoscope Hemera Photo-Object of a tourist, we'll bring photography into the 3D world as an element of the scene and create a 3D composited scene of a tourist listening to a sea shell in the ocean. Then we'll take a quick look at modeling water from a fountain with metaballs, and finally, you will model a doll's head from a series of 20 photos using a process known as photogrammetry.

You will cover the following two "best practices" issues in this chapter:

Object, material and selection naming: While your models will construct correctly and render well without having each hierarchy, material, and selection named, naming them provides the structure required to manage complex scenes, scenes developed between team members, and scenes developed over long periods of time.

Efficient Objects Manager hierarchies (parent–child structures): Though it is ultimately possible to create any project with minimal use of hierarchical structures, it would not only make for an inefficient work flow, but would likely result in less attractive models and animation. If you worked with poseable mannequins in a department store window, just imagine what it would be like if you didn't have the hierarchical structure of the mannequins. You would have to pose the forearm independently of the upper arm. When you turn the torso, you would then have to turn the head, legs, and arms. For this reason and for the efficient distribution of material, the control of object element display, and the application of deformer objects, well-thought-out and efficient hierarchies are valuable friends to the 3D modeler and animator.

Now let's look at the issues involved in modeling two real-world objects (a cell phone and a building) with reference photos, compositing a photo into a 3D scene and modeling with meta balls. These tutorials are also on the accompanying DVD-ROM as video tutorials, along with the tutorial project files.

ON THE DVD

Remember, as you make progress in each tutorial, to save your Cinema 4D projects.

TUTORIAL 1   THE PROTOTYPE CELL PHONE

FIGURE 3.1   A finished render of the cell phone modeled in this tutorial.

Covered in this tutorial:

- Compound Booleans
- Phong tags
- Loop Selection
- 3D text
- Multidocument operation
- Point-based modeling
- HyperNURBS weighting adjustment
- Compositing tag
- Efficient effective hierarchies

Start by building a prototype cell phone polygon model based on reference photos of a real cell phone. Though the reference photos provide us with a design guide, you will take stylistic creative detours from the reference photo design to come up with your prototype model.

This tutorial will be divided into four sections: (1) base plate and keypad keys; (2) joypad (start), materials, and keypad text; (3) joypad (end), poles, and lights; (4) display and product posing. Finished project files for many sections of this tutorial are included on the accompanying DVD-ROM in the tutorials folder. All of the images used in this tutorial are

ON THE DVD

located in "Tutorials/ProjectFiles/Chapter 03/Tutorial-01" on the Projects DVD-ROM. Figure 3.2 provides labeled reference views of the real cell phone against which you will model.

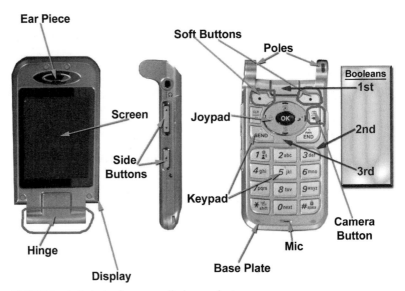

FIGURE 3.2   Labeled reference cell phone photos.

Base Plate and Keypad Keys

1. To model our cell phone based on the reference image of Figure 3.2, you start by adding the reference image "**Tutorials/ProjectFiles/ Chapter 03/Tutorial-01/Keypad-1.png**" to the front viewport and "**Tutorials/ProjectFiles/Chapter 03/Tutorial-01/RightSide-1. png**" to the right viewport and use the local menu to set both front and right viewports to **Gouraud Shading**. Add a primitive **Cube** and check the **X-Ray** and **Fillet** options. Then in the front view, shape the cube to match the width and height of the cell phone base plate in the reference image and make the cube editable. Only the bottom of this fillet cube will match the reference image at this point.

 To add a reference image to a viewport, in the viewport's local menu, choose Edit/ Configure. In the Attributes Manager, Back tab, Image field, Browse to select the image you wish to add to that viewport.

 If the cube's corner parametric handle cannot be moved past the point where you need it, increase the depth of the cube in the right view.

2. In **Default** mode (not Tweak mode), in **Point** mode and still in the front view, use the **Rectangle Selection** tool (**Only Select Visible Elements** unchecked) to select the upper fillet points and delete them. In the right view, delete all points in the left and right fillets, leaving only one center row of points (shown in Figure 3.3).

3. Then move those points in the front view to match the base plate in the reference image (shown in Figure 3.4).

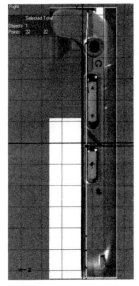

FIGURE 3.3   One row of points remains.

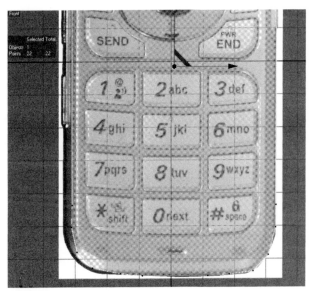

FIGURE 3.4   Points moved to match the reference image base plate.

4. Move the top points to the top of the base plate and from the Main menu, choose **Structure/Add Point** to add eight points as shown in Figure 3.5.

5. With the **Move** tool, switch to **Tweak** mode and move the points at the bottom of the base plate to match the reference image. Then use the **Create Polygon** tool (from the **Structure** menu) to connect the points along the edge of the reference image in the front view. This will form an N-gon (polygon with more than four sides).

6. In **Polygon** mode extrude this base plate polygon to be one-quarter as thick as the cell phone base plate in the right view.

Holding the "v" key on the keyboard brings up floating menu access to many of the modeling tools. Pressing the "M" key once pops up a menu to access tools as well. For example M~S would mean press the M key once and then press S to get the Bevel tool.

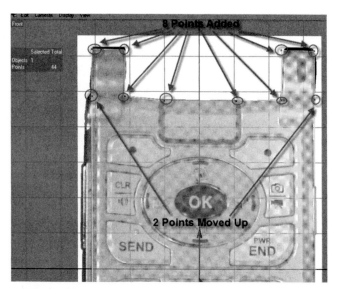

FIGURE 3.5   Add eight points to match the reference image base plate and poles.

7. To straighten the edges of the base plate polygon, six groups of points must be selected and straightened with the **Set Point Value** tool (**Structure** menu). For the first set of points, in the front view with the **Live Selection** tool (**Only Select Visible Elements** unchecked), switch to **Point** mode. Select the first three sets of points (point group 1; Figure 3.6) on the right side of the extruded polygon, going from the top down. They should form a straight vertical line but are currently not centered with each other because of the difference between the reference photo and the orthogonal (having no perspective visual scaling) front viewport. From the **Structure** menu, choose **Set Point Value** and set the **X** to Center, ensuring that **Y** and **Z** are set to Leave, and then click **Apply**. Use this technique now to straighten the top three sets of points on the left side (point group 2), the top four sets of points of the poles (point group 3), the bottom four sets of points of the poles (point group 4), the top two center sets of points of the base plate (point group 5), and the bottom two sets of points of the base plate (point group 6).

This centers the selected points in the X axis relative only to their position so they do not move to the center of the polygon or the work space but are centered at the same location in the X axis.

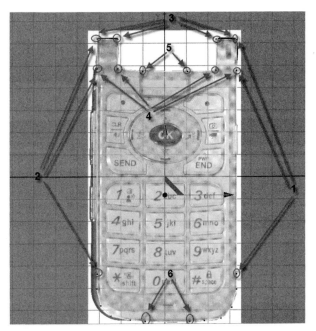

FIGURE 3.6   Select the points circled above and straighten them with Set Point Value.

8. To separate the two poles into two polygons, make a knife cut at the base of each pole (shown in Figure 3.7). This allows you to use modeling tools (such as beveling) on the large base plate polygons without causing interference on the small pole polygons.
9. In the right view, bevel (keyboard shortcut = M~S) the large front base plate polygon so that the beveled polygon reaches the front of the base plate in the reference image. Then use **Extrude Inner** (**Structure** menu) to create a very defined edge for this new beveled polygon.
10. In the Objects Manager select the cube's **Phong tag** and in the Attributes Manager set the **Phong Angle** to 45 degrees. Then add a **HyperNURBS** as the cube's parent. In the HyperNURBS' Attributes Manager, change the **Type** to Catmull Clark.

The Phong tag allows you to control how smoothed polygons will look when rendered. Without this tag, even with lots of polygons, a ball could still look faceted close up when rendered. When modeling rigid geometry such as in architecture, reducing the phong angle allows for sharp edges and visibly flat surfaces. Phong coupled with HyperNURBS can make objects with few polygons appear to be very smooth and sophisticated.

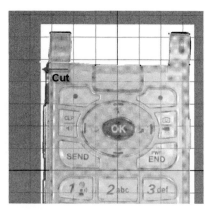

FIGURE 3.7 Two knife cuts at the base of the poles.

11. Add a primitive **Cube** and check its **X-Ray** and **Fillet** functions. Shape and position the cube at the top of the base plate at the first bevel (labeled earlier in Figure 3.2). In the right view, position the cube so that the fillet intersects with the base plate (shown in Figure 3.8).

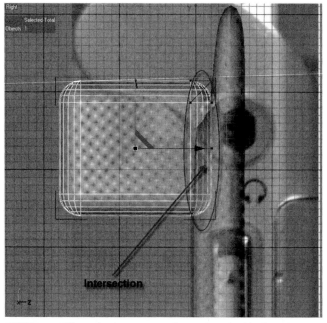

FIGURE 3.8 Fillet cube intersecting base plate for first bevel.

12. Now add a **Boolean**. Place the fillet cube into the Boolean first and then put in the HyperNURBS. Render the perspective view to see the result (shown in Figure 3.9).

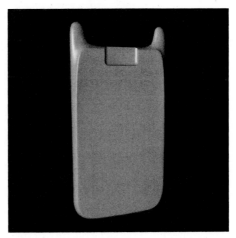

FIGURE 3.9   First Boolean.

13. Add a primitive **Cube** and check its **X-Ray** and **Fillet** functions. Shape and position the cube at the top of the base plate at the second bevel (shown earlier in Figure 3.2) and make the cube editable. In the right view, delete all points in the right side fillet.
14. In the front view, in **Polygon** mode, deselect all polygons. Then use the **Knife** tool to make a cut down the center (**Restrict To Selection**, **Visible Only** unchecked) from the top to the bottom of the cube (shown in Figure 3.10). In **Point** mode, use the **Live Selection** tool (**Only Select Visible Elements** unchecked) to drag the new bottom column of points (created by the last knife cut) down slightly to match the second Boolean in the reference image.
15. In the Objects Manager, turn off the Boolean's **Editor Display Switch** (red). Orbit the perspective view to see the hollow side of the cube that will cut the second Boolean. In **Polygon** mode, use the **Close Polygon Hole** tool (**Structure** menu) and hover over the hollow open cube until a large yellow polygon becomes highlighted. Click once to close the polygon hole. This creates a new polygon.

 An object must have volume in order to perform a Boolean cut, and the two objects must overlap each other.

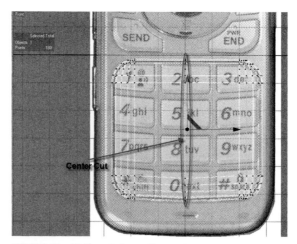

FIGURE 3.10 Knife cut down the center.

16. Using the **Live Selection** tool (**Only Select Visible Elements** checked), select the newly created polygon. Orbit your perspective view back to the original orientation so that the fillet side of the cube faces you. In the right view, in **Model** mode, move the fillet cube so that it touches the edge of the base plate. **Bevel** (**Structure** menu) the selected polygon to create the depth of the second Boolean (shown in Figure 3.11).

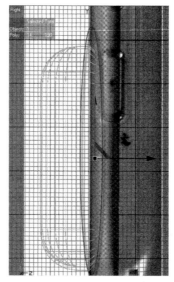

FIGURE 3.11 Bevel for second Boolean.

17. In the Objects Manager, group (**Alt-G**) the cubes from the first and second Booleans. This creates a new object called "**Null Object**." Make that null object the second child of the "Boole" to cause both cubes to boolean the HyperNURBS.

Because two objects cannot boolean with a third object, placing two or more objects into a null object allows any number of objects (collectively seen as a single null object) to boolean with another object. While this technique is effective, care should be taken to not have objects within a null overlap each other to avoid unpredictable results.

18. Set the second Boolean cube's Phong tag's **Phong Angle** to 25 degrees. This prevents the second Boolean from appearing to bulge when rendered.

19. From the **Main** menu, choose **Objects/Polygon Object** to add a Polygon object. Switch to **Point** mode in the front view. Use the shape of the third Boolean as your guide and add points symmetrically so that for every point on the left, there is a corresponding point on the right. Use the **Move** tool in **Tweak** mode to adjust the position of the points to more closely match the reference image as necessary. From the **Structure** menu, use **Create Polygon** and follow along, clicking on the points to make the polygon. To close and finish the polygon, make sure the last point you click on is also the first point you started with. Last, check the polygon's **X-Ray** option and switch to **Model** mode.

20. In the right view, move the polygon left to make room for an extrusion. **Extrude** (**Create Caps** checked) the polygon and **Bevel** so that it intersects with the base plate. Then drag the polygon into the hierarchy with the other two cubes (shown in Figure 3.12).

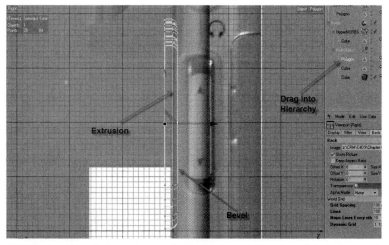

FIGURE 3.12   Extruded and beveled polygon for third Boolean (labeled earlier in Figure 3.2).

21. With the **Ctrl** key held down, drag a **Phong** tag from one of the other cube objects to this object and set the **Phong Angle** to 25 degrees.

22. In the front view, using the process performed in step 19, create a polygon to match the first soft button (Figure 3.13). Check the **X-Ray** option for this object.

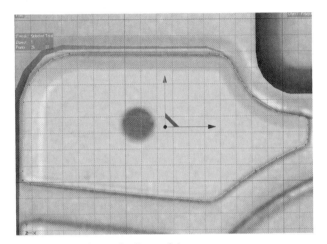

FIGURE 3.13   Polygon for first soft button.

23. **Bevel** this polygon and use the **Move** tool in **Tweak** mode to move the beveled polygon's points to match the bevel in the reference image. Then add a slight **Extrude Inner** (**Structure** menu) to sharpen the top edge (shown in Figure 3.14).

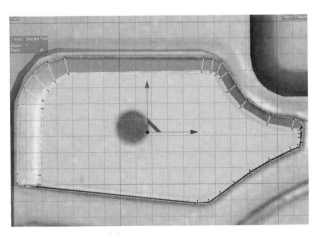

FIGURE 3.14   First soft button.

24. Copy a **Phong** tag to this object and set the **Phong Angle** to 25 degrees. Add a **HyperNURBS** object as parent and set the **Type** to Catmull-Clark. Now model all the remaining keypad keys using the technique shown in steps 22 to 24 (Figure 3.15). This would be a great time to save your work so far. In the main menu, while using the **File/Save As** will allow you to save your project, using **File/Save Project** puts all image files and 3D data into a folder so that you won't have to go hunting for the required images later.

 Getting in the habit of saving incremental versions (Cellphone-01, Cellphone-02, Cellphone-03) of your projects not only allows you to revert to an earlier version to recover your steps, but it also provides a way to use the elements of a project in future projects before those elements are irreversibly converted (e.g., a parametric object to a polygon object).

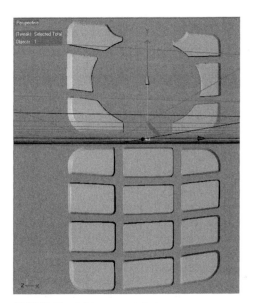

FIGURE 3.15   All keys modeled.

Joypad (start), Materials, and Keypad Text

25. In the Objects Manager, with the **Shift** key held down, select the polygon object for each of the keypad keys. Then from the **Functions** menu, choose **Connect** to create a new object at the top of the hierarchy named "**Polygon**." This new polygon object contains the polygons from all of the keypad keys. You can now delete all of the original polygon objects and their HyperNURBS to clean up the hierarchy.

26. Now you will create a new material named "**Sky**." It will be seen later in reflections on the cell phone. In the **Color** channel, select "**Tutorials/ProjectFiles/Chapter 03/Tutorial-01/CLOUD_01.jpg**" from the Chapter 03/Tutorial-01 folder on the DVD-ROM. Uncheck the **Specular** channel and close the Material Editor. From the main menu, add a **Sky** object (**Objects/Scene/Sky**) and drag the Sky material onto the Sky object in the Objects Manager. In the Objects Manager, from the File menu choose **CINEMA 4D Tags/Compositing** to add a compositing tag to the sky object. In the Attributes Manager, uncheck **Seen by Camera**, **Cast Shadows**, and **Receive Shadows**.

ON THE DVD

27. To create the main cell phone metallic material, create a new material named "**Main**" and set the **Color** channel **Color** to **Red** = 255, **Green** = 243, and **Blue** = 206. In the **Reflection** channel, set the **Brightness** to 10% to reflect the sky object. In the **Environment** channel, select the "**Tutorials/ProjectFiles/Chapter 03/Tutorial-01 /Desert-1.jpg**" from the Chapter 03/Tutorial-01 folder on the DVD-ROM for the Texture. Set the **Environment Color** to **Red** = 255, **Green** = 237, and **Blue** = 235. To cause this metallic material to reflect without showing what is being reflected, set the **Blur Offset** to 98% and **Blur Scale** to 22%. In the **Specular** channel, set the **Mode** to Metal and the **Height** to 58%, then close the Material Editor.

28. In the Objects Manager, rename "Boole" as "**BasePlate**" and "HyperNURBS" as "**Keys**." Group Keys and BasePlate and name the new null object "**Cell Phone**."

It's OK to use spaces and non-alphanumeric characters in object names in Cinema 4D. These names are used internally in the program and do not affect file names when saving the project to disk.

29. Drag the metallic material onto Cell Phone in the Objects Manager.

30. Near the Objects Manager, click on the **Browser** tab and use the menu **File/Import File** and browse to the file "**Tutorials/ProjectFiles/Chapter 03/Tutorial-01 /Keypad-1.png**" (shown in Figure 3.16).

31. To build the text for the SEND button, use the main menu **Objects/ Spline Primitive/Text** to add a text object. In the **Object** tab of the Attributes Manager, change "Text" to "**SEND**." In the top view, use the **Move** tool to position the text object to be just slightly in front of the keys in the keypad. With the text object selected and with the **Alt** key held down, add an **Extrude NURBS** object to make the text object its child. In the Objects Manager, rename "Extrude NURBS" as "**SEND**" and rename "Text" as "**SEND**."

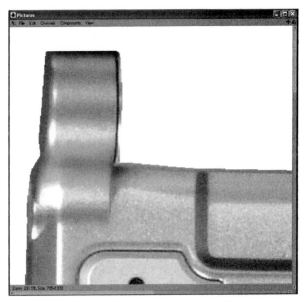

FIGURE 3.16   Cinema 4D browser displays a reference image.

The reason for adding an Extrude NURBS object as the parent of a text object is that it makes the text visible in the renderer since splines are 2D and have no surface or volume.

32. Make sure that **X-Ray** is checked for the Keys object so that you can see the reference image through the keys. This is necessary for positioning and scaling the text objects to match the reference image. In the front view, use the **Move** and **Scale** tools to shape and position the text object to match the text on the SEND key in the reference image.
33. In the Objects Manager, select the SEND Extrude NURBS object. In the Attributes Manager, in the **Objects** tab, change the **Z** (third field to the right in the top row) from 20 to 0.5 to create flat text, like the thickness of paint (shown in Figure 3.17).

While an image of text could be loaded, modeling text gives the sharpest letters that render perfectly at any resolution and from any distance.

FIGURE 3.17   Extrude NURBS text object over reference image.

34. Now add a **Light** from the main toolbar. Use the top and front views to position the light above and to the right of the cell phone (shown in Figure 3.18). In the Attributes Manager, set the **Shadow** to Soft.

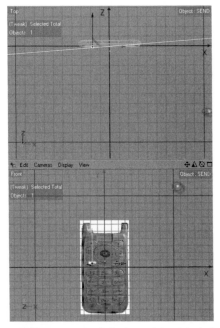

FIGURE 3.18   Point light in position (circled above).

35. With the **Ctrl** key held down, in the Objects Manager, drag a copy of the **Compositing** tag from the Sky object onto the SEND Extrude NURBS object. In the Attributes Manager **Tag** tab, check **Seen by Camera** and uncheck **Cast Shadows** and **Receive Shadows**. In the perspective view, position the SEND Extrude NURBS to be just slightly above the surface of its key in the keypad and render (shown in Figure 3.19).

FIGURE 3.19   Well-positioned SEND Extrude NURBS.

36. Next you'll need to create the material for the keypad text. Create a new material named "**Text**" and set the **Color** channel **Brightness** to 8%. Close the Material Editor and drag this new material to the SEND Extrude NURBS in the Objects Manager.

37. In the Objects Manager, make a copy of the SEND object. Name the copy "**END**" and edit the text content to END as well. In the front view, position the END Extrude NURBS object to match the END button in the reference image.

38. **Ctrl** drag (hold the **Ctrl** key down and drag) a copy of the END Extrude NURBS object into its Text object so that the END hierarchy becomes four levels deep (shown in Figure 3.19). Rename this new Extrude NURBS "**PWR**" and edit its text object contents to PWR. Move and scale the PWR Extrude NURBS to match the reference image (shown in Figure 3.20).

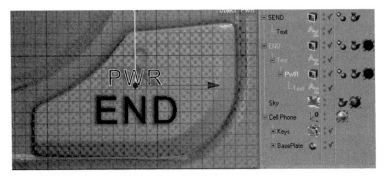

FIGURE 3.20   Extrude NURBS and text within Extrude NURBS and text.

39. Build and position the remaining text objects (shown in Figure 3.21). Don't worry about the two soft buttons and the camera button for now. We'll deal with those shortly.

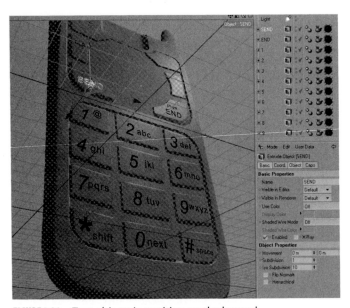

FIGURE 3.21   Text objects in position on the keypad.

40. In the Objects Manager, drag a selection rectangle (shown in Figure 3.21), selecting the Extrude NURBS objects for all text on the cell phone keypad and group (**Alt-g**) them together. Name the new group "**Key Text**" and drag it into the Cell Phone object.

41. Now you'll create the rest of the soft buttons. To create the first button add a primitive **Disc** from the tool bar and check its **X-Ray** function. Set the **Disc Segments** to 1 and **Orientation** to –Z. In the front view, shape and position the disc to match the small black circle in the first soft button in the reference image. Make a copy of this disc and position it on the second soft button, matching the reference image. Drag these two discs into the Key Text in the Objects Manager and drag the Black material from the Materials Manager to the Key Text in the Objects Manager. In the perspective view, with both of the discs in the Key Text selected, hold the Z axis (blue arrow) and position the discs to be just above the surface of the soft buttons. Render the perspective view as you make adjustments to check their proper placement.

42. To create the camera button, go into the Key Text hierarchy and make a copy of the first disc. Rename the disc "**Transmit**" and position it on the camera button (shown in Figure 3.22). In the Materials Manager, make a copy of the Black material and name it "**Red**." Set its **Color** channel **Brightness** to 100%, **Red** = 255, **Green** = 0, and **Blue** = 0 and close the Material Editor.

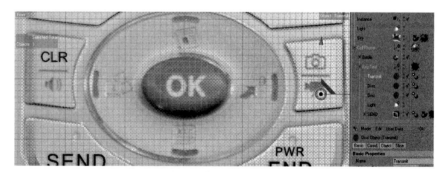

FIGURE 3.22   First Transmit disc in place.

43. For this next step make sure you are in **Default** mode and not Tweak mode (as some tools are not available in Tweak mode). From the **Functions** menu, choose **Duplicate**. Then in the Attributes Manager, **Duplicate** tab, set the **Copies** to 3 (**Generate Instances** checked). In the **Options** tab, set the **Mode** to Linear. Under **Position**, Enable should be checked and **Y** (the second position field) should be set to 25. Under **Scale**, Enable Scale should be checked and the **X** and **Y** (first and second fields) should be set to 50% (half the original scale). In the **Tool** tab, click on **Apply** to activate the object duplication. Until you leave this tool, the settings update instantly and are interactive. In the Objects Manager, you should now

see the Transmit object as well as the Transmit_copies object containing the duplicated instances of Transmit. Your front view and Objects Manager should now look like Figure 3.23.

FIGURE 3.23 Duplication of the Transmit disc.

44. Now group Transmit and "Transmit_copies together and name the new group "**Transmit.**" Drag the **Red** material onto the Transmit object. In the perspective view, with the Transmit group selected and holding the Z axis (blue arrow), position the discs to be just above the surface of the camera button. Render the perspective view as you make adjustments to check their proper placement.

 Remember to adjust the axis position of your objects to give you control over moving, scaling, and rotating them.

45. Now it's time to build the joypad. Start by adding a **Disc** object and set its **Orientation** to –Z with the **X-Ray** function on and make it editable. In the front view, position and shape the disc to match the reference image. In **Point** mode, select the second row of points from the outside (shown in Figure 3.24) and scale them out to make the outer edge of the joypad sharper. Then select the third row of points in and shape their scaling in the **Y** axis. In **Polygon** mode select the two inner rows of polygons and in the perspective view, extrude them with **Create Caps** unchecked (shown in Figure 3.25).

46. To add a little more bulge to the center of the joypad, select the innermost row of points and the center point. Then, with the Z axis in the perspective view, pull them back and slightly away from the cell phone.

47. From the right-hand view select all points in the joypad bulge and drag to the right slightly to pull the points. This causes a depression in the joypad, making the shape more interesting (shown in Figure 3.26).

48. Now add a **HyperNURBS** as parent and then apply the Cellphone material to the joypad Disc object.

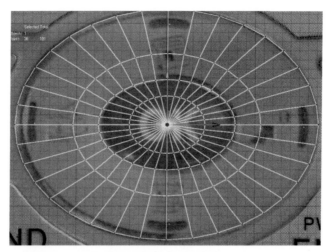

FIGURE 3.24   Second row of points moved close to outer edge.

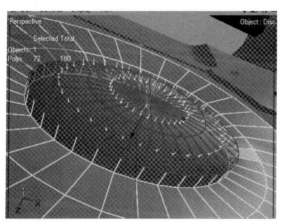

FIGURE 3.25   Inner polygons extruded to make the joypad bulge.

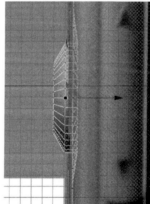

FIGURE 3.26   Joypad depression.

49. Switch to **Polygon** mode and select all polygons in the bulge. Use the **Selection** menu **Set Selection** and name the selection "**glass**." Also, in the Materials Manager menu, choose **File/Shader/Banji** to create a Banji shader and name it "**Glass**." In the **Diffuse** channel, set the **Surface Color** and the **Volume Color** to 128, 255, 128. Apply the new Glass material to the joypad disc and drag the glass selection to the **Selection** field in the Attributes Manager. Your rendered perspective view should now look like Figure 3.27.

FIGURE 3.27   Glass bulge on the joypad.

50. Create a text object (text content = "**OK**", **Font** = Arial Black, **Z depth** = 0.5) and add an **Extrude NURBS** as its parent. Name the Extrude NURBS "**OK**." Then rename the joypad HyperNURBS "**Joypad**." Using the front and right views, position and scale the Extrude NURBS text ("OK") to fit within the joypad bulge. Match this to the reference image. Make the OK text render brightly by adding a **Compositing** tag, unchecking **Cast Shadows** and **Receive shadows**, and checking **Compositing Background** and **Seen by Camera**. Now render the perspective view (shown in Figure 3.28).

FIGURE 3.28   Text object ("OK") within joypad bulge.

In the Compositing tag, the Compositing Background causes the object to render without shading, so its color remains constant. This is an easy way to make objects appear to be self-illuminated. In the material's Luminance channel, increased Brightness values can also be used to make objects appear to be self-illuminated.

51. Now's a good time to clean up your hierarchy. Do so by putting/dragging the OK into the Joypad and then the Joypad into the Cell Phone. Now would also be a good time to save your project to protect the work you've done so far.

Joypad (end), Poles, and Lights

52. To create the four curved cuts around the edge of the joypad, add a primitive **Cube** and check the **X-Ray** function. Then set **Segments X** and **Y** to 2. In the front view, position and shape the cube to match the top joypad cut in the reference image. Press "**o**" to frame the cube in the front view. In the right view adjust the depth of the cube to intersect with the base plate (shown in Figure 3.29).

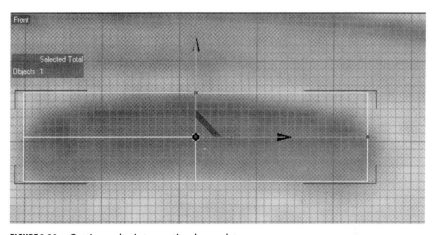

FIGURE 3.29   Cutting cube intersecting base plate.

53. Make the cube editable. In **Point** mode, in the front view, move the center points up (shown in Figure 3.30). At this point you'll want to add a **HyperNURBS** as parent and check the HyperNURBS **X-Ray**.
54. Make three copies of the HyperNURBS and position and rotate them so all four HyperNURBS match the slotted cut holes in the reference image.

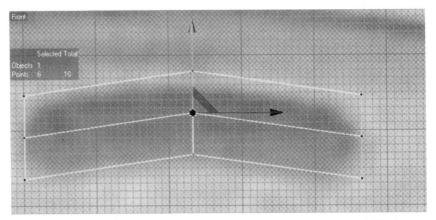

FIGURE 3.30   Cube center row of points moved up to create a curve once within the HyperHURBS.

55. Group (**Alt-g**) the four HyperNURBS objects and place the group within the Cell Phone object. Add a **Boole** object and check its **X-Ray**. Place first the HyperNURBS group into the Boolean, then the joypad. Frame the Boolean in the perspective view and render. At this point you will see a HyperNURBS problem (shown in Figure 3.31). The "OK" text is smooth, but the joypad is not. This is because the HyperNURBS object can only operate on one child object. This means you need to change the joypad hierarchy (shown in Figure 3.31). Move the Disc object to be the first child object in the Hyper-NURBS to correct this.

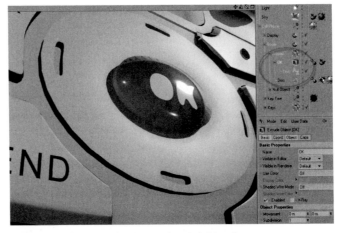

FIGURE 3.31   HyperNURBS hierarchical child order error.

56. Now, to finish modeling the base plate, add some detail to the model by adding a thin vertical gap in the base plate. Select the base plate cube (shown in Figure 3.32). Switch to **Polygon** mode and the **Live Selection** tool (**Only Select Visible Elements** checked) and orbit the perspective view to see the back of the cell phone plate. Select only the single large back polygon. **Extrude Inner** just a little bit (shown in Figure 3.33) to define the depth of the gap. Then **Extrude** a little to define the width of the gap. Go back to **Extrude Inner**, but make the extruded polygon larger this time to match the original size of the back plate. To make sure this last Extrude Inner is the correct size, do it from the front view. Then apply a **Bevel** and **Extrude Inner** to the selected back polygon to match Figure 3.34.

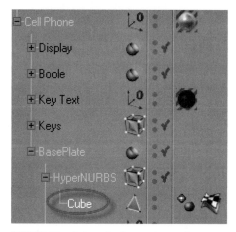

FIGURE 3.32   Select the base plate cube.

FIGURE 3.33   First Extrude Inner applied to base plate back polygon.

57. Next, add a point **Light** above and to the right of the cell phone. Use the front and top views to establish proper placement of the light. In the Attributes Manager, in the **General** tab, set the **Shadow** to Soft. In the **Shadow** tab, set the **Shadow Map** to 1000 × 1000, **Sample Radius** to 4, and **BIAS** (Abs) to 4 for a shadow that casts closely and more realistically in our scene. Add two **Instances** of the light, placing one instance in front the object, across from the original light. Center the second instance of the light behind the cell phone. Check that your light placement matches Figure 3.35.

58. To finish building the two poles, in the front view, in **Polygon** mode, use the **Live Selection** tool (**Only Select Visible Elements** unchecked) and select all of the polygons for the two poles. Use the **Knife** (**Restrict To Selection**, **Visible Only** unchecked) to make two cuts (shown in Figure 3.36).

FIGURE 3.34 Bevel and last Extrude
Inner applied to base plate back
polygon.

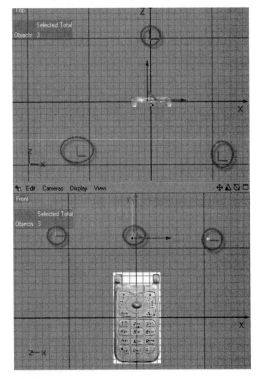

FIGURE 3.35 One light and two instances (circled in
the above image).

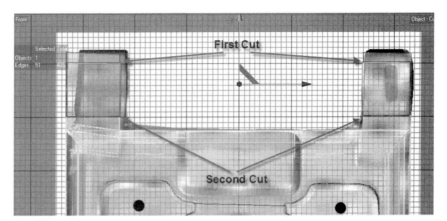

FIGURE 3.36   Two cuts on the two poles.

59. With the **Live Selection** tool (**Only Select Visible Elements** checked), select the main center polygon on each pole in the front view. **Extrude** the polygons in the perspective view. Make sure the BasePlate HyperNURBS is on (green check mark) and use the extruded polygon's Z axis in the perspective view (blue arrow) to position the extruded end of the poles to match Figure 3.37.

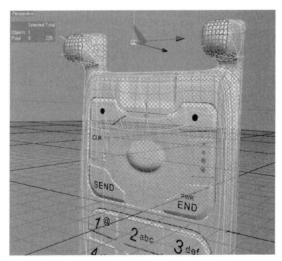

FIGURE 3.37   Extruded pole polygons in position.

60. To give the poles more definition, from the **Functions** menu, choose **Subdivide** (Subdivision 1) and click **OK**. Turn the HyperNURBS off and select the poles' center end points and position them as shown in Figure 3.38.

When subdividing polygon objects in HyperNURBs, to make them appear more detailed and defined, use a higher subdivision value.

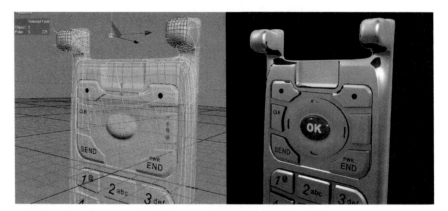

FIGURE 3.38   Poles' center end points moved into position.

Display and Product Posing

61. Now it's time to model the display unit for our cell phone. In the **Main** menu, go to the **File** menu and choose **New** to create a new document. In the top view, set the reference image to "**Tutorials/ProjectFiles/ Chapter 03/Tutorial-01/Display-1.png.**"(local menu **Edit/Configure—Attributes Manager, Back** tab **Image**). Add a primitive **Cube**. Shape and position it (with **Fillet** and **X-Ray** checked) to match the reference image shown in Figure 3.39).

The cube matches only to top of the reference image at this point.

62. Make the cube editable. Then in the front view, switch to **Point** mode and delete the top and bottom points, leaving only the middle two rows of points that form the flat row of polygons (shown in Figure 3.40).

63. In the right view delete the polygons to the left, leaving the polygon object open on the left side. To close these polygons, switch to **Edge** mode and select the two edges on the left open end of the object and **Bridge** (**Structure** menu) them together (shown in Figure 3.41). From the **Structure** menu, choose the **Close Polygon Hole** tool and close the inside bottom and top polygons (shown in Figure 3.41).

64. In the top view, drag the bottom polygon (created by bridging the two edges) to the bottom of the display in the reference image (not to the bottom of the hinge).

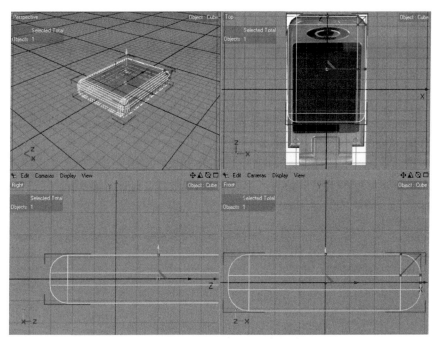

FIGURE 3.39   The fillet cube matches the top of the display (top view) and is shaped to have a flat side row (right view).

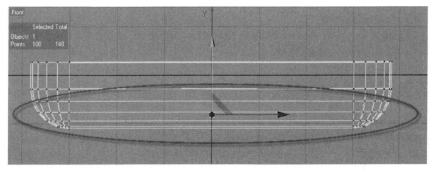

FIGURE 3.40   The top points have been deleted. The bottom points (circled above) are about to be deleted, leaving only the two center rows of points.

65. In the top view, with the **Live Selection** tool (**Only Select Visible Elements** checked), select the large flat polygon over the blue screen in the reference image. **Bevel** and **Extrude Inner** to create edges similar to that of the base plate.

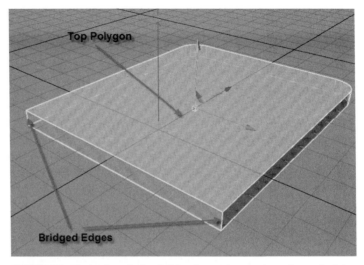

FIGURE 3.41   Two edges being bridged together to close the end of the object. The top polygon being closed by the Close Polygon Hole tool.

66. With the perspective view on the left and the top view on the right, select the bottom polygon. Use the **Knife** tool (**Restrict To Selection**, **Visible Only** unchecked) and in the top view, make two vertical cuts to this end polygon just along the edge of the hinge in the reference image (shown in Figure 3.42).

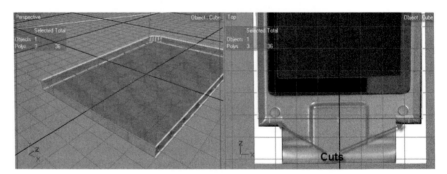

FIGURE 3.42   The display polygon that leads to the hinge gets two cuts.

67. Now, from those three end polygons, select the center polygon and **Extrude** it the length of the hinge in the reference image. At this time you'll need more geometry to work with so in the Attributes Manager, in the **Options** tab, set the **Subdivision** value to 3. Deselect all polygons and hit "**k**" to get the **Knife** tool and cut the hinge polygons

along the inside of the Boolean in the reference image. In our prototype cell phone, you will not be making a Boolean here. You will add
some unique style.

68. In the top view, on the hinge, select the two outer sets of polygons
and scale them down (shown in Figure 3.43).

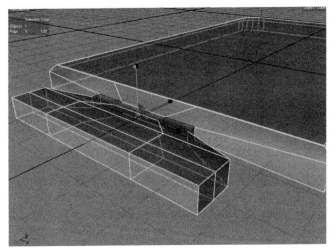

FIGURE 3.43   The two outer sets of polygons scaled down.

69. In the right view, select points that form the left-most polygons at the
end of the hinge and scale them down so they taper. Then add a **HyperNURBS** as parent and set the **Type** to Catmull-Clark.

70. In the top view, with the **Knife** tool (**Restrict To Selection** unchecked, **Visible Only** checked) make a horizontal cut across the entire display at the top of the chrome that borders the blue screen.
Make a similar cut at the bottom of the chrome as well. This divides
the large display polygon into three pieces. Make a vertical cut from
the top to the bottom of the chrome surrounding the blue screen
(along the inner edge that borders the blue screen). Do this on both
the left and right sides. This divides the screen polygon into three
pieces. Then select the polygon that now covers the chrome and blue
screen and use the **Extrude Inner** tool to create a new polygon
(dragging the mouse until the new polygon's vertical lines touch the
vertical edges of the blue screen). Move the points of this new screen
polygon so the new center polygon matches the shape of the screen
in the reference image. In the perspective view, select and **Extrude**
the center screen polygon down (shown in Figure 3.44).

FIGURE 3.44 Display screen modeled.

71. Select all polygons for the screen and the chrome frame (shown in Figure 3.45). **Subdivide** the selected polygons with a **Subdivision** value of 2 (shown in Figure 3.45).

 It may be necessary to alternate the HyperNURBS between on and off (Q) while selecting these polygons in the perspective view to be sure that they (and only they) are all selected.

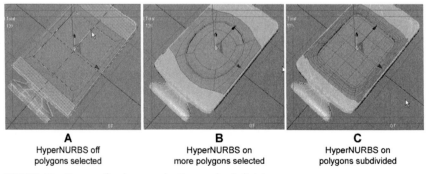

| **A** | **B** | **C** |
| HyperNURBS off polygons selected | HyperNURBS on more polygons selected | HyperNURBS on polygons subdivided |

FIGURE 3.45 Stages of polygon selection and subdivision.

72. In **Polygon** mode and in the right view, select the polygons at the left end of the hinge. These are the polygons that don't scale down to connect to the display. On the keyboard, hold the **period** key down

and drag to the right to see the HyperNURBS decrease the smoothing influence on the selected polygons. You are making this adjustment so that the point where the display connects to the cell phone will look functional and attractive.

73. To define which area of the display will show the communications data, select the 16 polygons in the screen area as well as the row of polygons immediately outside of them and create a polygon selection named "**screen.**"

74. To model the ear piece, start by adding a primitive **Cylinder**. Set the **Rotation Segments** to 16, **X-Ray** on, and make it editable. Switch to the **Model** mode in the top view and use the **Move** and **Scale** tool to match the cylinder to the basic shape of the ear piece in the reference image. Using the **Live Selection** tool (**Only Select Visible Elements** unchecked) and the **Scale** tool, select and scale the rows of points to more closely match the ear piece in the reference image. In **Polygon** mode, select the second row of polygons from the outside and the center row of polygons (shown in Figure 3.46).

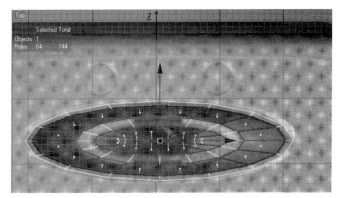

FIGURE 3.46   Ear piece early modeling steps.

75. In the right view, drag the selected polygons down just enough to cause the indentation seen in the top view reference image. Then add a **HyperNURBS** as parent. Name this new HyperNURBS "**Earpiece**" and the original HyperNURBS "**Display.**" In the right view position the ear piece so it intersects with the display but does not pass the second line (shown in Figure 3.47).

76. Add a Boolean object and name it "**Display.**" Then drag the ear piece into the display.

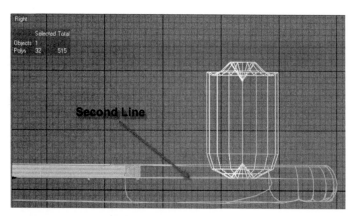

FIGURE 3.47 Ear piece positioned for Boolean.

By default, Cinema 4D turns on High Quality on new Booleans. To speed up your display while modeling, uncheck High Quality. It is best to turn it back on before final rendering. If you are not using a video card with great performance, this may speed up your work flow.

77. Copy the Boolean display object and go back to the original cell phone document (project) and paste to add the display to the cell phone. Turn off all reference images. Move and scale the display to make necessary adjustments so the hinge of the display fits in between the cell phone poles. Make sure the Display axis is at the end of the hinge so that the display will be able to rotate predictably just like a real flip cell phone (shown in Figure 3.48).

78. Now it's time to pose the display as though you were making an ad for this prototype cell phone. In the perspective view, use the **Rotate** tool and drag the **X** axis (red band) to rotate the display. Play around with it until you find an attractive pose. Orbit the perspective view to a pleasing presentation angle, then drag the display into the cell phone. Uncheck **X-Ray** on all objects to speed up Cinema 4D's display.

79. To bring the display screen to life, add a new material named **"Screen"** and load **"Tutorials/ProjectFiles/Chapter 03/Tutorial-01/DisplayScreen-2.jpg"** from the DVD-ROM into the Texture of the Color channel. To make the screen appear to be lit, in the **Luminance** channel, set the **Texture** to **"DisplayScreen-2.jpg,"** **Brightness** to 0, and **Mix Strength** to 50%. Drag this new material to the cube within the HyperNURBS in the Display Boolean. Drag the polygon selection screen into the **Selection** field in the Attributes Manager to limit this image map to the screen.

ON THE DVD

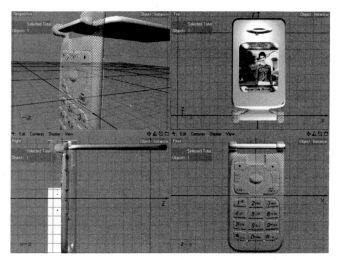

FIGURE 3.48   Display and its axis in final position before posing.

80. If you render the perspective view, you will notice that the orientation of the material is not yet correct, so first, in the Objects Manager,
turn off the editor and renderer display switches for the rest of the
cell phone. Make sure that you are in **Model** mode and select the
Display object. Use the Coordinates Manager to set its **Bank** to 90
degrees. On the cube within the Display Boolean, select the Screen
material, and in the Attributes Manager, change the **Projection
Type** to Flat and uncheck **Tiling**. Select the **Object Axis** tool, and in
the Coordinate Manager, set **P** to −90 degrees. In the front view,
switch to the **Use Texture** tool and use the **Move** and **Scale** tools to
correct the position and scale of the image map on the screen. A front
view render of the display model is shown in Figure 3.49.
81. Turn all display switches back on and switch to **Model** mode. Then
pose the display again with the rotate tool.
82. To add a microphone to the cell phone, add a primitive **Cylinder**
and drag it into the cell phone and set its **Height Segments** to 1 and
Orientation to –Z. Shape and position the cylinder in the front and
right view. Be sure the cylinder does not protrude through the bottom of the base plate. Name the cylinder "**Mic**" and drag it into the
group of objects that cut the three Booleans in the base plate. (The
mic now also cuts into the base plate.)
83. Add a **Floor** object and rotate it 90 degrees in the pitch (**P** in the Coordinates Manager) and move it to be a floor for the cell phone. Render
and adjust the original light brightness to get the scene mood that you
wish. The perspective view render should look like Figure 3.50 now.

FIGURE 3.49   Front view render of the display with the corrected image map.

FIGURE 3.50   Finished prototype cell phone.

Summary

Depending on the level of detail required for the finished image, a carefully created material can be more efficient than modeling lots of detailed geometry. Still, depending on the material you create, the memory and CPU resources required to render the final image can prove as challenging as detailed geometry, so planning which method of modeling and texturing each project requires becomes more crucial as the demand for higher-quality 3D images increases.

A close look at the structure of the hierarchy of this tutorial demonstrates why proper planning and hierarchies are so important. Also note that though you may have to deviate from the photo perspective distortion when modeling against a reference image, it's important to develop consistent rules of how you will deviate. This is essential to creating great real-world production 3D models.

TUTORIAL 2   **ROTOSCOPE—THE TOURIST**

FIGURE 3.51   Finished render of the tourist Photo-Object composited into the 3D ocean scene.

Covered in this tutorial:

- Creating seamless image textures in Photoshop
- Compositing 2D photos in 3D space
- Subpolygon displacement mapping

- Render effects: Highlights
- Volumetric lighting
- Hemera Photo-Objects

In this tutorial, you will composite a Hemera Photo-Object (*http://www.hemera.com*) of a tourist listening to a sea shell into a 3D scene of ocean, sky, and the visible sun in Cinema 4D. This powerful technique will be used to create an image that combines reality and digital fantasy to produce a commercial-grade believable image.

While photographs provide believable imagery, it isn't always possible to photograph a scene to perfection. Photo retouching adds some possibilities, but rotoscoping the photo into the 3D world for an immersive composite offers levels of control that can produce imagery previously only imagined.

A rotoscope is a device that enabled animators to trace live action movement, frame by frame, for use in animation. The rotoscope was invented around 1914 by Max Fleischer and influenced many modern animation support technologies such as motion capture. For the scope of this tutorial, rotoscoping will be limited to the image of a person extracted from a photo and placed into 3D space.

In this tutorial, you will use a Photo-Object from the online subscription service at *http://www.hemera.com*. At this online service, you can search the photo object database to find high-quality photo art useful in both 2D and 3D work. These Photo-Objects are provided as both JPG files for the photo and PNG files for the mask. When using the Hemera.com site, always get both the color and the mask image for working in Cinema 4D.

ON THE DVD

All of the images used in this tutorial are located in "Tutorials/Project-Files/Chapter 03/Tutorial-02" on the DVD-ROM included with this book. Now let's make some magic!

1. You begin by adding a primitive **Plane** and set its **Orientation** to –Z axis, **Width** to 247, and **Height** to 497. The numbers for the width and height are factors of the pixel resolution of the image of the tourist (Photo-Object). Entering the pixel resolution into the Z axis of the primitive plane ensures that your image will maintain its aspect ratio and will not squash or stretch from the original likeness. Since there is no need for detailed geometry in the plane, set the **Width Segments** and the **Height Segments** to 1. Rename this plane "Tourist."

2. Next, create a new material and name it "**Tourist**." Load the "**Tutorials/ProjectFiles/Chapter 03/Tutorial-02/Tutorial-03-src/tex/22519300-Tourist.jpg**" image from the Goodies/Hemera folder on the DVD-ROM into the **Color** channel **Texture**. Load the "**Tutorials/ProjectFiles/Chapter 03/Tutorial-02/Tutorial-03-src/tex/22519319-msk-Tourist.png**" image from the Goodies/Hemera folder on the DVD-ROM into the **Alpha** channel **Texture**. When the Cin-

ON THE DVD

ema 4D requester ("**This image is not in the document search**

path. Do you want to create a copy at the document location?") appears, choose **Yes**. Now change the preview type to **Plane** to see the tourist mapped without a surrounding background. Uncheck the **Specular** channel and drag the Tourist material to the Tourist object in the Objects Manager to see the rotoscope on the perspective view.

3. Now that the tourist is done, let's create the ocean that he's standing in. Start by adding another primitive **Plane**. Set the **Width** to 6500 and the **Height** to 4500. In the Coordinates Manager, set the **Z** to 1700. Rename this plane "**Ocean**" and make it editable. In the perspective view, position the ocean to be at the tourist's knees (shown in Figure 3.52).

FIGURE 3.52   Ocean plane at tourist's knees.

4. To light your scene, start by adding a **Light** and set the **Shadow Type** to Soft and set its position to **X** = 250, **Y** = 300, and **Z** = −240. Name this first light "**Main**" and add another **Light** and set **Visible Light** to Volumetric. Set its position to **X** = −1475, **Y** = 1550, and **Z** = −1925 and rename the light "**Back.**" Set its **Brightness** to 70%, and to make this light add some visibly organic disturbance, set **Noise** to Visibility. In the **Visibility** tab, set the **Outer Distance** to 959 m. Add a third **Light** and set the **Type** to Parallel Spot Square and name it "**Sun.**" To choose the glowing warmth and color of the sun, set the **Color** to **R** = 255, **G** = 128, and **B** = 0 and set **Brightness** to 70. To make this light visible, set the **Visible Light** to Volumetric. In the **Details** tab, set the **Outer Radius** to 819 m and **Aspect Ratio** to

0.1. In the **Visibility** tab, set the **Outer Radius** to 4500 and the **Inner Radius** to 4000. In the Coordinates Manager, rotate the sunlight 180 degrees in the pitch (**P**) and position the sun at **X** = 0, **Y** = 0, and **Z** = 6135. In the top view, make sure that the sunlight is as wide as the ocean (shown in Figure 3.53).

 When creating water, it is important to use multiple lighting sources to cause enough interaction with the refraction (bending of light) in the water.

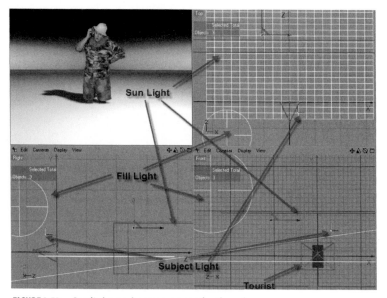

FIGURE 3.53   Sunlight and ocean properly placed.

ON THE DVD

5. To create the clouds, add a primitive **Sphere** and name it "**Clouds**" and set its **Radius** to 6400. Then create a new material and name it "**Clouds.**" Load the "**Tutorials/ProjectFiles/Chapter 03/Tutorial-02/Tutorial-03-src/tex/SUNRIS01.jpg**" from the "**Tutorials/ProjectFiles/Chapter 03/Tutorial-02/Tutorial-03-Rotoscope/Tutorial-03-Rotoscope-01.c4d**" folder on the DVD-ROM into the **Texture** of the **Color** channel and the **Diffusion** channel. Then uncheck the **Specular** channel. To apply this material, drag it onto the clouds object.

6. You've already created the Ocean plane, but now you need to add the material. Create a new material and name it "**Ocean**" and then load the "**Tutorials/ProjectFiles/Chapter 03/Tutorial-02/Tutorial-03-src/tex/Ocean.jpg**" from the "**Tutorials/Project-**

Files/Chapter 03/Tutorial-02/Tutorial-03-Rotoscope/Tutorial-03-Rotoscope-01.c4d" folder on the DVD-ROM to the **Color** channel **Texture** and apply this material to the ocean object. In the Attributes Manager, set the **Length X** and **Length Y** to 25% so that the ocean size looks right.

7. A render of the perspective view (shown in Figure 3.54) shows that you have a problem with the ocean. The image isn't seamless, which creates an unattractive visible repeating pattern.

FIGURE 3.54   Ocean image map repeating pattern.

8. To fix this problem you will use Photoshop CS2. Load the "**Tutorials/ ProjectFiles/Chapter 03/Tutorial-02/Tutorial-03-src/tex/Ocean. jpg**" image into Photoshop and select all (**Ctrl-A**), copy (**Ctrl-C**) and paste four times. Position these four new layers so that their edges meet in the center of the image (shown in Figure 3.55).

9. Now Merge the four linked layers and use the **Erase** tool with a wide soft brush (86 pixels) and erase the seams and fade to reveal the original layer below (shown in Figure 3.56). Save this new image as "**OceanSL-1.jpg**" and exit Photoshop CS2.

10. Now replace the ocean image in the Ocean material with the new seamless image created in Photoshop CS2. To complete the Ocean material, in the **Transparency** channel, load the "**Tutorials/ProjectFiles/ Chapter 03/Tutorial-02/Tutorial-03-src/tex/OceanSL-1.jpg**" from the "**Tutorials/ProjectFiles/Chapter 03/Tutorial-02/Tutorial-03-Rotoscope/Tutorial-03-Rotoscope-01.c4d**" folder on the DVD-ROM as the **Texture** and set the **Refraction** to 1.26. In the **Reflection**

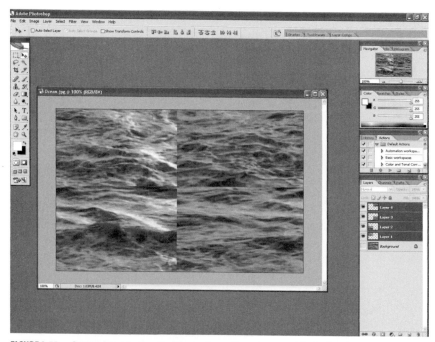

FIGURE 3.55 Ocean image map in Photoshop. Four layers with their edges meeting in the center of the image.

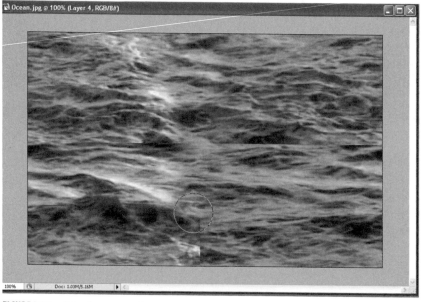

FIGURE 3.56 Seamless ocean image.

channel, set the **Brightness** to 52%. In the **Environment** channel, load the "**Tutorials/ProjectFiles/Chapter 03/Tutorial-02/Tutorial-03-src/tex/Desert-1.jpg**" from the "**Tutorials/ProjectFiles/Chapter 03/Tutorial-02/Tutorial-03-Rotoscope/Tutorial-03-Rotoscope-01.c4d**" folder on the DVD-ROM as the **Texture** and set the **Color** to **R** = 25, **G** = 138, and **B** = 255 and set the **Brightness** to 39. In the **Specular** channel, set the **Width** to 39 and **Height** to 61. In the **Displacement** channel, load "**Tutorials/ProjectFiles/Chapter 03/Tutorial-02/Tutorial-03-src/tex/OceanSL-1.jpg**" as the **Texture** and check the **Sub-Polygon Displacement** and set the **Height** to 15 m.

ON THE DVD

11. The ocean now needs a floor to complete the richness of its color depth. To create this, add a **Floor** object and name it "**Ocean Floor.**" In the front view, position the floor at the bottom of the tourist. Create a new material named "**Ocean Floor.**" Set the **Color** channel to Noise and set the **Noise** to Displaced Voronoi. Set **Color 1** to **R** = 128, **G** = 255, and **B** = 255 and **Color 2** to **R** = 0, **G** = 66, and **B** = 0. Set **Octaves** to 4 and **Global Scale** to 400. Apply this new material to the ocean floor object. In the Attributes Manager, set the **Length X** and **Length Y** to 500. Render the perspective view to see an image similar to Figure 3.57.

FIGURE 3.57   Textures, lighting, and objects completed.

12. For the final touch, add some sparkles to the ocean by clicking the
Render Options icon. In the **Effects** page, in **Post Effects**, select
Highlights. Set **Threshold** to 100%, **Minimum Flare Intensity** to
35%, **Maximum Flare Intensity** to 75%, **Flare Size** to 5%, and
Preset to Sun. Your rendered perspective view should now look like
Figure 3.58.

*Try changing other photo objects from the accompanying DVD-ROM or the
Hemera.com Web site to turn this tutorial into a production project. Increasing the
level of subpolygon displacement in the ocean material can improve the image
quality. Be aware that higher values here demand exponentially higher amounts
of RAM and processing time.*

FIGURE 3.58   Finished tutorial, complete with sparkles.

Summary

This tutorial demonstrates a valuable truth that seemingly complex
scenes are often constructed of a few simple, well-defined parts. Master-
ing materials and lighting can sometimes reduce the need for complex
modeling solutions.

TUTORIAL 3 ### THE METABALL PARTICLE FOUNTAIN

FIGURE 3.59 Finished render of the metaball-based fountain water created in this tutorial.

Covered in this tutorial:

- Metaballs
- Particle emitter
- Particle gravity
- Particle deflectors
- Particle wind
- Particle turbulence
- Motion for modeling

In this tutorial you will build a static shot of fountain water. You will focus on creating a single image of this fountain water but will do so by creating a fully animated environment from which you will choose one great frame.

There are times when motion is a critical and necessary component of a still image. For example, if you were working on a magazine ad and were tasked with creating the image of a flock of birds flying into a gymnasium, it's actually much easier to animate this and then select the best frame and the best viewing angle for your still shot.

We'll be combining particle animation, metaball modeling and the Banji shader to create the illusion of the water in the fountain. As we've previously covered the basic modeling techniques used to construct the objects and environment in the scene, our focus is the water and not the other objects, so you will load the rest of the scene and build the water only.

Particles is probably one of the most mesmerizing and hypnotic areas of 3D animation. After completing this tutorial, take some time to play with the various settings and try placing different objects into the particle emitter just to see what comes out. It's pretty cool!

ON THE DVD

Finished project files of this tutorial are included on the accompanying DVD-ROM in the tutorials folder. All of the images used in this tutorial are located in "Tutorials/ProjectFiles/Chapter 03/Tutorial-03" on the Projects DVD. There is one saved project on the DVD-ROM for this tutorial.

1. To begin, load "Tutorial-03-Fountain.c4d" from the "**Tutorials/ ProjectFiles/Chapter 03/Tutorial-03/**" folder on the DVD-ROM. This loads the sky, ground, fountain step, and fountain base into Cinema 4D. You should render the perspective view to get a sense of the environment before you start building the fountain's water.

2. To make sure that our animation is long enough for the water to get to its full flow of motion, you will set the number of frames in the project to 600 by going to **Edit/Project Settings** in the **Main** menu. Then set **Maximum F** to 600.

3. Create the motion that drives the water by adding a **Particle Emitter** from **Objects** in the main menu. This adds a particle emitter that creates a stream of particles traveling horizontally (click the play button in your Transport Control to see this). To make the stream flow vertically, set the emitter's pitch (**P**) to 90 (degrees) in the Coordinates Manager. The particles will now stream up vertically so that our water will shoot into the air. Also, check the **Emitter** tab in the Attributes Manager and make sure that the **Emitter Type** is Pyramid, **X-Size** and **Y-Size** = 100 m and **Angle Horizontal** and **Angle Vertical** = 0.

4. In the **Particle** tab, set the **Birthrate Editor** (birthrate of particles you will see in Cinema 4D while working on this project) to 150 so that 150 particles (drops of water) will be emitted per second. Do the same for the **Birthrate Renderer** (birthrate of particles you will see in the finished render).

Because the higher the particle birthrate, the slower your software will function, it's usually a good idea to set the editor to a lower number of particles than the renderer so that your screen updates faster. However, in this project, because you will combine metaballs and particles, it's essential that the editor and renderer have the same number of particles. Otherwise it would be very difficult to interactively set up the water to match the final image.

5. Set the **Stop Emission** (when to stop emitting particles) and the **Lifetime** (how long the particles live) to 600 and set the **Speed** to 415 so the water will have a stronger force. You might want to play a little here and see how the emitter works at various speeds. Be sure to set the speed back to 415.

6. Although the particles are moving, they're too uniform and predictable. Water is more organic and algorithmic, so to the right of Lifetime, set the **Variation** to 75% and do the same for the **Speed Variation** and **Scaling Variation**. In the **Emitter** tab, setting the **Angle Horizontal** and **Angle Vertical** both to 5 degrees causes the speed and lifetime variations to be more visible. Play the animation to see a view similar to Figure 3.60.

Because the emitted particles update to reflect changes in the emitter parameters, it's a good idea to first let the emitter emit many particles and then make changes to the emitter parameters. This way, you can have instant feedback to better understand what the various parameters do.

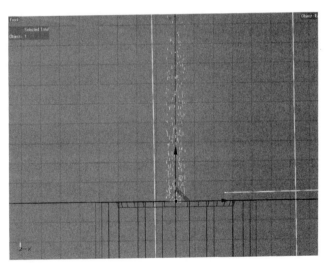

FIGURE 3.60   Fountain particles emitting up.

7. To make the water fall back down to the fountain, you add **Objects/Particle/Gravity** from the main menu. This adds a gravity object that affects only particles and only those within the gravity object's bounding box.

Unlike Earth's gravity, which pulls on all objects on Earth, Cinema 4D's particle gravity operates within a definable space and is seen in the viewport as a yellow box outline. This makes for some interesting animation possibilities where you can have one gravity object causing water to fall to the ground while another gravity object causes some water to fall into the ceiling. The sci-fi applications are endless.

8. In the **Objects** tab in the Attributes Manager, set the **Size** to 5000 m, 2500 m, and 5000 m so that the gravity object will be large enough to affect the particles. Position the gravity object at 740 m in the **Y** axis. Play the animation to see a view similar to Figure 3.61.

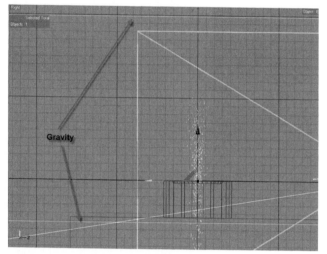

FIGURE 3.61 Fountain particles emitting up and then being pulled down by gravity.

9. In Figure 3.61, you can see that the particles fall right through the fountain. You haven't yet instructed the particles to collide with the fountain or any other objects. So, using the **Main** menu, choose **Objects/Particle/Deflector** to create a plane that the particles can bounce off of. Deflectors act like walls for the particles. So that the deflector matches the size of the base of the fountain, in the Attributes Manager, **Object** tab, set the **Size X** and **Size Y** to 1715 m. Rotate the deflector's **Pitch** 90 degrees and set its **Y** position to –440. When you play the animation now, the particles will fall and bounce on the deflector (shown in Figure 3.62).

10. Now, to make deflectors for the top of the fountain, copy and paste the current deflector. Make this new deflector 600 m in the **X** and **Y**. From

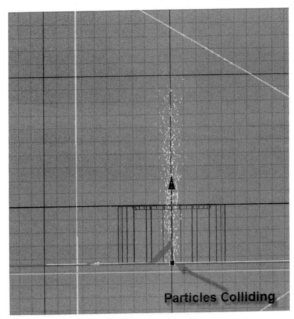

FIGURE 3.62   Particles colliding with the deflector.

the top view, the deflector is overlayed on the fountain. Make three copies of this new deflector and rotate them so that all four of these deflectors now match the shape of the fountain (shown in Figure 3.63).

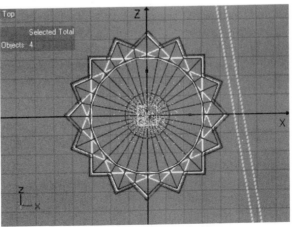

FIGURE 3.63   Four deflectors now match the shape of the fountain.

11. Next, finish shaping the original deflector using the **Scale** tool. Select the first deflector. In the top view, scale the deflector to match Figure 3.64. Then group all deflectors, gravity, and emitter. Name that group **"Particles."**

You can shape the particle objects both by their parameters and by the Scale tool. Depending on where you are in your project, it makes sense to use different methods.

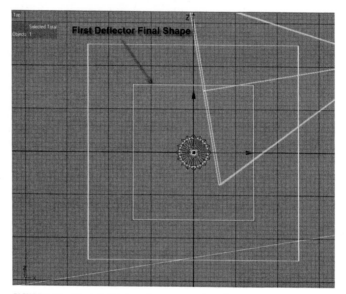

FIGURE 3.64   First deflector shape completed.

12. Group the Particles group with the Disc, Cylinder, and Cube objects and name the new group **"Fountain."**
13. Next we'll add some wind to the scene for a more natural look. To add Earth's elements to the particles, from the **Main** menu choose **Objects/Particle/Wind**. In the Attributes Manager **Object** tab, set the **Wind Size** to 1500 m, 1500 m, and 1500 m and set the **Wind Speed** to 20 for a more dramatic effect (shown in Figure 3.65). Position the wind object to −200 M in the **Z** axis.
14. From the **Main** menu, choose **Objects/Particle/Turbulence**. In the Attributes Manager **Object** tab, set the **Turbulence Size** to 2000 m, 2000 m, and 2000 m. Then drag the wind and turbulence objects into the particles hierarchy in the Objects Manager.

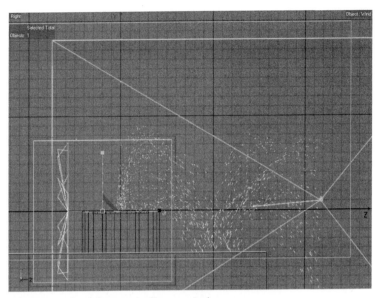

FIGURE 3.65   Particles responding to wind.

Unlike many other object types in Cinema 4D, maintaining the particle hierarchy doesn't affect their interactive performance. It is still a very good practice to structure your hierarchies to reflect operational relationships so that it is effortless to test your options, troubleshoot problems, and integrate various projects together.

15. Although the particles are now moving well, if you render the perspective view, you will see the fountain and the environment but you will not see any particles (shown in Figure 3.66). Particles need to move other objects. It is those objects moved by the particles which can be rendered.

16. To make the particles visible, add a primitive **Sphere** and drag it into the Emitter object within the particle hierarchy. Then in the emitter's attributes, check **Show Objects**. You can see the result immediately. It's interesting, but it's not water. Your fountain now emits spheres and they're much too large. To correct this, set the Sphere **Radius** in the Attributes Manager to 25 m. Render your perspective view to see results similar to Figure 3.67.

To make these spheres look like water, in the Materials Manager, you need to use metaballs and a **Banji shader**.

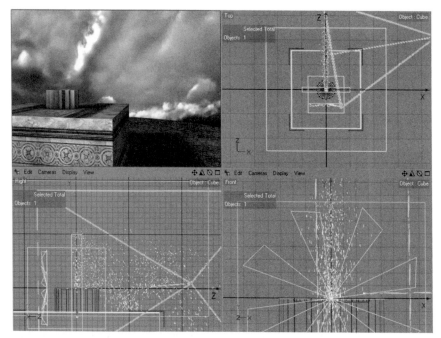

FIGURE 3.66   Particles cannot be rendered.

FIGURE 3.67   Fountain emitting spheres.

17. Start by adding a **Metaball** object from the toolbar (shown in Figure 3.68).

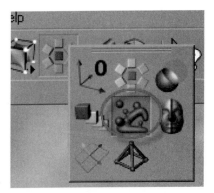

FIGURE 3.68   Selecting the Metaball
object in the toolbar.

18. In the Objects Manager drag the Metaball into the Particles hierarchy
    and drag the Emitter into the Metaball. The result is something a bit
    crazy (shown in Figure 3.69). If this is water, it's mad water.

FIGURE 3.69   Fountain emitting uncontrolled metaball water.

19. Select the metaball object and set its **Editor Subdivision** and **Ren-
    derer Subdivision** to 30 m and check **Exponential Falloff**. Cinema
    4D will take a few moments to calculate the new mesh geometry cre-
    ated by the metaball and then you will see the balls behaving more
    like water. They group together when close together and form indi-
    vidual drops when they travel apart.

20. Drag the Water material on to the metaball object. Rendering your perspective view will give you a sense of how the water renders now (shown in Figure 3.70).

FIGURE 3.70   Fountain emitting water.

21. Last, to get the final image in this project, you will need to go back to frame zero on your transport control and play to about frame 366, but you will quickly find out that because of the very heavy internal math computations required, metaballs can drag even a top of the line workstation to a crawl. So, uncheck the metaball's green check mark in the Objects Manager. It will become a red X. Also, uncheck the sphere inside the emitter and uncheck Show Objects in the Emitter. Then play to frame 366. This allows you to get to frame 366 very quickly. Now check Show Objects in the emitter and turn the sphere and metaball objects back on. Render your perspective view to see the final image of the fountain and water (shown in Figure 3.71).

If you simply try go directly to frame 366, the particles will not be computed correctly and the result will be unpredictable. Particles animation builds each frame of motion based on the parameters set and the position of the particles in the previous frame. That's why it is necessary to play from the start of the animation.

FIGURE 3.71   Fountain final shot.

Summary

In this tutorial, we've seen that not all objects are modeled by moving, dragging, and shaping object elements. We've also seen how it is sometimes necessary to create an animation in order to create a still image. This concept could also be applied to later chapters where you explore using dynamics to apply the Newtonian laws of physics to animation.

Particles are fascinating generator objects. Not only can they emit as we've just seen in the fountain, but they can be animated in their location, scale, rotation, and parameters. Metaballs provide organic dynamic mesh creation that can change shape from frame to frame. Experimenting with the combination of metaballs and particles can prepare you to produce elegant solutions to seemingly daunting real-world production challenges.

TUTORIAL 4   **iMODELLER 3D PRO 2.6 AND THE DOLL HEAD**

Covered in this tutorial:

- Automatic and manual image pattern calibration
- Photoshop masking
- Photogrammetric modeling

FIGURE 3.72 Final Cinema 4D render of the doll head modeled in iModeller 3D using a photogrammetric modeling process

In this tutorial you will model a polygonal doll head for use in Cinema 4D. You won't use any of the modeling tools and techniques covered in the previous tutorials. This time, you'll start with a series of 20 photos of a real doll head placed on a printed calibration pattern and brought into iModeller 3D Pro for processing before you will bring it into a Cinema 4D scene. This tutorial will allow you to explore a completely different method of modeling. This concept should become yet another tool in your arsenal of power skills to handle real-world production challenges.

You'll be working with iModeller 3D Pro, Photoshop CS2, and Cinema 4D for this project. Though the final Cinema 4D scene will include other elements, the tutorial will focus mainly on the photogrammetric modeling of the doll head. Toward the end, you will load the doll head into the rest of the scene in Cinema 4D and render it all for the final image.

The finished project file of this tutorial is included on the accompanying DVD-ROM in the tutorials folder. A demo version of iModeller 3D Professional can be downloaded by going to *http://www.imodeller.com/en/* or can be found on the DVD-ROM accompanying this book. iModeller 3D Professional is available for Windows ME/2000/XP and Mac OS X (10.2+). All of the images used in this tutorial are located in "Tutorials/ ProjectFiles/Chapter 03/Tutorial-04" on the Projects DVD-ROM. There is one saved project on the DVD-ROM for this tutorial.

ON THE DVD

When using iModeller 3D Pro in production, you would begin by printing the calibration pattern and taking several reference photos of an object placed on the printed calibration pattern. This tutorial begins immediately after those images have been transferred to your computer. For further information on the iModeller 3D calibration process, see the documentation accompanying iModeller 3D Pro.

ON THE DVD

1. First, you start in iModeller 3D Pro. From the **Choose Your Activity** windows, choose **Open Images**. Find the "**Tutorials/Project-Files/Chapter 03/Tutorial-04/Half**" folder in the DVD-ROM and choose "**DSCF0001.jpg**" to "**DSCF0020.jpg**" and select **Open**. Then with "**a new group**" selected, name the group and select **OK**. The 20 images will now load into iModeller 3D Pro.

2. The first thing you need to do is to click the **Calibrate** button (middle top) for iModeller to run the auto calibration routine on all 20 images. Each image will show a percentage of accuracy as well as a color bar. A green bar means the image will be very useful in both the voxel (volumetric pixel) modeling and image texturing process. A white bar means the image will not be considered for the voxel modeling but will be used in the image texturing of the model.

3. When the calibration progress bar at the bottom of the screen has reached 100%, it's time to check the accuracy that each image achieved during the auto calibration. Looking at the first image (DSCF0001.jpg), you'll see that its accuracy is 81%. Though the bar is green, you can improve the accuracy. To do this, select the first image. With the mouse in the main image area, right-click and select **Manual Calibration** (or select the **Manual Calibration** icon from the top tool bar). Hitting the **period** key zooms in so you can see more closely. Find the marker circled in Figure 3.73 and observe how the entire black round printed marker cannot be seen. It's overlapped by the wooden doll mount. So iModeller can't get a calibration lock on that marker, and that's contributing to the auto calibration accuracy of 81%. Since you're already in manual calibration mode, place the cursor over the defective marker and left-click it to delete it.

It is better to have fewer markers than to have any defective markers. iModeller was designed to create excellent models with only a portion of the pattern markers visible in images.

4. Sometimes, though a marker is basically following the contour of the printed pattern, if the marker appears to be slightly off, it's better to rebuild it by deleting the marker and then clicking again to recreate it. This makes better markers and improves the calibration accuracy of the image. So, look at the remaining markers and rebuild any that look like they could be improved.

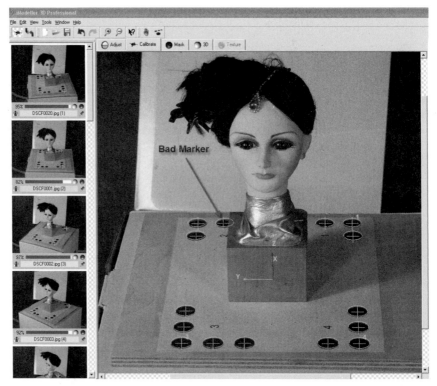

FIGURE 3.73   Defective marker causing 81% accuracy on the first image (DSCF0001.jpg).

5. When you're done rebuilding markers, right-click and choose **Calibrate** (or choose the icon in the tool bar to the right of the Manual Calibration icon) and look at the accuracy for DSCF0001.jpg improve.

6. Go through the remaining images and delete defective markers and rebuild makers that could be improved. Don't forget to calibrate each image when you're done with the markers. Try to get the accuracy of each image calibration to at least 95% so the voxel modeling will reflect the original doll head well. Then using the **File** menu, choose **Save As** and save the project.

7. For iModeller to know which parts of the object are to be built, you need to create a mask. To do this, start Photoshop CS2 and load the first image (**Tutorials/ProjectFiles/Chapter 03/Tutorial-04/Half/DSCF0001.jpg**). To put the image into a new layer, Select All (**Ctrl-A**), then Cut (**Ctrl-X**), and then Paste (**Ctrl-V**). Now turn off the background layer. Get the **Magic Wand** tool and set the **Tolerance** to 30. Be sure **Anti-alias** and **Contiguous** are checked (shown in Figure 3.74).

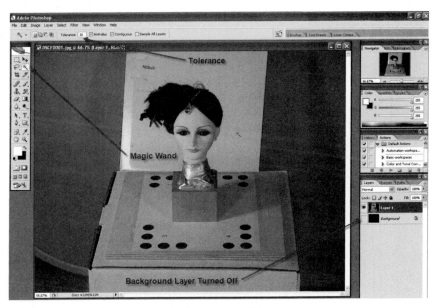

FIGURE 3.74   Magic Wand selected in Photoshop CS2.

8. With the magic wand, select the major areas of the image that don't include the doll head or its wooden mount. While being careful not to include the doll head or mount in the selection process, don't worry about being perfect about selecting everything outside the doll head and mount for now.

9. Zoom in and switch to the **Polygon** selection tool (shown in Figure 3.75). Hold the **Alt** key down and make polygon selections of the areas outside the doll head and mount that were not selected by the magic wand. If you make a mistake, hold the **Shift** key down and make a polygon selection within the doll head or mount to correct any areas that should not have been selected.

For further clarification on this selection process, see the accompanying video tutorial on the DVD-ROM.

ON THE DVD

10. Next, hold the **Polygon Selection** icon down, which allows you to choose the **Lasso Selection** tool. Using the Lasso, look around the contour of the doll head and switch between using **Alt** and **Shift** to make sure the selection stays just outside the doll head. Use the **Alt** key with the lasso to include any stray fine hairs in the selection. Such tiny hairs (shown in Figure 3.76) will be troublemakers later, so get rid of them now.

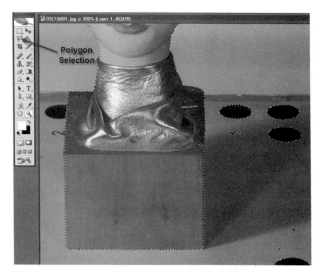

FIGURE 3.75   Polygon Selection tool in Photoshop CS2.

FIGURE 3.76   Stray hairs added to the selection to be deleted.

11. Cut (**Ctrl-X**) to leave only the doll head and mount. Some of the surrounding areas of the image still remain, so use the Lasso and select the doll head and mount and then invert the selection (**Shift-Ctrl-I**) and cut to get rid of the extra surrounding image.

12. Finally, to do the fine detailed cleanup, use the **Eraser** tool (shown in Figure 3.77) and zoom in and clean up any areas that still show parts that are not the doll head or mount. Adjust the size and softness

of the eraser to get this cleanup done without damaging the doll head and mount.

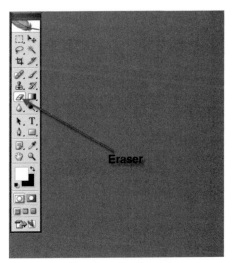

FIGURE 3.77   Eraser tool in Photoshop.

13. To select the mask of Layer 1, hold the **Ctrl** key and click on the picture icon of Layer 1. The mask is selected and looks like marching ants along the contour of the image. Now turn on the Background layer and use the **Eraser** to erase any remaining stray pixels.

 Because the background is black, stray pixels show up either as stray dark masked areas or lighter stray pixels.

14. Now you need to turn the doll image completely white for iModeller to be able to use it as a mask, so choose the **Paint Bucket** icon and on the top parameter bar, set the **Tolerance** to 255 and make sure **Anti-Alias** and **Contiguous** are both checked. Click the **Fore-ground Color** and set it to pure white as shown in Figure 3.78 (**R** = 255, **G** = 255, **B** = 255). Zoom out to see the whole object and click to fill it with the paint bucket.

15. Save the image as a .PNG file and name it "**Masked-DSCF0001 copy.png**." In the PNG Options, check **None** and click **OK**.

ON THE DVD

16. Repeat steps 7–14 on the remaining 19 images or go to step 17 and load the masked images from the tutorial DVD-ROM.

FIGURE 3.78 Paint Bucket tool in Photoshop.

17. Back in iModeller, if not already loaded, load the previously saved scene (in step 6) and click on **Mask** icon (middle top). iModeller may try to create an auto mask, but you will use the mask images created in Photoshop.

18. From the **Tools** menu, select **Import Mask** and then find and load "**Tutorials/ProjectFiles/Chapter 03/Tutorial-04/Half/Masked-DSCF0001 copy.png**." The red area (shown in Figure 3.79) shows the mask applied to the first image. When iModeller starts to build the 3D model, only the red masked areas will be built.

19. Repeat this process (step 18) and apply each mask to its related image.

20. Now, with the calibration and masking complete, iModeller is ready to build the 3D model, so click on the **3D Mode** icon and watch iModeller build the 3D model. First the model is built, then the texture is automatically applied. Drag the model around to inspect the completed photogrammetry process.

21. In the **Main** menu, use the **File/Export** and set the **Save as Type** to Cinema 4D Files; name the file "**Sherazard-01**" and click **Save**. Now, in the **Object Export** window, set the **Texture Quality** to 100 and click **OK**. Save your final iModeller project and exit iModeller.

22. In Cinema 4D 9, load the "Tutorials/ProjectFiles/Chapter 03/Tutorial-04/Tutorial-04-Photometry-End/Tutorial-04-Photometry-End.c4d" project and render the perspective view to see the finished scene with the photogrammetry model (shown in Figure 3.80).

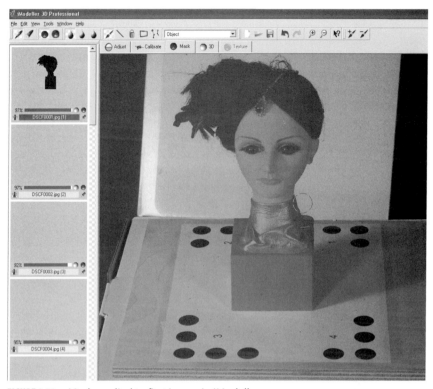

FIGURE 3.79   Mask applied to first image in iModeller.

FIGURE 3.80   Finished iModeller model rendered in Cinema 4D.

SUMMARY

Sometimes the challenge is to model an object (or some objects) in a short amount of time. Sometimes it's a matter of faithfully recreating a real object in 3D. At other times it's modeling something that can be animated very efficiently. Some times it's all of the above.

The modeling techniques we've covered so far approach modeling from different perspectives using different tools and applications. We hope to inspire you to maintain the commitment to grow your ability to be flexible and inventive in your approach to modeling. This way, when the impossible task comes, you will be ready both in skill and in your adaptability to problem solving.

4

BODYPAINT 3D 2

In This Chapter

- Tutorial 1: The SUV
- Tutorial 2: Species

 Software used: Cinema 4D 9 Studio Bundle, Photoshop CS2

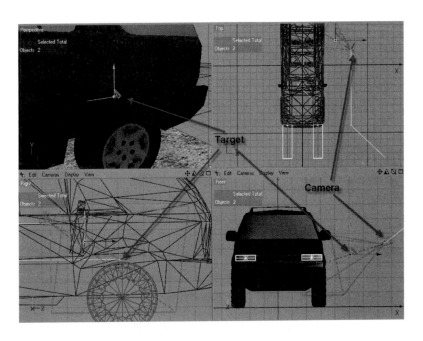

In this chapter, we'll explore the link between painting and 3D modeling. We will see how BodyPaint extends your ability to not only create fantasy, but also to control the realism of how image maps relate to the objects to which they are assigned.

One very important concept you will be exposed to is "**UV Polygons.**" Up to this point, polygons have been discussed as the smallest pieces of an object, which combine to create a visible surface that can be rendered. In BodyPaint, you will be introduced to the polygon's cousin known as the **UV Poly**gon.

In Figure 4.1, the middle and right sphere have some points moved to stretch the object and cause some polygon deformation. The middle sphere uses UVW Mapping, so its UV polys maintain their shape with the object polygons and the texture follows the object deformation closely. The right sphere uses Spherical Mapping so there is no UV poly relationship to the object polygons. The texture therefore cannot follow the deformation closely.

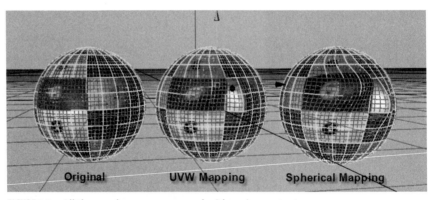

FIGURE 4.1   All three spheres are mapped with an image texture.

When working in BodyPaint, for every polygon in an object there is a corresponding UV poly. It is the UV poly that actually gets the paint texture. The UV poly then projects its texture onto the polygon. UV polys can be manipulated independently of their related polygons in BodyPaint. UV polys can be rotated, scaled, and moved and can even have their points reshaped to look very different. When manipulating UV polys, the original object polygons don't change their shape. Instead, as the UV poly is manipulated, the area of the painted texture covered by the UV poly is changed, and that new texture information is seen on the object polygons. If you think of the polygons as walls and the UV polys as wallpaper, moving the wallpaper on the walls can change how the wall surfaces look but can't change the shape of the walls.

Not to worry. If you are now totally confused by all of the "poly" talk, when we start painting, you won't be able to miss how UV polys relate to polygons.

To demonstrate, we will work with BodyPaint in two tutorials, addressing two very different uses of BodyPaint. First we'll look at adjusting the way that the texture on a model of an SUV covers the object polygons. This SUV is from the MarlinStudios.com object library in the Goodies folder of the DVD-ROM accompanying this book. Then we'll look at how to transform a plain human head into an alien species by painting and using many BodyPaint features. These tutorials are also on the accompanying DVD-ROM as video tutorials, along with the tutorial project files.

ON THE DVD

Remember, as you make progress in each tutorial, to save your Cinema 4D projects.

TUTORIAL 1   **THE SUV**

FIGURE 4.2   Finished render of the SUV after texture editing in BodyPaint 3D 2.

Covered in this tutorial:

- BodyPaint setup wizard
- UV poly editing
- Camera key framing
- UV mesh texture painting

As the focus of this tutorial is manipulating the SUV's texture in BodyPaint, you will be working from a scene that is almost ready to go. So now you get to be the texture artist in the production of a high-quality 3D image.

ON THE DVD

Finished project files for many sections of this tutorial are included on the accompanying DVD-ROM in the tutorials folder. All of the images used in this tutorial are located on the DVD-ROM.

1. To begin, from the Chapter 4 Tutorial 1 folder on the DVD-ROM, load the "**Tutorials/ProjectFiles/Chapter 04/Tutorial-01/SUV-Start/SUV-Start.c4d**" project and render the perspective view to inspect the initial state of the body and window textures applied to the SUV. Notice how the texture isn't quite to the edge of the polygons at the front and rear fenders. The window glass isn't transparent everywhere. Edit the "**CBGlass**" material and in the **Transparency** channel, change the **Refraction** from 1.5 to 1.05 to reduce the distortion.

This object was originally imported into Cinema 4D from the Marlin Studios "Traffic" library in the Lightwave 3D format. This is not a native MAXON format, and that's OK. Sometimes material settings such as refraction aren't handled the same way in different 3D applications and must therefore be set once imported into Cinema 4D. In 3D animation production, you will frequently use various file formats with ease. Some adjustment in the placement of the texture is necessary and will be performed in this tutorial. This SUV is also located in the Goodies folder on the

ON THE DVD

DVD-ROM.

To work on the SUV, you will need to set up the scene camera in three key-framed positions over time. The first will be the initial starting position. The second will be close-up to the front driver's side fender. The third will be close-up to the driver's side rear fender. To do this, you will create key frames on the timeline so that by simply moving between the key frames, you will be changing what the camera in the perspective view is seeing.

2. To create the first key frame of the camera and target position, select both the camera and target in the Objects Manager. Now, with the time slider at frame 0 (0 F—the first frame), hit the **Record Key Frame** button (shown in Figure 4.3) on the transport control to create a key frame for the camera and target.

The camera isn't looking at the SUV. It is looking at the camera target. Wherever that target is placed is where the camera will face.

FIGURE 4.3   Record key fame icon.

3. Drag the time slider to the next frame (1 F) and position the camera and target for a close-up shot of the front fender as shown in Figure 4.4. With both the camera and the target selected, hit the **Record Key Frame** button to create the first key frame in which the camera views the front fender.

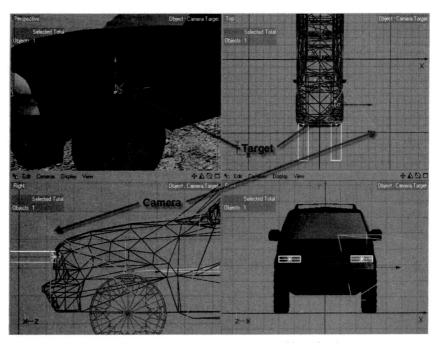

FIGURE 4.4   Second key frame position to view close-up of front fender.

4. Drag the time slider to the next frame (2 F) and with the camera and target still selected, in the top view, move them to the rear for a close-up shot of the rear fender as shown in Figure 4.5. With both the camera and the target selected, hit the **Record Key Frame** button to create the first key frame in which the camera views the rear fender.

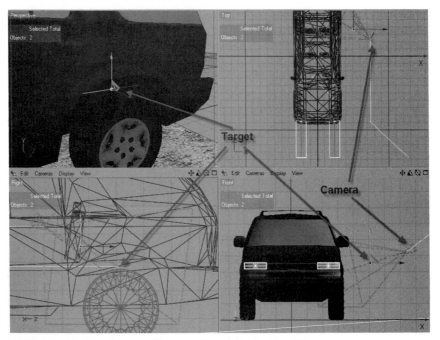

FIGURE 4.5   Third key frame position to view close-up of rear fender.

5. Now, to test your key frames, press "**g**" on the keyboard to go to the next key frame and press "**f**" to go to the previous key frame. This is how you will be able to predictably move between the three views of the SUV in BodyPaint.
6. Go to the first frame (0 F) and select the **BP UV Edit** layout (shown in Figure 4.6). To prepare BodyPaint to work on the SUV textures, choose the **Paint Setup Wizard** from the **Tools** menu. In the **Materials** page, choose which materials you will be able to paint on from a vertical list of materials. Because you will only be working on the body and the glass windows, uncheck all materials except for **CB-Glass** and **CBRed**. Because in Cinema 4D you can apply a material to several objects, it is necessary to also tell BodyPaint's setup wizard which objects you wish to be paintable. To do this, click on the Objects page and uncheck all objects except for **CBRed**, which is the object name of the SUV's body. Then click **Next**.

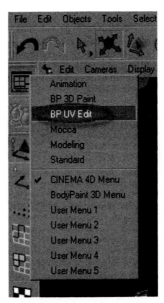

FIGURE 4.6   Change the layout
to BP UV Edit.

7. Because you only want to make slight corrections to the textures, uncheck **Recalculate UVs**. Then click **Next**, **Finish**, and then **Close**.

Leaving Recalculate UVs checked will cause BodyPaint to adjust the UV polys to make them easier to paint. However, when you wish to simply adjust how the texture covers the object polygons, you would only increase the complexity of the texture correction task by allowing BodyPaint to recalculate the UVs. In the next tutorial, we will use this option.

8. From the upper right canvas's local menu, choose **UV Mesh/Show UV Mesh**. UV Mesh equals UV Poly. In the local menu, next to the UV Mesh, choose **Textures/cbredd.jpg**. If you don't see the UV polys, use the canvas's **Zoom** icon to zoom out to see the UV polys overlayed on the texture of the body of the SUV. Using the **Pan** and **Zoom** icons, set the canvas to the driver's side front fender (Figure 4.7). While the model of the SUV is 3D, the UV polys are presented in 2D. This is what makes them so easy to work on.

The areas of BodyPaint where textures are manipulated may look and act like viewports in some ways. MAXON (creator of Cinema 4D and BodyPaint) distinguishes them from the regular 3D manipulation views (viewports) by calling them a canvas, as they relate more closely to the painting process.

FIGURE 4.7   UV polys for the SUV body material zoomed in on the driver's side front fender.

9. Use the "**f**" and "**g**" keys to go to the key frame of the close-up view of the driver's side front fender, set in step 3. Now would be a great time to render the perspective view and look closely at how the texture covers the object polygons.

10. In order to manipulate the UV mesh points to adjust how the texture covers the SUV front fender, from the **Main** menu, choose **Tools/UV Tools/UV Points**. Now the UV polys are light blue and their points can be selected (shown in Figure 4.8). The object modeling polygons are also visible in the perspective view, and their points can be selected as well. Selecting a point in either view selects the corresponding point in the other view.

11. Get the **Move** tool from the left tool bar and select and move the UV poly points around the fender as shown in Figure 4.9.

If you have a dual monitor system, click the thumb tack in the upper left corner of the UV Mesh canvas and Undock it. Then move it to the second display and maximize it to gain maximum access to the UV mesh details.

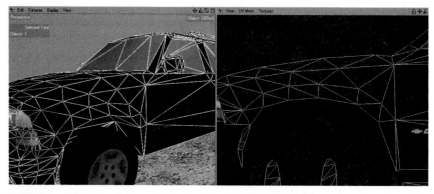

FIGURE 4.8   UV poly points and object polygon points can now be selected and moved.

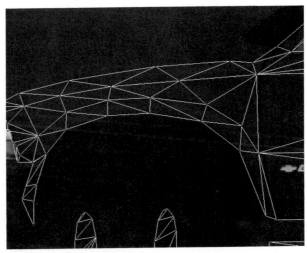

FIGURE 4.9 UV polys for the front fender adjusted.

12. Hit "**g**" on the keyboard to go to the next key frame and see the rear fender. Move the points in the UV mesh as you just did in the front fender.

This is just like regular modeling, in that pressing the spacebar allows you to toggle between Live Selection and Move.

13. Now, with both fender textures adjusted, render the perspective view to see an image similar to Figure 4.10.

FIGURE 4.10 Both fender UV polys adjusted.

14. To work on the SUV glass, from the canvas's **Textures** menu, choose **cbglass.jpg**. Be sure that in the **UV Mesh** menu "**CBRed [Tag Texture]**" is selected. Choose the **Brush** tool (shown in Figure 4.11).

FIGURE 4.11 Brush tool.

15. In the brush **Attributes** page, set the **Size** to 80, **Hardness** to 0, **Spacing** to 18, and **Squeeze** to 100. In the **Color** tab set **R**, **G**, and **B** to 204. Paint the texture in the UV mesh as shown in Figure 4.12. Render the perspective view to see the result (also shown in Figure 4.12).

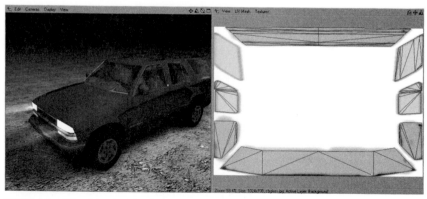

FIGURE 4.12 The driver's side glass and windshield are now adjusted.

Summary

Gaining control over the placement of textures using BodyPaint offers you one more solution for some troublesome situations you will likely face in 3D animation production.

TUTORIAL 2   **SPECIES**

FIGURE 4.13   Finished render of a 3D head painted in BodyPaint 3D 2.

Covered in this tutorial:

- BodyPaint setup wizard
- 3D Painting
- Multiple channel painting
- Material layers
- Painting with textures
- Creating textures in Photoshop

In this tutorial, you will be painting a 3D model of a human head to create another species. This will require you to use many of BodyPaint's tools and further explore the connection between materials in Cinema 4D and BodyPaint.

Finished project files for several sections of this tutorial are included on the accompanying DVD-ROM in the tutorials folder. All of the images used in this tutorial are located in "Tutorials/ProjectFiles/Chapter 04/Tutorial-02" on the Projects DVD-ROM.

ON THE DVD

1. To begin, from the Chapter 4 Tutorial 2 folder on the DVD-ROM, load the **"Tutorials/ProjectFiles/Chapter 04/Tutorial-02/Meg-Start/Meg-Start.c4d"** project and render the perspective view to see the initial image of the human head. Then switch the layout to **BP UV Edit**.

2. From the **Tools** menu, choose the **Paint Setup Wizard**. This time, leave all of the objects and materials selected and click **Next**. Select **Recalculate UV**, **Single Material**, and **Optimal Cubic Mapping**. Then click **Next**, **Finish**, and **Close**.

The Width/Height values in Step 3 of the BodyPaint Setup Wizard determine the resolution of the texture that will be applied to your object, so you should be aware that using small values may result in highly aliased coarse textures. Using very high values will look crisp and clear at the expense of requiring more RAM.

3. First, select the **Head** object in the Objects Manager. Then, in the top right UV mesh canvas's local menu, be sure to choose **UV Mesh/ Show UV Mesh**. In the UV mesh view, zoom out to see the entire mesh (shown in Figure 4.14).

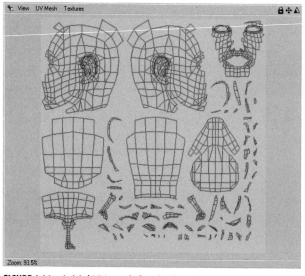

FIGURE 4.14   Initial UV mesh for the head.

4. To paint the head, we need to rearrange how the UV polys connect to each other. In the perspective view, draw a few brush strokes along the surface of the head and see how the strokes jump between groups of UV polys. Be sure to undo those strokes. Now, to correct this UV poly mess, in the **Tools** menu, choose **UV Tools/UV Polygons**. The UV polys turn light blue and can now be manipulated. Below the UV mesh, click on the **UV Mapping** page and choose the **Projection** tab and then **Sphere**. The UV polys are now all connected, but some of the mesh is now off of the texture.

5. To correct this, press **Ctrl-A** to select all the UV polys. Then use the **Scale** and **Move** tools from the left tool bar to fit all of the mesh on the texture (except for the two points that extend way off to the right). Then from the **Tools** menu, choose **UV Tools/UV Points**, and with the **Move** tool active, click each of the two points that are off the texture to the right and move them onto the texture (shown in Figure 4.15).

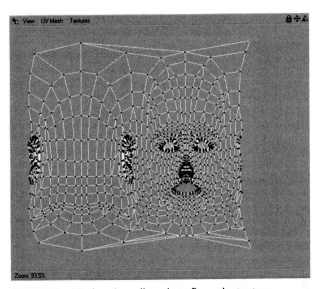

FIGURE 4.15   Mesh points all made to fit on the texture.

Click the blue thumb tack in the upper left corner of the UV mesh and use Undock to float this window. You can then maximize this window full screen or, better yet, place it on the second monitor of a dual display system for detailed access to the UV polys and textures.

6. To add color to the head, choose the **Brush** tool from the left toolbar, and in the bottom right palette, choose the **Colors** tab and set the color to **R** = 18, **G** = 119, and **B** = 242. Because you can choose any of 16.7 million colors from the color palette, it would be easier to store this color now so that when you wish to use it again, you can simply select it. Click the arrowhead at the bottom left of the color palette and choose **Show Quick Storage** and drag the vertical color sample into an available color well (shown in Figure 4.16).

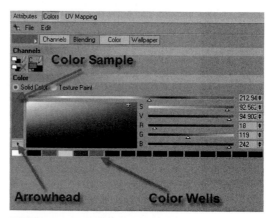

FIGURE 4.16   Sample color in color well.

7. Since you will start by painting a large area, set the **Size** to 284 in the **Attributes** tab. For a soft brush, set the **Hardness** to 5.
8. On the UV mesh canvas, paint the head blue. The 3D model is simultaneously being painted blue.

 Some benefits of painting the UV mesh canvas instead of the 3D model are that you can see the whole head when painting it and you can paint without concern for accidentally painting the eyes, eye brows, and lips because they are separate UV meshes.

9. Immediately below the Brush tool, choose the **Eraser** tool and erase blue around the eyes (shown in Figure 4.17).

 To erase to a different color, change the background color in the Colors page.

10. To add scars to the cheeks, double-click the "**skin**" material and check the **Bump** channel. This doesn't allow you to start painting yet. In the **Bump Texture**, click the arrowhead and choose **Create**

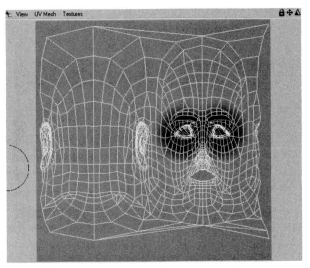

FIGURE 4.17   Dark eye wells created with the eraser tool.

> **New Texture** . . . and then click **OK**. Set the **Strength** to 56 and
> close the material requester.

11. In the UV mesh, view the **Textures** menu and choose **Skin_
    Bump_1.tif**. Click the **Color** channel to turn it off so that the pencil
    is turned off. Click the **Bump** channel so that the pencil is turned on
    (shown in Figure 4.18).

*Depending on your personal presets in the Main menu Edit/Preferences (Body-
Paint/Default Format) you may see a different file format such as .b3d or .psd.
That's OK.*

To paint on both color and bump at the same time, turn on both channels here.

12. Set the brush **Size** to 12. Draw three scar strokes on the UV mesh
    (Figure 4.19).
13. To fade the start and end of the scar strokes, choose the **Eyedropper**
    tool (to the right of the Eraser tool) and click on a gray area of the
    bump texture in the UV mesh. This changes the drawing color to
    gray. Set the brush **Size** to 73 and **Hardness** to 0. Draw slowly and
    carefully at the ends of the scars to fade their starts and ends.

*Even though we paint the bump and color channels separately in this tutorial to
create an additional analog sense to the design, it is also common to paint with several channels in the same stroke.*

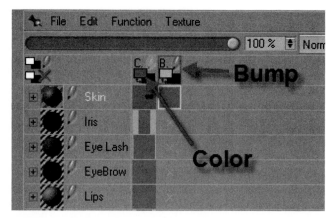

FIGURE 4.18 Only the Bump channel is turned on for painting now.

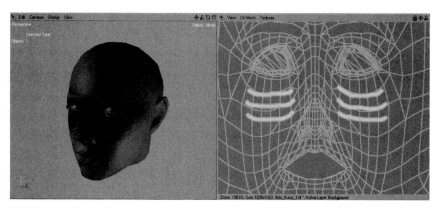

FIGURE 4.19 Scar strokes painted in the Bump channel.

14. Now turn off the **Bump** channel and turn on the **Color** channel and set the brush **Size** to 13 and **Hardness** to 20. Set the **Color** to **R** = 144, **G** = 94, and **B** = 44. Paint color onto the bumped scars on the 3D head.

Because the bumped scars are using the material's Bump channel, when working with this object in Cinema 4D later on, the apparent elevation of the scars can be adjusted by setting the Bump Strength.

15. To fade the start and end of the scar's color, choose the **Freehand Selection** tool and select the end of one set of scars (shown in Figure 4.20).

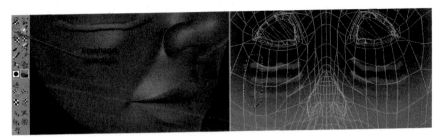

FIGURE 4.20   One end of the scars is selected.

16. From the **Main** menu, choose **Filter/Blur/Gaussian Blur…**, set the **Radius** to 12 and click **OK**. From the **Main** menu, choose **Render/ Raybrush Render View** to get a live rendered update of your work and freehand select and blur the other ends of the scars.

The Raybrush rendered view remains active and live until you change the view by actions such as moving or scaling an object or zooming, panning, or rotating a view. This means you don't have to re-render to see updated strokes.

17. To add some further detail to the scar's color, set the brush **Color** to a darker brown such as **R** = 79, **G** = 48, and **B** = 17. Set the brush **Size** to 3 and **Hardness** to 90. Zoom in to see the scars on the UV mesh and paint some dark dots on the scars.
18. Now it's time to add the cranial ridges. Fit the forehead and eyes in the UV mesh view. In the **Main** menu, choose **Window/Layer Manager**. Then in the **Layer Manager** menu, choose **Functions/New Layer** to create a new layer in the skin material just like when working in Photoshop. With the new layer selected, make a temporary guide vertical stroke to define the vertical area to be covered by the cranial ridges (shown in Figure 4.21).

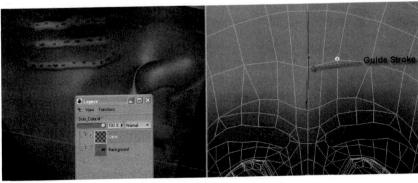

FIGURE 4.21   Temporary vertical guide stroke for cranial ridges.

19. Turn on only the **Bump** channel and set the brush **Size** to 21 and **Hardness** to 5 and set the **Color** to pure white (**R** = 255, **G** = 255, **B** = 255). Now draw three cranial ridges in the UV mesh.

20. To fade the ends of the ridges, use the **Eyedropper** to change the color to the gray default color of the texture. Also change the brush **Size** to 90 and the **Hardness** to 0. Now gently paint the ends of the cranial edges to fade them out.

21. Turn off the **Bump** channel and turn on the **Color** channel (be sure you have the color channel selected) to see the blue skin material in the UV mesh view. Since you no longer need the temporary guideline for the cranial ridges, choose the new layer in the **Layers Manager**. From the **Functions** menu, choose **Delete Layer** and close the Layer Manager.

22. To paint the eyebrows, start by choosing the blue skin color from the color well. To avoid interfering with the skin color detail, paint the eyebrows in the UV texture view. Directly under the Eraser tool, choose the **Fill Bitmap** tool and click in the eyebrow texture in the UV mesh view to fill the eyebrows with blue.

23. To paint the hairs of the eyebrow, switch to Photoshop CS2. Choose **File/Open** and navigate to your Cinema 4D 9 folder and enter the "**C:/Program Files/Maxon/CINEMA 4D R9/library/pattern**" folder and open the file "**eyebrow2.jpg**." With the **Move** tool, drag the horizontal and vertical markers off (shown in Figure 4.22).

24. To extract the eyebrow hairs from the image, use the **Magic Wand** tool (directly below the Move tool) with **Tolerance** set to 5 and **Contiguous** unchecked to click the black area of the image and cut (**Ctrl-X**). Then to adjust the levels select **Ctrl-L** and drag the leftmost marker so the **Input Levels** reads 208, 1.00, and 255 and then click **OK**. Use the **Crop** tool (first row, second icon down in the left toolbar) to crop the image, keeping only the area of the image containing the hairs of the eyebrow. Then choose **File/Save** as a PNG file and name it "**eyebrowB**." In the **PNG Options**, click **OK**. In Photoshop, the image should look like Figure 4.23.

25. Now back in BodyPaint, in the **Colors** page with the **Brush** tool selected, change **Solid Color** to Texture Paint. Choose the arrowhead now beneath Solid Color to choose the texture pattern. Choose **Load From Disc...** and choose **eyebrowB.png**. Change the **Dest X/Y** (destination method) from Locked to **Mouse Hit** and set the **Scale** to 61. Now paint the hairs onto the eyebrows in the UV texture view.

To fill in the gaps in the texture paint, adjust the two Source X/Y values and paint the area again. This creates an offset from the previous stroke, which helps fill the unpainted gaps.

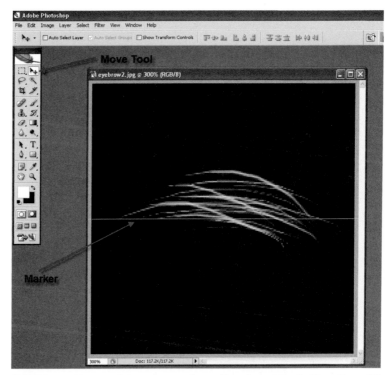

FIGURE 4.22   Move tool dragging markers off eyebrow2.jpg in Photoshop CS2.

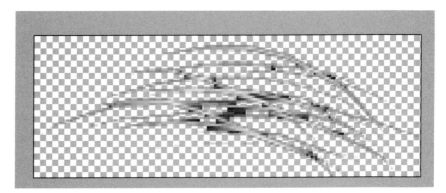

FIGURE 4.23   Finished eyebrow pattern image in Photoshop CS2.

26. To paint the lips, zoom in on the lips in the perspective view and choose the **Lips** material. This changes the selected texture in the UV mesh view to the Lips_Color.tif. With the **Fill Bitmap** tool selected, in the **Colors** page, choose **Solid Color** and set the color to a dark

blue color of **R** = 27, **G** = 60, and **B** = 119. Fill the lips texture with the dark blue color. Double-click the **Lips** material and turn on the **Specular** channel and set the **Width** to 36 and the **Height** to 78. Turn on the **Bump** channel. In the **Texture**, choose **Create New Texture…** and choose **OK** and close the Material Editor.

27. To paint the bumped lines on the lips, choose the **Brush** tool and set the **Size** to 1 and **Hardness** to 20 and **Color** to white. With only the **Bump** channel turned on and selected, in the perspective view draw some lines on the lips (shown in Figure 4.24).

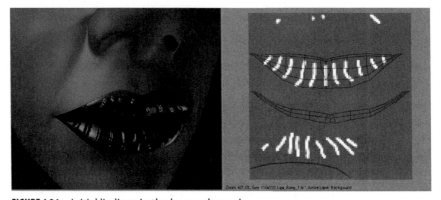

FIGURE 4.24   Initial lip lines in the bump channel.

28. It may look too harsh, so to soften the lip lines, in the UV mesh view use the **Eyedropper** tool to choose the texture default color. Set the brush **Size** to 42 and the **Hardness** to 100. Use the **Brush** to fade the ends of the lip lines. Then, from the main menu, choose **Filter/ Blur/Gaussian blur** and set the **Radius** to 3 to smooth the lines (shown in Figure 4.25).

29. To paint the eyes, be sure only the **Color** channel is selected and active. Choose the **White** material and be sure that the UV mesh view Textures menu has White_Color.tif selected. Change the painting color to **R** = 216, **G** = 233, and **B** = 255. Paint the whole texture white.

30. We will finish the eyes by coloring in the iris and the pupil. Go to the Objects Manager (between the materials and colors) and choose the **L_Iris** object. This makes the Iris_Color.tif the active texture in the UV mesh view. Change the color to **R** = 87, **G** = 147, and **B** = 221, the brush **Size** to 42, and **Hardness** to 50. Then paint the whole **L_Iris** texture.

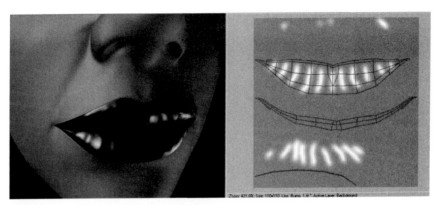

FIGURE 4.25   Gaussian Blur–smoothed lip lines.

31. For the pupils, select **L_Pupil** in the Objects Manager. Then change the color to **R** = 27, **G** = 60, and **B** = 119 and paint the whole pupil texture. Double-click the **Pupil** material and set the **Specular** channel **Width** to 47 and **Height** to 78.

Because both pupils share a texture, selecting either pupil and painting the pupil texture paints both pupils. The same is true for the iris's objects and texture.

32. To finish off our creation we'll apply some red color to the cheeks. Start by selecting the **skin** material and zoom the texture in the UV mesh view to see both cheeks. Set the color to **R** = 150, **G** = 10, **B** = 66. To independently control the opacity of this redness in the cheeks, add a new layer in the Layers Manager. Set the brush **Size** to 54 and **Hardness** to 0. Paint the cheeks and apply a **Gaussian Blur** with a **Radius** of 20. To soften the edges for a more natural looking blush choose the **Smear** tool, to the right of the Brush tool, and mess-up the clean edges of the red color on the cheeks so they look a bit more irregular. In the Layers Manager, change the **Opacity** to 66. Then apply a final **Gaussian Blur** with a **Radius** of 67. Last, in the Layers Manager, **Flatten** the layers to combine the redness of the cheeks with the blue skin color.

33. Change the layout to **Standard** to return to Cinema 4D. Add a **Sky** object and render to see the final result of this tutorial (Figure 4.26).

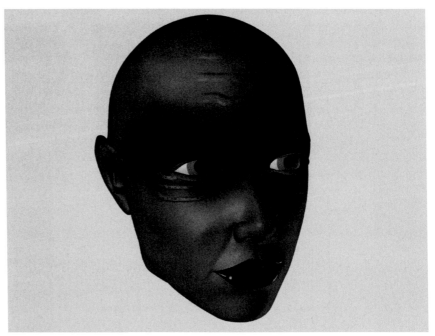

FIGURE 4.26   Gaussian Blur–smoothed lip lines.

Summary

With a working knowledge of how UV polys and modeling polygons are related, and with some hands-on experience of how BodyPaint can be used to add or change the personality of your models, your view of how to apply materials to models for use in production should be a bit more expanded and expansive.

Thinking back on these BodyPaint tutorials, when looking at 3D animation in movies and television, try to break down how you could replicate the imagery you see or how you can apply the inspiration from such great 3D animation to build better models with tools such as Cinema 4D 9 and BodyPaint 3D 2.

5

3D ANIMATION

In This Chapter

- Tutorial 1: Drive
- Tutorial 2: Wood Chipper
- Tutorial 3: Burn
- Tutorial 4: People N Motion

 Software used: Cinema 4D 9 Studio XL, Photoshop CS2, Adobe After Effects 6.5 ProS

In this chapter we begin to work with various aspects of 3D animation in Cinema 4D 9. A beautifully modeled scene is still void of life until you animate it, And just as there are many ways to approach modeling challenges, there are many ways to approach animation challenges. Because the objective of animation is to mimic life through illusion, we must think very creatively about how to move both the objects and the viewer when animating in 3D.

There is an unbreakable link between 2D cell animation and 3D animation. In 2D, the key frames (poses and shots) are drawn and either people or software work to create the in-between frames that we call tweens. This method is very straightforward and highly effective (as Saturday morning cartoons have shown). As we move further into the world of 3D animation, however, we quickly learn that the tools that give us the added third dimension implement the 2D concept of key framing differently. This is particularly obvious when people draw the tweens, as one can draw any action from the human mind in those tweens. In comparison, the 3D implementation of tweening is more linear and limited in that an object is simply transformed between two key frames. This may make 3D animation seem more limited at first, until you discover that in 3D, there are actually many methods of animation.

When we mimic life in 3D animation, we use key frames and tweening along with several other methods. Table 5.1 is a listing of some of these methods.

TABLE 5.1   3D Animation Methods

METHOD	DESCRIPTION
Key Frame	An object's position, rotation and scale are changed and recorded over time. The 3D software then fills in the motion in-between these recorded key frames. This is digital process is analogous to the hand drawn process used to generate cartoon animation.
Path	A curve is used to define a motion path. An object is then attached to that motion path and travels on that path. A path can be defined through a city and a car can be animated along that path.
Expression	Relationships between objects' properties define their animation, so a bicycle moving forward could cause the rider's feet to pedal.
Dynamics	3D objects react to Newton's laws of physics. A bowling ball collides with the bowling pins, accurately triggering many collisions.
Particles	A generator emits many copies of a source object. One bird added to a particle emitter can become a flock of birds.

To imagine applying these animation methods in addition to key frame animation is to better appreciate just how powerful animating in 3D can be. In this chapter, we take a look at some real-world applications of these animation methods to solve production challenges.

First, we will look at a solution to animating a car driving along a winding road with hills. This would be an absolute nightmare to animate using only key frames. It would be very difficult to keep the tires from floating above the road or from penetrating the road as the road elevation changes. It would also be difficult to maintain the proper rotation of the tires as they must both corner and drive. To solve all of this, we will use path animation, XPresso, and key frame animation. We will create a production solution that allows you (the animator) to interactively adjust to changes in road contour and vehicle speed. This kind of flexibility dramatically increases the production value to the rest of the production staff.

Then we will look at a solution for making a wood chipper that spits out wood chips when you drag a log into it. The issues to be resolved here are basically building the illusions that the log disappears into the chipper and the wood chips fly out in response to this. These two separate illusions will connect through the magic of XPresso.

Next we will take on one of the great challenges of 3D animation. We create the illusion of fire in a column of smoke. The fire and the smoke are two separate illusions that visually interact with and enhance each other. Particles, volumetric lighting, and PyroCluster combine to bring this illusion to life.

Last, we will take a look at a method for adding moving video-captured people into a 3D scene in Cinema 4D 9. This tutorial will focus on integrating the video clips into the 3D scene. This simple but very powerful technique is used to create the suspension of disbelief, which is key to storytelling in sci-fi.

Rather than exploring the rudimentary implementation of these animation methods, we will go step by step in tutorials that apply these methods in practical ways that build on the interaction between the animation methods.

XPresso is a node-based solution for creating expressions in Cinema 4D. With XPresso, unlike several other 3D applications, both simple and complex relationships between objects can be created without writing any code. XPresso is available in the Standard, XL, and Studio versions of Cinema 4D 9. PyroCluster is a volumetric shader, driven by particles to create smoke, fire, clouds, and other gaseous substances. PyroCluster is available in the XL and Studio versions of Cinema 4D 9.

ON THE DVD

These tutorials are also on the accompanying DVD-ROM as video tutorials, along with the tutorial project files. Remember, as you make progress in each tutorial, to save your Cinema 4D projects.

TUTORIAL 1   **DRIVE**

FIGURE 5.1   Finished render of the SUV driving on the road.

Covered in this tutorial:

- Edge to spline
- Spline deformer
- Magnet tool
- Extracting a spline from a mesh
- Align to spline
- XPresso: range mapper

Although this is your first animation project, it will be a cross-over project where you start by modeling the road with some techniques not yet covered in previous chapters. You'll then load in the SUV finished in a previous chapter and use modeling tools to prepare the tires for animation. Then you'll put it all together with a motion path spline extracted from the road and control the rotation of the four tires with XPresso.

ON THE DVD

Finished project files for seven sections of this tutorial are included on the accompanying DVD-ROM in the tutorials folder. All of the images used in this tutorial are located in Tutorials/ProjectFiles/Chapter 05/Tutorial-01 on the Projects DVD-ROM.

1. To start building the road, add a primitive **Plane** and set the **Width** to 10, the **Height** to 600, **Width Segments** to 6, and **Height Segments** to 40. Now convert this to a polygon object with the **Make Editable** icon.

The width segments define how much geometry detail can define the shape of the width of the road. The height segments are much higher because this road will be winding and will have hills.

2. Working in the top view, switch to the **Edge** mode. From the **Selection** menu, choose **Loop Selection** and select the third and fourth edge loops (shown in Figure 5.2). Using the **Live Selection** tool (**Only Select Visible Elements** unchecked) in the front view, hold the **Ctrl** key down and deselect the fourth edge loop. Your top view should now look like the second image in Figure 5.2.

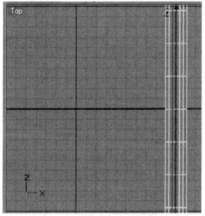 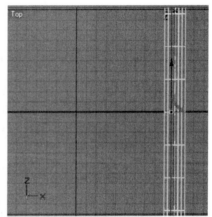

3rd and 4th edge loops selected   *4th edge loop de-selected*

FIGURE 5.2   Edge loop selection.

3. In the main menu choose **Structure/Edit Spline/Edge to Spline**. This creates a new spline object. A spline is a curve object and cannot be rendered. In the Objects Manager, drag the spline out of the plane hierarchy and name the spline "**Original.Spline**." Make a copy of this spline and name the copy "**Modifying.Spline**." These two splines will define the shape of the road. In the Attributes Manager, change the **Type** for each spline to **B-Spline**. This ensures that they will produce smooth interpolation (bending).

 Splines are used to define NURBS (Non-Uniform Rational B-Spline) objects. Splines can also be used to create motion paths for animation and manipulators or guides for modeling.

4. In the **Main** menu choose **Objects/Deformation/Spline Deformer**. In the Attributes Manager **Object** tab, drag the Original.Spline and Modifying.Spline from the Objects Manager into the fields named **Original.Spline** and **Modifying.Spline**, respectively. With the spline deformer selected, in the Attributes Manager set the **Radius** to 200. Now, when you move the modifying spline's points, the full width of the road will be affected.

5. In the Objects Manager, drag the Spline Deformer onto the Plane and rename Plane "**Road.**" With the modifying spline selected, switch to **Point** mode. In the **Main** menu, choose **Structure/Magnet**. In the perspective view, use the magnet to shape the modifying spline and thereby shape the road by adding hills. Switch to the top view and use the magnet to add a few bends in the road (shown in Figure 5.3).

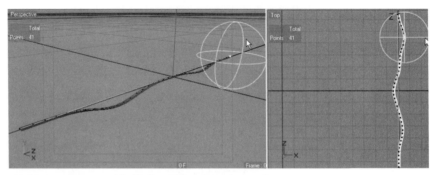

FIGURE 5.3   Magnet-added hills and bends in the road.

6. Create a new material and name it "**Road.**" In the **Color** channel **Texture**, browse to open "**Goodies/MarlinStudios/Seamless Textures 2—Rustic Exterior Surfaces/grnd01M2.jpg.**" Uncheck the **Specular** channel. In the **Bump** channel **Texture**, from the DVD-ROM, browse and open "**Goodies/MarlinStudios/Seamless Textures 2—Rustic Exterior Surfaces/grnd01M.jpg**" and set the **Strength** to 100.

7. Drag the new road material to the **road** object in the Objects Manager. In the Objects Manager, select the road material. In the Attributes Manager, set the **Length Y** to 2 to unstretch the texture on the road.

8. To build some grass along the road, switch to **Edge** mode and the perspective view. Selecting the outer edge loops (**Selection/Loop Selection**) on either side of the road also selects loops one row in as well. Hold the **Ctrl** key down and deselect these inner rows of edges until only the outmost loop of edges is selected (shown in Figure 5.4).

9. **Extrude** the selected edges. In the **Options**, set the **Offset** to 30 and set the **Subdivision** to 2. Switch to the **Polygon** mode. In the top view, using the **Loop Selection**, hold the **Shift** key down and select

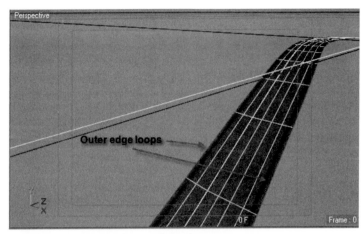

FIGURE 5.4   Outer edge loops selected.

all new polygons that were not part of the original road object (shown in Figure 5.5). In the **Main** menu, choose **Selection/Set Selection** and name the new selection "**Grass.**"

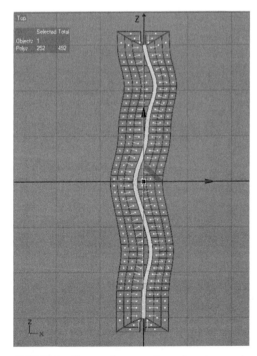

FIGURE 5.5   Grass polygons selected and named.

10. Switch to **Point** mode and, using **Loop Selection**, select all points that are not part of the road. Then move them down and make them wider by scaling them out using only the **X** axis (shown in Figure 5.6)

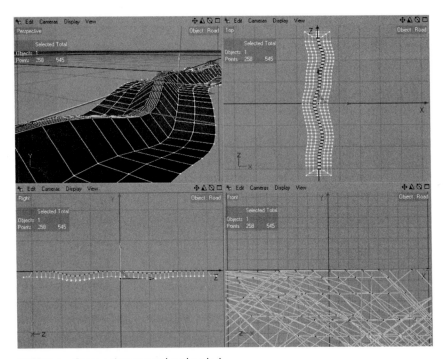

FIGURE 5.6   Grass points moved and scaled.

ON THE DVD

11. Create a new material and name it "**Grass.**" In the **Color** channel Texture, on the DVD-ROM, browse to open "**Goodies/Marlin Studios/Seamless Textures 1—General Purpose Surfaces/ shrb01L.jpg.**" Use this image for the **Bump** channel **Texture** as well and set the **Strength** to 100. Apply this new material to the road and drag the grass polygon selection to the **Selection** field in the Attributes Manager. Also set the **Length X** and **Length Y** to 20. From the **Main** menu, choose **Objects/Scene/Sky** to get rid of the black area in the scene. This fills the black area of the screen with a light gray.

Because the order of the material tags is important, make sure that the grass material tag is to the right of the road material tag in the Objects Manager.

12. Switch to **Model** mode and add a light and set the shadow **Type** to Hard. Position it in the Coordinates Manager at **X** = 265, **Y** = 155, and **Z** = −390 and make an **Instance** copy of the light. Position the light instance copy at **X** = 300, **Y** = 155, and **Z** = 490. Your rendered perspective view should now look like Figure 5.7.

FIGURE 5.7   Road and grass modeled.

ON THE DVD

13. Now it's time to prepare the vehicle for the road. From the DVD-ROM, load the "**Tutorials/ProjectFiles/Chapter 04/Tutorial-01/SUV-GlassDone/SUV-GlassDone.c4d**." This opens the SUV into a new document. Before this SUV will drive, we must first separate the tires into four individual objects and place their object axis at the center of each tire. In the Objects Manager rename CBRed "**SUV-Body**." Toggle the editor display switch off so that the SUV body is hidden and the tires are visible.

14. Frame the CBRed-Tires in the top view. In the Objects Manager make three copies of the CBRed-Tires so that there are now four polygon objects named CBRed-Tires. Use the following names to give each tire a unique name: **FrontLeft-Tires, FrontRight-Tires, RearLeft-Tires, RearRight-Tires**.

15. Switch to **Point** mode and select the **FrontLeft-Tires** object. Hold down the **Live Selection** icon to get the **Rectangle Selection** tool (**Only Select Visible Elements** unchecked) and select the front right tire and the rear tires and delete them. This leaves only the front left tire polygons within the FrontLeft-Tires object. Using this technique, edit the remaining three tires so they contain the polygons for the appropriately named tire.

16. These tires still aren't ready for the road. Because each tire object originally contained all four tires, the object axis (pivot rotation point) for each tire is not placed in the center of that tire. To correct this, select a tire and switch to **Use Object Axis** mode. Now with the **Move** tool, use at least two orthogonal views (top, front, or right) and center the axis on the tire both horizontally and vertically. Do this to all four tires. Then in the Objects Manager, drag all four tires into the SUV-Body object's hierarchy. Toggle the SUV-Body editor display switch back on so that the entire SUV can be seen in the viewport again.

17. Now with the SUV-Body selected, use the Objects Manager menu **Objects/Group Objects**. This gives the SUV-Body a new null object as its parent. This will come in handy later as we place the SUV on the road. **Copy** the null object and use the **Window** menu to select and switch back to the original project. Then **Paste** to add the SUV null object to the Objects Manager.

18. Switch to the **Use Object tool** and select the SUV-Body in the null object. If you frame the SUV in the top view, you will see that the SUV is much too large for the road. In the Coordinates Manager, change the **Scale** to 0.004 for **X**, **Y**, and **Z**.

For purposes of this tutorial, the scale of the SUV with reference to the road is chosen for visual appeal and not technical accuracy.

19. In the front view, frame ("**o**") the SUV and then zoom out to see where it is in relation to the road. Use the **Move** tool to move the SUV down to the road. The actual position isn't very important for now. That will be set up later.

When merging documents or copying and pasting objects from other documents object sizes, positions and orientations can be incorrectly set. Selecting the merged or pasted object, then framing it and zooming out will give you a sense of what actions must be taken to match the position, scale, or orientation of the merged or pasted object with the rest of the scene.

20. In this tutorial, the SUV will be traveling in the positive Z axis. If you frame the SUV in the perspective view, you can see that it is currently facing the negative Z axis (shown in Figure 5.8). To correct this, in the Coordinates Manager, change the Pitch (**P**) to 180.

The Z axis is the blue line parallel to the SUV. Positive Z travels into the monitor. Negative Z travels out of the monitor.

FIGURE 5.8   SUV is facing the reversed direction.

21. If you try to render the perspective view, you will get texture errors (shown in Figure 5.9). These texture errors occur because the images for the SUV textures are not yet loaded into this project. In the Materials Manager, double-click on the **CBTire** material sample and in the **Color** channel **Texture**, browse to the "**Tutorials/Project-Files/Chapter 05/Tutorial-01/Driving-04/tex**" folder and open the "**cbtired.jpg**" file. Repeat this process for the texture images in the CBInterior, CBGlass, and CBRed materials.

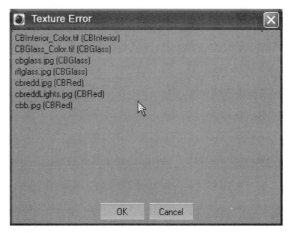

FIGURE 5.9   Texture error when first rendering the scene with the SUV.

22. Now it's time to put the SUV on the road. First, rename the null object **"SUV."** In the right view, with the SUV selected, zoom out until you see both the SUV (null) and the SUV-Body. Switch to the **Use Axis** tool and use the **Move** tool to position the SUV (null) at the bottom of the SUV-Body.

It's not necessary to get this positioned perfectly. You'll adjust the SUV so the tires touch the road later.

23. Switch to **Model** mode. In the Objects Manager, right-click on the SUV (null) and choose **Cinema 4D Tags/Align To Spline**. In the Attributes Manager, in the **Tag** tab, drag the Modifying.Spline into the **Spline Path** field. The SUV immediately disappears. The SUV has actually moved to the start of the Modifying.Spline, which is the start of the road. To find the SUV, select it and in the top view, press **"o"** to frame it in the view. Then zoom out to see the SUV at the start of the road.

24. With the SUV's **Align To Spline** tag selected, in the Attributes Manager, drag the up/down arrows for the Position to see the SUV move along the road. The SUV isn't really driving yet. It's just following the Modifying.Spline to travel the contour of the road. You might want to play with this in the perspective view as well to get a real sense of how the Align To Spline really works. Zoom in for a close look at an area where the road goes up and adjust the Align To Spline position to see what happens to the SUV when it starts to climb the road (shown in Figure 5.10). To correct the orientation error shown in Figure 5.10, check the **Tangential** option in the **Tag** tab.

FIGURE 5.10   The SUV is not orienting correctly to climb the road.

25. Now it's time to place the SUV on the road so the tires actually touch it. With the SUV selected, in the perspective view, frame the SUV. Orbit the view until you can see a close-up side view of the SUV. Since the position of the SUV (null) is controlled by the Align To Spline tag, select the SUV-Body and use the **Move** tool to position it on the road. Orbit the view to get an angular view of the SUV and render the frame to see if the tires are touching the road. Adjust the height of the SUV-Body and test render until the placement on the road is good.

26. In the **Main** menu, choose **Edit/Project Settings** and change **Maximum** to 600.

Since the frame rate is 30 (frames per second = rendered images per second of video) and since the project is now 600 frames long, when rendered, this animation will take 20 seconds to play from start to end.

27. Now the SUV can travel with the right orientation and at the right elevation along the road, but the tires still don't roll. To get the tires rolling, right-click on the SUV-Body and choose **CINEMA 4D Tags/ XPresso**. The empty XPresso Editor opens. From the Objects Manager, drag the Align To Spline tag into XPresso and then drag all four tires in as well.

28. Five nodes are now visible in XPresso. To arrange the nodes so they don't overlap each other, drag them by the white text area. So their titles can be read, position the mouse over their corners until it becomes a four-way cursor (shown in Figure 5.11).

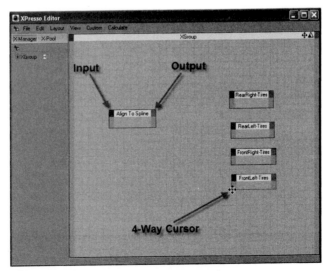

FIGURE 5.11   XPresso nodes being arranged.

29. In XPresso, you're going to set up a relationship between the position parameter of the Align To Spline and the pitch rotation of each tire. The Align To Spline tag has many parameters. In order to select which one will be used to control the rotation of the tires, left-click on the red corner of the Align To Spline node and choose **Tag Properties/Position**. The output of the position node is now equal to the Align To Spline's current Position value.

30. Working with the tire node, left-click the blue corner and choose **Coordinates/Rotation/Rotation.P**. This means that any node connecting to this tire's node's input will be able to control how this tire rotates in the pitch (around its local X axis). Set the remaining tires' nodes' inputs like this as well.

You could connect the output of the Align To Spline to the input of the tires. But the result would be that as the SUV travels from 0% to 100% on the Align To Spline's Modifying.Spline path, the tires would roll only 100 degrees, so they would just appear to slide along the road.

31. Right-click in XPresso and choose **New Node/XPresso/Calculate/Range Mapper**. This new node will translate the Align To Spline's output into something useful to drive the tire's pitch rotation.

Each selected node displays its parameters in the Attributes Manager. The available parameters depend entirely on what type of node is selected in XPresso.

32. With the **Range Mapper** selected in XPresso, in the Attributes Manager, change the **Output Upper** to 480. This means that for every percent the SUV travels on the Align To Spline, the tires will turn 480 degrees in the pitch. To create the first wire connection, drag from the Align To Spline's position node output (red circle) to the Range Mapper node input (blue circle). Just before you release, the wire turns green to indicate that the connection can be made. Now connect the output of the Range Mapper node with the input of each tire node (red circle to blue circles). Your XPresso should now look like Figure 5.12. Close the XPresso Editor window.

33. In the perspective view, with the **Align To Spline** tag and the **SUV-Body** selected, drag the Align To Spline **Position** to 0 and frame the SUV. The SUV is still not completely on the road. Set the **Position** to 0.25 so that the SUV is completely on the road. Make sure that you are on frame 0. With the **Ctrl** key held down, left-click (**Ctrl-click**) the **Position** key frame dot to set the starting position of the SUV animation (Figure 5.13).

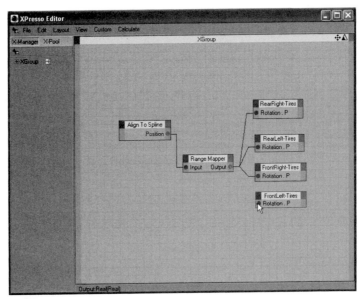

FIGURE 5.12   XPresso setup now complete. The tires now roll based on where the SUV is on the road.

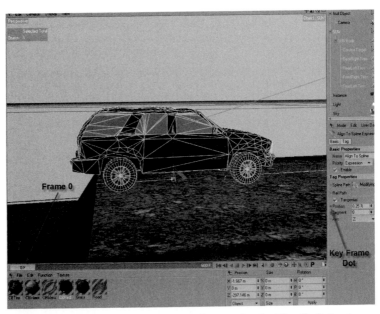

FIGURE 5.13   The first key frame is set at frame 0 for the Align To Spline tag. This establishes where the SUV will be positioned at the start of the animation.

34. Now, to determine where the SUV will be at the end of the animation, drag the playback head to frame 600 and set the Align To Spline **Position** to 99.5. Frame the SUV to see that it is completely on the road. **Ctrl-click** the **Position** key frame to record this end position. You will notice that although the SUV is now animated over 600 frames, traveling along the road it's difficult to see it.

35. In the **Main** menu, choose **Objects/Scene/Target Camera** and in the perspective view local menu, choose **Camera/Scene Camera/ Camera** to start using this new target camera. In the Attributes Manager, with the **Camera** selected, set the **Projection Type** to Perspective in the **Objects** page. Use the top and right views to place the camera.target in the SUV-Body. Then in the Objects Manager, drag the camera.target into the SUV-Body hierarchy. Using the **Move** tool in **Model** mode, with the camera selected, use the top and right views to position the camera until your perspective view looks similar to Figure 5.14.

FIGURE 5.14   Camera placed in starting position.

36. In the Objects Manager, select the camera and group it so that it now has a null object as its parent. Then right-click the null object and choose **Cinema 4D Tags/Align To Spline**. Continue by dragging the Modifying.Spline into the **Spline Path** field. The perspective view immediately gets very dark (Figure 5.15). This is due to the camera being under the road, because its null object parent just

moved to the start of the Modifying.Spline attached to its Align To Spline tag. No problem!

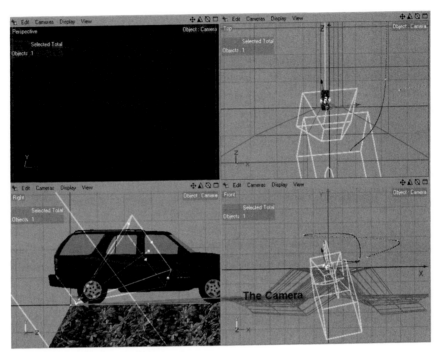

FIGURE 5.15   The camera is under the road.

37. Because only the camera's null parent is aligned to the spline, you can now use the Move tool and move the camera above the road and off to the passenger side to see the SUV. With the camera's null parent's **Align To Spline** tag selected, **Ctrl-click** a key frame at frame 0 and 0% percent in the **Position**. Now go to frame 600 and set the **Position** to 100 and **Ctrl-click** to set the end position of the camera's null parent. Now press the **Play** button on the transport control to see that the camera follows perfectly. The camera actually follows the SUV too perfectly now. Because the camera is in perfect sync with the SUV, it almost looks like the SUV is staying still and the road is moving. What would be cool here is if the camera could move like it is part of a helicopter camera crew—a helicam.

38. To breathe some life into the camera, in the top view, zoom out to see the entire road. Be sure the camera is selected (not the null parent). At frame 0, press the **Key Frame Record** button on the Transport Control

to record the first camera key frame. Change to a desired camera position and set a key frame at frames 90, 180, 270, 415, and 600. Along with the first key frame, you should now have a total of six key frames on the camera. Switch to just the perspective view and play the animation to see how your choice of key frames worked out. If you think some of those camera key frames would make the director of this production unhappy, adjust them and record another key frame.

39. Working in just the perspective view, with the **Modifying.Spline** selected, switch to **Point** mode and use the **Magnet** tool (**Structure/Magnet**) and drag the spline to change its shape (shown in Figure 5.16). Because this single spline has been used to modify the shape of the road, by attaching the SUV and the camera's null parent to the road, changing the shape of the spline allows you to reshape the animation so it can now be adapted to another project. Cool!

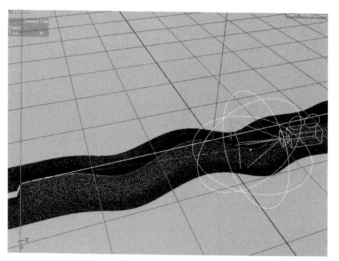

FIGURE 5.16   The Modifying.Spline being manipulated by the magnet tool after all animation is already set up.

Summary

This tutorial provides a very good example of the difference it can make to choose a method of modeling that gives a great level of animation control. This is particularly important to consider as the road could have been modeled several different ways. Similarly, the rotation of the SUV tires could have been set up using different methods with different advantages and drawbacks.

In the end, factors such as those listed below help define which modeling and animating method will work best:

- Do the animation changes have to be handled interactively?
- What level of visual realism and accuracy is required?
- How much time do you have to set up the scene?
- Are you setting up the scene for someone else to animate?

TUTORIAL 2   **WOOD CHIPPER**

FIGURE 5.17   Chips fly out of the wood chipper animated in this tutorial.

Covered in this tutorial:

- Animated Boolean
- Particle animation
- XPresso
- Scene motion blur
- Protection tag

For this tutorial, let's imagine that you're the senior animator at a production facility. The modeler and junior animator have prepared the scene for you. Everyone is just waiting to see you work your digital magic.

In the scene, you must drag a log on a wooden table through a wood chipper. In response to this, the wood chips must come flying out. If this sounds a little advanced to you now, just wait until you see the break-down of the steps. You'll be the master of the wood chipper in no time, and your production team will once again be assured that you do walk on water on Wednesdays.

The magic that you will perform here is the apparent merging of two visual illusions. Illusion 1 is that the log disappears when it moves into the wood chipper. Illusion 2 is that moving the log into the wood chipper causes wood chips to come flying out the other side.

ON THE DVD

Finished project files for two sections of this tutorial are included on the accompanying DVD-ROM in the tutorials folder. All of the images used in this tutorial are located in Tutorials/ProjectFiles/Chapter 05/ Tutorial-02 on the Projects DVD-ROM.

1. Begin by loading the "**Tutorials/ProjectFiles/Chapter 05/Tutorial-02/WoodChipper-Start/WoodChipper-Start.c4d project**." The first object to animate will be the wood chipper blade. In the Objects Manager, select the **HyperNURBS** object named **Blade**. Make sure that you're currently on frame 0. Also, be sure that only the **Rotation** channel is **active** to record key frames (shown in Figure 5.18). Press the **Record Key Frame** button on the Transport Control to record the key frame for the initial state of the wood chipper blade's rotation. This is where its rotation begins.

Pressing the Record Key Frame button records key frames for several channels depending on whether position, scaling, rotation, parametric, or PLA (point level animation) are enabled. For example, with position enabled, recording a key frame for the selected object stores the x, y, and z position information for that object in separate channels so that they can be manipulated independently later in the Timeline or F-Curve editors.

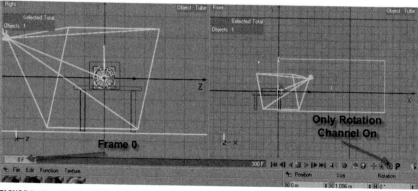

FIGURE 5.18   Playback head at frame 0 and rotation is the only active channel to record key frames.

2. Drag the playback head to change the current frame to 300. In the Attributes Manager, **Coordinates** tab, change the pitch (**P**) to −24,000. This is the number of degrees the blade will rotate during this 10-second animation. Press the **Record Key Frame** button (small red ball) to set another key frame for the blade. The blade is now instructed to start at 0 degrees in the pitch and end at −24,000 degrees in the pitch. You're done animating the blade. You can now hit the Play button or drag the playback head to see the blade rotating over time.

3. In preparation for animating the log, in the Objects Manager, in the **Boole** object, select the **Cylinder** and name it "**Log.**" If you try to move the log in the perspective view, you might find it a little difficult to not grab the blade or some other object by mistake. To make it easy, and prevent moving the wrong objects accidentally, **Ctrl-click** the emitter **Protection** tag and drag a copy and release it to the right of the blade's Material tag (Figure 5.19). **Ctrl-drag** a Protection tag to the table, floor, gravity, deflector, and camera target as well.

If the Protection tag is applied to an object, the object cannot be accidentally transformed (moved, scaled or rotated).

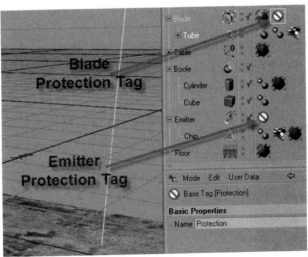

FIGURE 5.19   The emitter's Protection tag being copied to the blade.

4. To further restrict the movement of the log, in the top toolbar, activate the **Y** and **Z Axis Locks**. This prevents movement in the Y and Z axis; you can only move the log in the X axis. Selecting the log in the Objects Manager and using the **Move** tool moving back and forth in the perspective view safely moves the log without selecting any other objects

and without moving the log off of its track to go through the wood chipper. As you may already have noticed, illusion 1 seems like it's working already. That's because the log is in a boolean object and is being subtracted by the second object in the boolean hierarchy, the Cube.

The Protection tag and Axis Locks are particularly useful when teams of people must work on an animation project. These protective measures can help ensure that certain scene elements will be manipulated in a common manner according to a single production plan.

You may remember learning how to create simple and compound Booleans in Chapter 3. In this tutorial, you get to animate a Boolean. This feature is something that separates Cinema 4D from most other 3D packages in that Booleans can be freely and interactively animated.

5. To set up the relationship between the log's movement and the chips flying out, in the Objects Manager, right-click on the log and choose **CINEMA 4D Tags/XPresso**. From the Objects Manager, drag the log and the emitter into the XPresso Editor. In XPresso, place the log node on the left and the emitter node on the right. With the left button held down on the log's output (the red corner), choose **Coordinates/Position/Position.X**. As the log is moved in the X axis, the numeric value of its position in the X axis is available in XPresso in the log node at this newly created output.

6. To create illusion 2, you need to cause the emitter to send out wood chip particles when the log has moved to a certain position in the X axis. To predetermine what this certain position is, right-click in XPresso and choose **New Node/XPresso/General/Constant**. With the **Constant** node selected, in the Attributes Manager, in the **Node** tab, set the **Value** to –100.

7. You must now compare the current position of the log with the –100 you just set in the constant. To do this, right-click in XPresso and choose **New Node/XPresso/Logic/Compare**. Drag the **Position.X** output (red dot) from the log to the **Input 1** of the Compare, and drag the **Real ()** output from the Constant to **Input 2** of the Compare (Figure 5.20). The Compare node will now be triggered to do something when the log moves to –100 in the X axis. With the **Compare** node selected, in the Attributes Manager, in the **Node** tab, set the **Data Type** to Integer and set the **Function** to >=. As the Compare node can output several data types and compare based on different math functions, these settings make it easy to communicate when the log's position should cause an event. So, the Compare node's output will be changed if the log's position on the X axis is greater than or equal to –100.

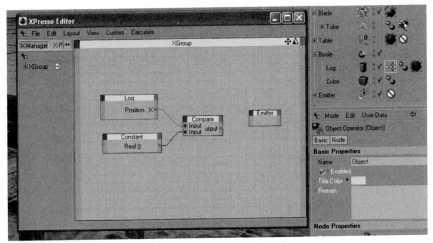

FIGURE 5.20   The log and Constant nodes are connected to the Compare node, and the Compare node's Node attributes are set.

8. In XPresso, add the new node **New Node/XPresso/Bool/Bool**, and in the Attributes Manager, **Node** tab, set the **Function** to OR. Connect the Compare **Output** to the Bool top **Input**. This creates a state change (true or false) rather than a numeric value.

9. Although the boolean output is ultimately very useful to trigger the emitter to emit wood chips, the emitter itself can't accept a boolean input, so in XPresso, add a new node **New Node/XPresso/Adapter/ Universal**. In the Attributes Manager, in the **Node** tab, set the **Data Type** to Real. Connect the Bool **Output** to the Universal **Input**.

It may seem contrived and extraneous to go from numbers to true/false and back to numbers, but there is a very important reason. The log can smoothly move along the X axis. This XPresso setup converts that smooth movement into a sudden numeric jump in the speed of the emitter. This setup is ultimately the conversion of smooth numeric movement of the log into sudden speed in the emitter.

10. The final node to be added is **New Node/XPresso/Calculate/Range Mapper**. The Range Mapper's job is to convert the output of the universal node (which is 0 −1) to a user-controllable numeric value that can create the desired performance of speed in the emitter. With the Range Mapper selected, in the Attributes Manager, **Parameter** tab, set the **Output Upper** to 500. This means that when the log's position is greater than or equal to −100 in the X axis, the emitter speed will be set to 500 meters per second. Connect the Universal **Output** to the Range Mapper **Input**.

11. Set the emitter input (blue corner) to **Particle/Speed**. Connect the Range Mapper **Output** to the Emitter **Speed**. Your XPresso editor should now look like Figure 5.21.

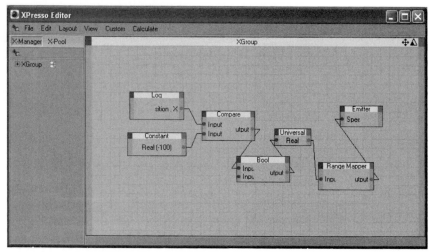

FIGURE 5.21 Completed XPresso setup.

12. To test the XPresso setup, in the perspective view, with the log selected, play the animation and drag the log into the wood chipper to see the wood chips fly out. If your video card has difficulty doing this interactively, position the log in the wood chipper and then press the Play button or drag the log while the animation is playing, but do this only in the front view.

13. In the front view, at frame 0, with the log selected, zoom in to see the log and the wood chipper. To the right of the key frame record buttons, activate only the **Position** channel and position the log as shown in Figure 5.22. **Record** a key frame.

14. Activate **Automatic Keyframing** (shown in Figure 5.23). Go to frame 60 and position the log as shown in Figure 5.23.

Using automatic keyframing when animating single objects speeds up work flow. You can quickly find the previous key frame for an object with the keyboard shortcut Ctrl-F and the next key frame with Ctrl-G.

15. At frame 230, move the log all the way through the wood chipper. In the Objects Manager, remove the protection tag from the blade so that it can spin in the animation. Play the animation to see everything working now.

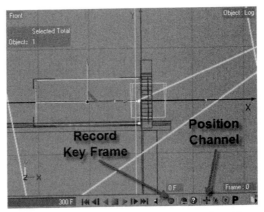

FIGURE 5.22   Playback head at frame 0 and position is the only active channel to record key frames.

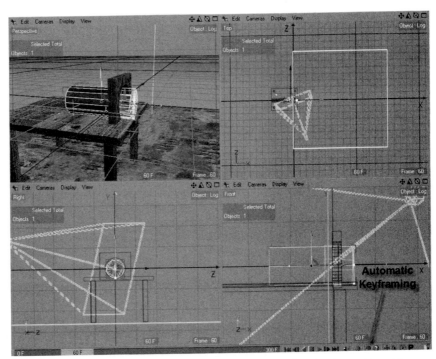

FIGURE 5.23   Playback head at frame 60 and automatic keyframing is used to set key frames. The log is now being cut by the wood chipper.

Take a moment to inspect your scene. There is a gravity object that pulls the wood chips down from the emitter. This gravity object can only affect particles. A deflector object is positioned on the floor to cause the wood chips to collide and bounce back up. This deflector object only affects particles. Inside the emitter, there is a chip object. Any objects placed in the emitter will fly out the wood chipper when the log enters the wood chipper. Select the emitter and in the Attributes Manager, **Particle** tab, notice that the **Birthrate Editor** (which controls how many particles are shown in the editor while you work) is set to 150 particles per second. The **Birthrate Renderer** (which controls how many particle objects are actually rendered) is also set to 150 particles per second. If your graphics card has difficulty keeping up with the animation playback, reduce the Birthrate Editor value until you see smooth playback. This won't affect how the particle objects render when you output your final animation file.

16. To tweak the particles, set the **Rotation** to 35 (to make the wood chips tumble), **Speed Variation** to 80 (to offset the wood chips from each other so they don't look too uniform), and **End Scale Variation** to 60 (so the wood chips appear to be different sizes).

17. Go to frame 1 and render the perspective view. Since the blade is rotating at a constant high speed, you might expect it to look blurred here (like an airplane propeller in motion). Instead, this blade looks lifeless (shown in Figure 5.24).

FIGURE 5.24   Wood chipper blade rendered at frame 1.

18. This demonstrates just how much creative responsibility you have in creating digital imagery. By default, Cinema 4D acts like an ultra high–speed digital camera, able to render all motion as perfectly still life. As cool as that may be, to fool the human eye and make great images, some motion blur would help this scene create the illusion of a

blade rotating at very high speed. To add the motion blur, in the **Main menu**, choose **Render/Render Settings**. In the **Effects** page, at **Post Effect**, choose **Scene Motion Blur**. In the Scene Motion Blur **Basic Properties**, set the **Samples** to 9 Times.

The higher the samples, the smoother the blur and the more time required to render each frame of the animation.

19. Amazingly, if you render frame 1 once more, you won't see any motion blur applied to the image. That's because this effect is only rendered when rendering is done to the picture viewer. So in the top toolbar, click the **Render In Picture Viewer** icon to see the image rendered with motion blur applied (shown in Figure 5.25).

FIGURE 5.25   Motion blur is now applied and the blade renders like it is rotating at high speed.

Summary

In this tutorial, we've gone a little further into how relationships can be built with XPresso. Users of other 3D packages must use scripting to write cryptic lines of code to accomplish what you have just done by visually adding and connecting a few nodes in XPresso. Not only is this attractive to creative noncoding people, but it also makes it easier to debug the expression relationships created with XPresso.

In the Cinema 4D manual, take the time to look at the various node types so you can streamline your animation setup and be better prepared to produce some real-world 3D animation that offers your production team the added flexibility, efficiency, and adaptability gained from the use of expression-based animation.

TUTORIAL 3   **BURN**

FIGURE 5.26   Finished render of PyroCluster and volumetric light combining to create the illusion of smoke and fire.

Covered in this tutorial:

- PyroCluster shader setup
- Volumetric light
- Rendering a range of frames

In this tutorial you will add a column of burning smoke rising from an exhaust pipe on a sidewalk. To make this illusion believable, you will combine particles, PyroCluster, and a volumetric light.

Part of pulling off an illusion in 3D animation is having a great environment. The environment sets expectations of what the quality of the animation should be. Using a photographic sidewalk and windowed wall for this scene will add value to the end result. The materials in this project use images from the Goodies/MarlinStudios folder on the DVD-ROM ac-

ON THE DVD

companying this book. Feel free to experiment and use various images from that folder to see how they change the mode of the rendered image.

Finished project files for two sections of this tutorial are included on the accompanying DVD-ROM in the tutorials folder. All of the images used in this tutorial are located in Tutorials/ProjectFiles/Chapter 05/ Tutorial-03 on the Projects DVD-ROM.

ON THE DVD

1. Let's begin by loading the "**Tutorials/ProjectFiles/Chapter 05/ Tutorial-03/Burn-Start/Burn-Start.c4d**" project. To add the particle emitter that will move the smoke out of the exhaust pipe into the air, in the **Main** menu, choose **Objects/Particle/Emitter**. In the Coordinates Manager, rotate the emitter 90 degrees in the pitch (**P**). In the Attributes Manager, in the **Particle** tab, set the **Birthrate Editor** and **Birthrate Renderer** to 30 to set the number of particles per second that will be rising out of the exhaust pipe. As this animation has 250 frames, set the **Stop Emission** to 250 so that the smoke will not stop. To make sure the smoke rises slowly, lower the **Speed** to 75. To make sure that the smoke particles don't rise in perfect unison, set the **Speed Variation** to 100. To add some rotation to the smoke particles, set the **Rotation** to 57. To create variation between the sizes of the smoke particles, set the **End Scale Variation** to 72. Play the animation to see the particles emitting from within the exhaust pipe at the rate at which the smoke will rise.

2. As you learned in a previous tutorial (Fountain), while particles can move, they cannot be seen when you render the image. To see the particles as smoke, you will add PyroCluster shaders. In the Materials Manager menu, choose **File/PyroCluster/PyroCluster** and then choose **File/PyroCluster/Pyrocluster—VolumeTracer**. In the **Main** menu, choose **Objects/Scene/Environment** and drag the PyroCluster Volume Tracer to the Environment object in the Objects Manager.

Without the Volume Tracer, the PyroCluster shader cannot be rendered.

3. To control what the rendered smoke will look like, double-click the PyroCluster material sample. To change the color of the PyroCluster particle, in the **Globals** page, in the **Color**, double-click the first gradient handle and change the color to black. This changes the smoke particle from looking like a white puffy cloud to looking more like smoke (shown in Figure 5.27).

4. In the **Age** page, these parameters control the smoke at the birth and death of each particle. (Birth and death are "particle talk" for start and end.) In **Luminosity**, double-click the second gradient handle and change the color to black. This causes the smoke particles to turn darker as they rise away from the fire.

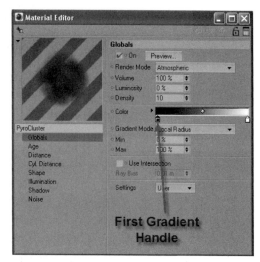

FIGURE 5.27 PyroCluster particle color gradient now starts as black.

5. In the **Illumination** page, check **Use Illumination**. This helps the smoke look more realistic and makes the illusion more believable. Then set the **Mode** to Diffuse. The diffuse mode distributes light hitting the smoke within each puff of smoke.

6. In the **Shadow** page, check **Receive Shadows** so that any item between the light and the smoke will cast a shadow on the smoke, **Cast Shadows** so the smoke can cast its shadow on objects in its environment, and **Self Shadows** so that the puffs of smoke cast shadows on each other. This again improves the realism of the illusion of smoke. Set the **Transparency** to 10. This will be particularly useful later when you add the volumetric light to create the fire within the smoke.

7. The parameters in the **Noise** page control the fractal characteristics of the smoke particles. Set the **Noise Type** to Fractal, **Scale** to 300, **Peak Blend** to 80, **Detail** to 5, **Phase** to 590, **Gain** to 60, and **Low Thres**. to 20. Your PyroCluster Material Editor should now look like Figure 5.28.

While other animations will require different settings to create smoke, these are the parameters for this visualization of smoke. Further experimentation could result in smoke more appropriate for a different environment or end goal.

8. Drag the PyroCluster material sample (just created) to the emitter in the Objects Manager. Go to frame 94 and render the perspective view to see the smoke particles rising from the exhaust pipe. Rendering

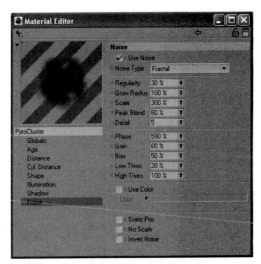

FIGURE 5.28   PyroCluster shader completely setup.

this one frame in the animation could take a few minutes. Both the parameters in the PyroCluster shader and the number of particles being emitted affect the render time. Remember, in 3D animation, quite often, great images require much patience, and mediocre images require less.

This is different from adding an object to an emitter, in that objects are added as a child of the emitter hierarchy and PyroCluster shaders are added directly to the emitter as a material tag.

9. Your smoke is starting to look good, but it's missing something to bring it alive. It's missing the illusion of fire. To create the fire, add a **Light** to the scene and rename it "**Fire**." In the Coordinates Manager, set the pitch (**P**) to 90 so the fire faces up. In the Attributes Manager, **General** tab, change the **Light Type** to Parallel Spot (Round) so the fire will be column shaped. Set the **Visible Light** to Volumetric so the fire can actually be seen. Set **Noise** to Both so there will be disturbance in the appearance and illumination of the fire. Set the **Color** to 255, 95, 0 so the fire color will be visually warm. Set the **Brightness** to 350 so the fire will be visually active enough within the smoke to appear to be burning hottest at the smoke's center.

10. In the **Details** tab, set the **Brightness** to 192 to increase the fire's visible brightness without making it cast more light. This also helps the fire shine through the obscuring smoke. In the perspective view, drag the fire's parametric handles to look like Figure 5.29.

Lighting in Cinema 4D mimics physics and reality. Amazingly (in the vein of power to the animators), lighting in Cinema 4D also provides functionality not available in reality. A light can be made bright and visible without illuminating a scene. For the sake of creating visual effects, this can be very useful. A light's brightness can be increased to increase the visibility of the light as well as to increase the illumination of the scene. Brightness can also be increased to only increase the apparent brightness (visibility) of the light.

FIGURE 5.29 The fire parameter handles moved into place.

11. In the **Noise** tab, set the **Wind** to 0, 0, 2. Because the light was initially rotated 90 degrees, the Z axis is now pointing up, so a value of 2 in the **Z** axis is needed to make the fire appear to be flowing up. Also set the **Wind Velocity** to 2. The Wind Velocity determines how strong the wind will blow. From the top toolbar in the **Render To Picture Viewer** icon, choose **Render Region** and draw a rectangle around the particles and exhaust pipe to see an image similar to Figure 5.30.

The main factors that control the visualization of the fire are its color, shape, brightness, and noise.

12. Because the fire is the same height for the entire animation and the smoke starts from within the exhaust pipe and rises up, when you render your final animation, to keep the smoke and fire synchronized,

FIGURE 5.30   The fire and smoke rendered together.

click the **Render Settings** icon and go to the **Output** page and set the **Frame** to 60 to 250 (shown in Figure 5.31). This way, the rendered animation always shows the smoke and fire as one visual effect.

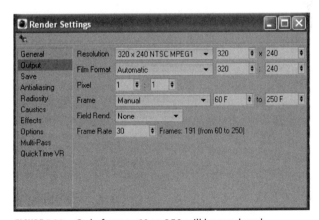

FIGURE 5.31   Only frames 60 to 250 will be rendered.

Summary

This tutorial demonstrated the power of animating seemingly unrelated objects (namely PyroCluster particles and the volumetric light) in concert to produce what appears visually to be a single animation event. In some cases PyroCluster shaders can be used with an emitter to create fire. The result is simply a different kind of fire visualization and may be great for certain animations. Changing Settings to Fire in the Globals page of the PyroCluster shader material creates a PyroCluster visualization of fire.

This tutorial also takes a sublevel look at how smoke is created and points to a very important aspect of being a good animator, modeler, or digital media producer. It's incredibly important to regularly dissect how things in the real world work and how they work visually. When at a restaurant that cooks with an open flame, pay attention to details such as:

- How does the fire really cast light on its surroundings?
- What do the edges of the fire look like?
- Is there little or much smoke?
- How far is the smoke from the fire?
- How is this smoke and fire relationship different from a bush fire in a field?

By paying attention to these questions you will learn to work efficiently and effectively to create digital visual illusions that suspend disbelief.

TUTORIAL 4   **PEOPLE N MOTION**

FIGURE 5.32   Mark and Lucia walking in a 3D office.

Covered in this tutorial:

- Animated textures
- Instance-controlled lighting
- Rendering an animation in Cinema 4D
- Adobe After Effects rendering

What you will learn in this tutorial is simple and very visually power-ful. You will learn how to put video image sequences of people in motion into the 3D animation world of Cinema 4D 9. Just think of the applications:

- Architectural previsualization
- Industrial videos and simulations
- Television commercials
- Instructional training videos

You will be working with a scene of a simple office filled with cubicles. One person will stand facing the camera, talking. Another will be walking by at an angle. Once you get the hang of this, you will quickly view pro-duction possibilities differently.

ON THE DVD

The image sequences of people used in this project are from the Good-ies/MarlinStudios folder on the DVD-ROM accompanying this book. Feel free to experiment and use various images from that folder to see how they change the mode of the rendered image. Finished project files for two sections of this tutorial are included on the accompanying DVD-ROM in the tutorials folder. All of the images used in this tutorial are located in Tutorials/ProjectFiles/Chapter 05/Tutorial-04 on the Projects DVD-ROM.

1. Let's begin by loading the **"Tutorials/ProjectFiles/Chapter 05/Tu-torial-04/PeopleInMotion/People-N-Motion-Start.c4d"** project. Now, add a **Light** to your scene. Position your light within the scene using Figure 5.33 as a guide. When positioning your light, occasion-ally select your ceiling object in the Objects Manager to ensure that you are not placing your light above the ceiling. Position the light at **X** = −1086, **Y** = 0, and **Z** = −1433.
2. With the light selected, in the Attributes Manager, set the **Shadow** to Soft and **Brightness** to 50. In the **Shadow** tab, set the **Shadow Map** to 750 × 750. This light is the original source light from which all the other eight office lights will be made. These other eight lights will be instances of the original light so that any changes made to the original will be applied immediately to the instance clones of the original light. To add an instance of the original light, make sure the light is selected and from the **Main** menu, choose **Objects/Model-ing/Instance**. Now copy and paste this instance of the light seven times. This means you now have nine lights in your scene. Working in the top view, arrange the light as shown in Figure 5.34 (the nine lights are circled).

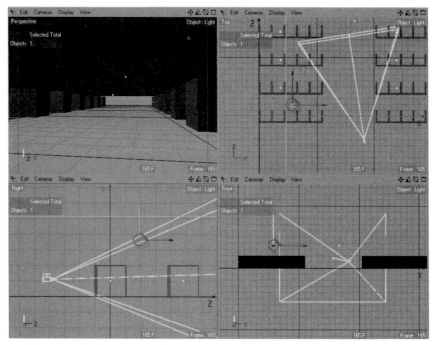

FIGURE 5.33   First light in position.

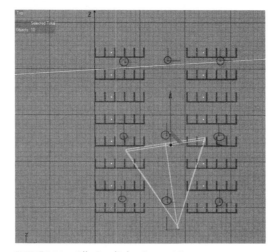

FIGURE 5.34   All nine lights in position.

3. Render the perspective view to see an image similar to Figure 5.35.
4. The lighting is a bit harsh, so with the original light selected, adjust its **Brightness** to 35. Now rendering the perspective view shows that all

FIGURE 5.35   All nine lights now light the office.

the lights have been turned down to a more bearable level. This is possible only because the eight lights are instances of the original light. Select all of the lights in the Objects Manager. In the Objects Manager menu, choose **Objects/Group Objects** (or use the **Alt-g** shortcut) and name the group "**Lights**."

Because you can only make an instance of one selected object, to make an instance of two or more selected objects, first group the objects and make an instance of the group.

5. Now, to add the first person, create a new material and name it "**Lucia**." In the **Color** channel **Texture**, browse to "**Goodies/MarlinStudios/PeopleInMotion/LuciaSmall/LuciaSmal/lr_color**" and Open "**lr_CS_Lucia0000.jpg**." This is a sequence of jpeg images taken from a video clip. When you are prompted with the question "**Do you want to create a copy at the document location?**" choose **No** (shown in Figure 5.36).

Choosing yes here will result in loading only the first image of the sequence. All additional images will be ignored.

6. The path of the sequence is displayed in the Color Channel Texture. Click on the displayed path to edit the setting for the image sequence and then choose the **Animation** tab. Change the **Timing** to Range. Since this animation project has 300 frames, set the **Range End** to

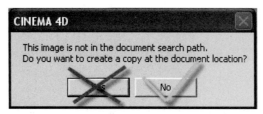

FIGURE 5.36   Choose **No**.

300 and then click **Calculate**. Cinema 4D now compares the number of frames in the image sequence to the number of frames in the range and configures to load each corresponding frame of the image sequence to the appropriate frame of the animation when rendered. At the top of the Material Editor window, press the up arrow (shown in Figure 3.37) to go back to the Texture.

 Because the image sequence is loaded when the scene is rendered, playing the animation will not update materials with animated textures.

FIGURE 5.37   Clicking the up arrow navigates back to the texture.

7. Right-click on **Texture** and choose **Copy**. This copies all the information within that texture so it can be pasted into another channel in this material without having to load the image sequence or calculate the frames in the texture settings. *This copy cannot be done from the Main menu.* Check the **Luminance** channel and right-click on the Luminance channel **Texture** and choose **Paste** to paste the Lucia color image sequence into the texture for this channel. Set the **Brightness** to 0 so that all luminance for the material will be based solely on the image sequence in the luminance texture. Set the **Mix Strength** to 50 so the material self-illumination will render halfway between the original image sequence brightness and the shading of the scene based on how the Lucia object is lit. Uncheck the **Specular** channel.

 The Luminance channel is a key point of adjustment in this kind of animation. If you feel the subject (person) is too dark and you don't wish to position lights just to compensate for that, adjusting the mix strength in the Luminance channel can get you some improvement in lighting of the subject. Leaving the luminance brightness at 100% will wash out the image sequence.

8. Right-click in the material preview in the top left corner of the Material Editor and choose **Plane**. The Lucia image sequence preview is now projected onto a flat plane. Don't be concerned if the image looks too wide here. All materials are projected in this same plane, so there is some stretching. You can also see a gradated background around Lucia. To pull off the illusion that Lucia really is in your 3D office, you will have to get rid of that background, so check the **Alpha** channel, and in **Texture**, browse to the "**Goodies/Marlin-Studios/PeopleInMotion/LuciaSmall/LuciaSmal/lr_alpha**" and **Open** "**lr_aCS_Lucia0000.jpg**." Again, when prompted with the question "**Do you want to create a copy at the document location?**" choose **No**. Enter the texture and on the **Animation** tab, set **Timing** to Range and **Range End** to 300 and click **Calculate**. Close the Material Editor window.

9. Add a **Plane** primitive to the scene and name it "**Lucia**." Set the **Orientation** to –Z so Lucia will face the camera. Set the **Width Segments** to 1 and **Height Segments** to 1 because you don't need the extra geometry. Set the **Width** to 89 and **Height** to 200 to match the resolution of the image sequence files. To position Lucia in front of the camera, in the Coordinates Manager, set the **Position X** to 1820, **Y** to 98.2, and **Z** to 138. Apply the Lucia material to the Lucia object. Render the perspective view to see a poorly lit Lucia (shown in Figure 5.38).

FIGURE 5.38   Lucia is poorly lit.

10. In the lights object, make a copy of the last instance object and position it at **X** = −100, **Y** = −74, and **Z** = −2080. Render again to see a well-lit Lucia.

11. To add the second image sequence (Mark), add a new material and name it "**Mark.**" In the **Color** channel **Texture**, browse to "**Goodies/MarlinStudios/PeopleInMotion/MarkSmall/MarkSmall/lr _color**" and Open "**lr_BW_Mark0000.jpg.**" When prompted with the question "**Do you want to create a copy at the document location?**" choose **No**. Enter the texture and on the **Animation** tab, set **Timing** to Range and **Range End** to 300 and click **Calculate**.

12. In the **Color** channel, right-click on **Texture** and choose **Copy**. Check the **Luminance** channel and right-click on the **Luminance** channel **Texture** and choose **Paste** to paste the Mark color image sequence into the texture for this channel. Set the **Brightness** to 0 so all luminance for the material will be based solely on the image sequence in the luminance texture. Set the **Mix Strength** to 50 so the material self-illumination will render halfway between the original image sequence brightness and the shading of the scene based on how the Mark object is lit. Uncheck the **Specular** channel.

13. Now, check the **Alpha** channel, and in **Texture**, browse to "**Goodies/MarlinStudios/PeopleInMotion/MarkSmall/MarkSmall/lr _alpha**" and Open "**lr_aBW_Mark0000.jpg.**" Again, when prompted with the question "**Do you want to create a copy at the document location?**" choose **No**. Enter the texture and on the **Animation** tab, set **Timing** to Range and **Range End** to 300 and click **Calculate**. Close the Material Editor window.

14. Just like you added Lucia to the office scene, add a **Plane** for Mark. Rename the plane "**Mark.**" In the Attributes Manager, set Mark's **Orientation** to –Z, **Width Segments** to 1, and **Height Segments** to 1. Based on the pixel resolution of the Mark image sequence, set the **Width** to 101 and the **Height** to 200. To position Mark to begin walking behind and to the left of Lucia, in the Coordinates Manager, set the position **X** to 2001, **Y** to 100, and **Z** to 314. Apply the Mark material to the Mark object.

When placing image sequences or still images on a floor in a 3D scene, the position in the Y axis is critical in building the illusion that the person (or object) is truly on the floor and not magically hovering over it, so it is customary to make a few test renders of the area where the image sequence or still image makes contact with the floor until it looks natural. Additionally, when placing people in a 3D scene, people standing with their feet at approximately the same distance from the camera will appear more natural.

15. Lucia will be standing in place, speaking and gesturing. Mark will be walking from left to right at a diagonal angle. Lucia will require no key frames, but Mark needs a start and end key frame. On the Transport Control, at frame 0, and with only the **Position** channel active, **Record** (red ball) a key frame for Mark's starting position. In **Model** mode, go to frame 300 and set Mark's position to **X** = 1444, **Y** = 100, and **Z** = 48. This positions Mark to Lucia's right and in front of her. **Record** a key frame. A motion path now shows where Mark will travel. Play the animation to see Mark magically sliding from the first to the second key frame.

Because there are only two key frames (0 and 300), the motion path is a straight line. A third key frame that alters the direction of the path would cause the path to curve. Even though the path is now a straight line between the first two key frames, adding a third key frame can cause the path between the first two key frames to curve because of something called interpolation. Without this characteristic built into key frames, it would be very difficult to avoid rigid motion.

16. To render this animation and see the final result, click the **Render Settings** icon. In the **Output** page, set the **Resolution** to 640 × 480 NTSC and set **Frame** to All Frames. In the **Save** page, set the **Format** to JPEG. Later, you will use Adobe After Effects to assemble the JPEG images into a video clip. Choose a Path where your rendered images will be saved and close the Render Settings window. Click the **Render In Picture Viewer** icon once to start the animation render.

Depending on the resources of your computer system, this will take between a few seconds per frame to a few minutes per frame to render.

17. When your animation render is complete in Cinema 4D, launch Adobe After Effects. From the **Main** menu, choose **File/Import** and navigate to the path where you saved your image sequence in Cinema 4D. Choose the first frame (image file) of your rendered sequence and check **JPEG Sequence**. To create a composition in this After Effects project, drag the icon for the loaded rendered sequence of images to the **Create a new Composition** icon (shown in Figure 5.39).

As Cinema 4D is capable of rendering animations directly to video files, the use of After Effects here is meant as an introduction to its integration into the Cinema 4D work flow. More on this in later chapters.

FIGURE 5.39 Cinema 4D rendered sequence being dragged to create a composition in Adobe After Effects.

18. In the **Main** menu, choose **Composition/Add To Render Queue**. This opens the Render Queue window (shown in Figure 5.40).

Up to this point, After Effects has no way to output this sequence of images.

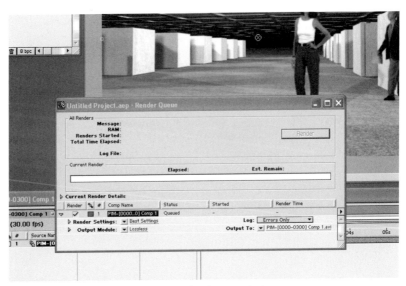

FIGURE 5.40   Adobe After Effects Render Queue window.

19. Click the **Output Module** and choose what video file **Format** and codec you will use for the final animation video file. At the top of the Output Module window, in **Based on "Lossless,"** in **Format**, choose a format based on what is available on your computer. The default format is Video For Windows. Your system may have Mpeg, Real Media, Quick Time Movie, Windows Media, and many others to choose from.

In this case, "format" refers to the file type of the video to be output from After Effects. "Codec" (compressor/decompressor) refers to the particular method of storing the data within the selected format.

20. In **Format** Options, choose what codec ("flavor") of the selected **format** will be used and adjust the codec's setting if necessary. Then click OK to close the Output Module window.

21. In **Output To:** enter the filename and choose the path where the final video will be saved. It's a good idea to save your project now by going to the **Main** menu and choosing **File/Save As...** and entering the file name and choosing the file path. This is only the After Effects project file. It cannot be loaded by Cinema 4D.

For purposes of this tutorial, you may never need this file again. It's just a safety measure at this time. This is important because some formats cannot be rendered at certain image resolutions. For example, some formats require the image width and/or height to be entered in powers of 2 or use only certain multiples (i.e., a width of 256 may work, but not 257). By saving you project now, if your choice of format cannot render because of the output resolution, you could simply reopen the saved project and select a different format, and then render.

After Effects will not let you undo if a render fails because of incompatibility between the file format and the output resolution. Your only recourse is to reload the project and select a different format. It's not an issue once you know this.

22. To finally output the video file, click **Render**. This step will take a few minutes.

Summary

Done well, this immersive compositing method can bring a static 3D scene to life in a way that can convince the viewer that the entire scene was videotaped or filmed.

This tutorial used video sequences for the People N Motion library from *http://www.MarlinStudios.com*. In a later chapter you will learn how to create your own video sequences to be used similarly in Cinema 4D.

When working on many projects, using a library such as People N Motion can be very quick and highly productive. When choosing whether to use a library video sequence or make your own, you should consider the following questions:

- Is the use of a specific person relevant for your project?
- Does the person need to walk in a specific and unique path?
- Must the person perform unique actions (i.e., lifting, climbing, rolling)?
- Does the person have to speak dialogue?

These are some critical questions to be answered before determining whether to use library people or produce your own.

CLOTH SIMULATION

In This Chapter

- Tutorial 1: Tablecloth
- Tutorial 2: Flag Day
- Tutorial 3: Drapes
- Tutorial 4: Tailor Made
- Tutorial 5: Jell-O

 Software used: Cinema 4D 9.5 Studio

When animating in 3D, it's often the real-world things that we take for granted that provide the greatest challenges. For example, watching the performance of a figure skater, very few people focus on how the material of her outfit moves and responds to her actions. The fact that the fabric of her outfit seems to have some predisposed memory recall of its default shape isn't something that gets much attention.

Attention to such overlooked nuances can provide a point of reference for defining how cloth materials should respond in 3D. In 3D animation, cloth simulation has long held a distinguished position as being illusive, complex, and generally out of reach of the average animator. And until recent breakthroughs in 3D animated cloth simulation software, even the financially endowed and experienced animation studios only did a passable emulation of cloth.

In Cinema 4D, cloth simulation is a component of the Mocca animation module. The cloth simulation is a specialized implementation: "soft body dynamics." Soft body dynamics is the accurate simulation of flexible objects. Examples of soft body dynamics include simulating hair, muscles, cloth, Jell-O™, and soft rubber. For 3D animation software to effectively provide a useful implementation of soft body dynamics, the software must handle large numbers of changing calculations internally while giving you, the user, intuitive control. This is in essence what Cinema 4D provides in its implementation of Mocca Cloth.

The Cloth section of the Mocca software manual focuses on helping you to simulate cloth. The tutorials in the chapter will help you quickly master cloth simulation beyond the software manual and will seek to engage you to think beyond the box. Rather than simply reserving the use of Mocca Cloth for simulating fabric, you will learn how to utilize the cloth simulation functions to simulate noncloth soft bodies.

From the perspective of creating an illusion, it's important to remember the value of creating great materials for your cloth objects. Choosing an inappropriate material for your cloth object may reduce your ability to sell the illusion and tell the story, so this chapter presents five cloth simulation tutorials, covering different aspects. In Tutorial 1 (Tablecloth), you will learn the basics of cloth simulation by placing a tablecloth on a round table and then applying a material to the tablecloth. In Tutorial 2 (Flag Day), you will learn about the forces such as wind and turbulence that can act on the fabric to bring some life to your cloth simulations. In the Tutorial 3 (Drapes), you will learn how to solve a real challenge in cloth simulation by creating two layered drapes that move in the wind. The two layers will interact with each other without intersecting each other. In Tutorial 4 (Tailor Made), you will learn how to create clothing for a 3D character based on a sketch of an outfit. This has obvious and far-reaching applications and gets into fascinating aspects of cloth simulation such as Dress-O-Matic and Belting. In Tutorial 5 (Jell-O), you will learn how to apply cloth simulation to the noncloth simulation of 12 Jell-O cubes falling through an obstacle and collecting in a bowl. This tutorial will also get into creating an advanced material that uses the principle of subsurface scattering. This will be an example of how you can use cloth outside of the applications normally thought of as cloth simulation.

ON THE DVD

These tutorials are also on the accompanying DVD-ROM as video tutorials, along with the tutorial project files.

Remember, as you make progress in each tutorial, to save your Cinema 4D projects.

TUTORIAL 1   **TABLECLOTH**

FIGURE 6.1   Finished render of the tablecloth draped on a round table.

Covered in this tutorial:

- Mocca Cloth tags
- Mocca Collider tag
- Simulation caching
- Negative frame simulation caching

ON THE DVD

Finished project files for three sections of this tutorial are included on the accompanying DVD-ROM in the tutorials folder. All of the images used in this tutorial are located in Tutorials/ProjectFiles/Chapter 05/Tutorial-01 on the Projects DVD-ROM.

1. Begin by loading the **"TableCloth-Start.c4d"** project from the **"Tutorials/ProjectFiles/Chapter 06/Tutorial 01/TableCloth-Start"** folder on the DVD-ROM. This loads a scene of a round table on a tiled wood floor. Two lights are already placed in the scene.

2. To create the tablecloth, first add a primitive **Plane** to the scene and rename the plane **"TableCloth."** Also, rename Cylinder **"Table."** In the Attributes Manager, set the tablecloth's **Width** and **Height** to 1300. Set the **Width Segments** and **Height Segments** to 40 and make the tablecloth object editable.

3. In the Coordinates Manager, move the tablecloth up by setting **Y** to 350. The tablecloth object is now floating above the table. To give the tablecloth enough time to settle into place on the table, from the **Main** menu choose **Edit/Project Settings** and change **Maximum** to 150.

4. In order for the table to catch the tablecloth when it falls, in the Objects Manager, right-click on table and choose **Clothlide Tags/Collider**. The table is now part of a cloth simulation.

Any object not having a collider tag cannot collide with a cloth object.

5. Select the **Collider** tag in the Objects Manager. Then in the Attributes Manager, set the **Bounce** to 5 and leave **Friction** at the default of 20. Setting the bounce to 5 limits the rebound energy between the tablecloth and the table and thereby allows the cloth to settle into place more quickly. The friction value also aids in the settling process by preventing slipping.

Setting the friction too high could cause the tablecloth to snag.

6. In the Objects Manager, right-click on the tablecloth and choose **Clothlide Tags/Cloth**. In the perspective view, play the animation to see the tablecloth fall onto the table (Figure 6.2).

7. To make the simulation more natural, select the **Cloth** tag in the Objects Manager; then in the Attributes Manager, **Tag** tab, set the **Stiffness** to 0 to allow the cloth to freely conform its shape to the collision with the table. Set the **Flexion** to 0 so that the tablecloth does not try to return to the original flat plane shape once it collides with the table. Set the **Rubber** to 10 to allow the tablecloth to be able to stretch a little, as most of them can. As this rubber value helps control the folding of the tablecloth under the table top, this value also helps the simulation settle down to bring the tablecloth simulation to rest. Set the **Bounce** to 5 to aid the simulation in settling down. Set the **Friction** to 70 so the tablecloth stays on the table. Set the **Mass** to 0.2 to cause the tablecloth to simulate a light material. This also causes the ends of the tablecloth to simulate with less inertia and therefore be less likely to gather beneath the table top.

FIGURE 6.2   Tablecloth fallen onto the table using default cloth tag parameters. Though the tablecloth is colliding with the table, the simulation seems a bit unnatural (particularly when the tablecloth collects beneath the table top).

Flexions are the springs that cause a cloth object to try to maintain its initial shape.

When creating a simulation of a napkin and chain-mail object of the same x, y, and z dimensions, setting the mass of the napkin cloth tag to a very small value, and setting the mass of the chain-mail cloth tag to a high value allows the objects to simulate realistically relative to each other.

8. In order to see the simulation play back at a faster frame rate, in the **Cache** tab, click **Calculate Cache**. This records every frame of the simulation of the selected cloth tag into memory. Once the simulation is cached, click the **Play** button on the Transport Control to see the tablecloth fluidly fall onto the table. Render the perspective view at frame 135 to see an image similar to Figure 6.3.

The speed of animation playback is affected by the selected playback frame rate, the speed of your CPU, the amount of RAM installed, your screen resolution, the selection of Open GL or Software in Edit/Preferences/Viewport, and the capabilities of your video card. The default frame rate in Cinema 4D is 30 frames per second.

Once a simulation is cached, you can scrub the playback head on the Transport Control to instantly view the animation at any point on the timeline.

FIGURE 6.3   Rendered image of the tablecloth fallen onto the table using altered cloth tag parameters. Although the simulation is more natural now, the tablecloth material displays some polygonal artifacts.

9. With the TableCloth polygon object selected in the Objects Manager, hold the **Alt** key down and in the **Main** menu choose **Plugins/Clothlide/Cloth Nurbs** to add a Cloth NURBS as the TableCloth's parent.

Cloth Nurbs affects cloth objects with visual smoothing properties similar to the way HyperNURBS affects polygon object surfaces when rendered.

10. With the Cloth Nurbs selected, in the Attributes Manager, set **Thickness** to 3 so that the tablecloth fabric no longer looks paper thin. Now when you play back the cached simulation, the tablecloth will have some thickness. This helps sell the illusion that this really is fabric and not just a large sheet of paper.

11. To define the surface material for the tablecloth, in the Materials Manager, create a new material and name it "**TableCloth.**" In the material's **Color** channel, browse the **Texture** and go to the "**Goodies/MarlinStudios/Seamless Textures 9—Fabulous Fabrics**" folder on the DVD-ROM and choose the "**Plaid21M.jpg.**" Set the **Brightness** and **Mix Strength** to 50 to lighten the image texture. Uncheck the **Specular** channel so that the tablecloth will not be shiny. Apply the TableCloth material to the TableCloth object.

ON THE DVD

When working with dense geometry like the tablecloth, to really see how a material looks on the tablecloth in the viewports, temporarily select another object such as a light. The polygons on the tablecloth will no longer be highlighted, and the applied texture will be more clearly displayed.

12. With the **Cloth** tag selected, in the Attributes Manager, in the **Cache** tab, click **Empty Cache** so that the simulation can once more be calculated. In the **Tag** tab, uncheck **Auto** and set the **Start** to −150 and the **End** to 150. In this animation, if you think of frame 0 as the present and frame 150 as the future, then frame −150 is the past. Before you overanalyze how this affects the "space–time continuum" of the universe, in the **Cache** tab, click **Calculate Cache** to see what happens. After clicking Calculate Cache, the timeline goes to −150 and counts up to 150. The result is that once cached, the animation plays from frame 0 to frame 150 so that it starts with the tablecloth already settled on the table with just minor settling to take place during the animation. It would be pretty unnatural to see an animation where each time you enter a restaurant, the tablecloths have to fall onto the tables.

To speed up playback, temporarily uncheck the Cloth Nurbs in the Objects Manager. Be sure the Cloth Nurbs is checked before you render the scene.

Summary

Although the technology driving cloth simulation is heavy duty and the results can be mesmerizing, remember, it's the story that drives an animation and not the technology. Use of the cloth as it aids in telling a story will help successfully sell the illusion of a real-world 3D animation. Also keep in mind the following two things when simulating cloth: (1) cloth properties such as Mass should be set according to the material you are trying to simulate, and (2) even though you may simulate a cloth object well, you can't effectively sell the illusion without applying an appropriate material that the viewer will associate with the cloth simulation.

TUTORIAL 2   FLAG DAY

FIGURE 6.4   Finished render of three flags flying in the wind.

Covered in this tutorial:

- Mocca Cloth tags
- Mocca Collider tag
- Simulation caching
- Fixing Points

In this tutorial, you will load a basic scene of a floor and wall and add three flagpoles with flags. You will then create three materials, apply them to the flags, and make the flags blow in the wind.

ON THE DVD

Finished project files for five sections of this tutorial are included on the accompanying DVD-ROM in the tutorials folder. All of the images used in this tutorial are located in Tutorials/ProjectFiles/Chapter 06/Tutorial-02 on the Projects DVD-ROM.

1. Begin by loading the "**FlagDay-Start.c4d**" project from the "**Tutorials/ProjectFiles/Chapter 06/Tutorial 02/FlagDay-01/FlagDay-Start**" folder on the DVD-ROM. This loads a scene of a round table on a tiled wood floor. Three lights are already placed in the scene.

2. To create the first flagpole, add a primitive **Cylinder** and rename it "**Flag Pole.**" Set its **Radius** to 25 and **Height** to 1040. To reduce the geometry to just what's needed, set the **Height Segments** to 1, **Ro-**

tation **Segments** to 20, and **Cap Segments** to 1. Position the flag-pole at **X** = –300, **Y** = 690, and **Z** = –200.

3. To create the first flag, add a primitive **Plane** and set the **Orientation** to –Z, **Width** to 590, and the **Width Segments** to 30. Position the plane at **X** = 24, **Y** = 1000, and **Z** = –200 so that the plane appears to be with the flagpole (shown in Figure 6.5).

FIGURE 6.5   First flag (plane) and flagpole in their initial positions.

4. Make the flag editable and drag it into the flagpole's hierarchy in the Objects Manager. Make sure you are in **Model** mode and that the flagpole is selected and set the pitch (**P**) to 30 so that the flag and flag-pole are hanging from the wall.

5. To create the second flag (and pole), with the flagpole still selected in the Objects Manager add an **Instance** object and set its **X** position to 570.

6. To create the third flag (and pole), copy and paste the instance copy of the flagpole and set its **X** position to 1440.

7. To create the material for the first flag, create a new material in the Materials Manager and name it "**Flag 1**." In the **Color** channel **Texture**, browse to the "**Tutorials/ProjectFiles/Chapter 06/Tutorial 02/FlagDay-01/FlagDay-Start/tex**" folder and open "**PlaidPower-01.jpg**." To assist the texture image brightness at render time, check the **Luminance** channel and **Texture**, then select the same Plaid-Power-01.jpg. Set the **Brightness** to 0 and the **Mix Strength** to 50. Uncheck the **Specular** channel so that the flag doesn't shine.

8. To create the material for the second flag, in the Materials Manager, copy Flag 1 and paste. Rename this material "**Flag 2**." In the **Color** channel **Texture** and **Luminance** channel **Texture**, browse to the "**Tutorials/ProjectFiles/Chapter 06/Tutorial 02/FlagDay-01/ FlagDay-Start/tex**" and open "**WA.jpg**."

This copy and paste method streamlines the production process because all three flags will use the same luminance channel method.

It is not necessary to close the Material Editor when copying and pasting new materials. Simply selecting a new material updates the contents of the Material Editor.

9. To create the material for the third flag, in the Materials Manager, copy Flag 1 and paste. Rename this material "**Flag 3**." In the **Color** channel **Texture** and **Luminance** channel **Texture**, browse to the "**Tutorials/ProjectFiles/Chapter 06/Tutorial 02/FlagDay-01/ FlagDay-Start/tex**" folder and open "**3D-Kanji.jpg**."
10. To create the material for the flagpole, add a new material and name it "**Flag Pole**." Check the **Environment** channel and in the **Texture**, browse to open "**Tutorials/ProjectFiles/Chapter 06/Tutorial 02/ FlagDay-01/FlagDay-Start/tex/Desert-1.jpg**." As you can see, this reflection is too bright, so set the **Brightness** to 30 and the **Mix Strength** to 70.
11. In the Objects Manager, select the two flag pole instance objects and make them editable to convert each of them into a polygon object hierarchy of a pole and a flag.

Without converting the instance objects to a polygon hierarchy, you cannot access the second and third flags independently of their flagpoles.

12. Now it's time to rename flags and flagpoles in the Objects Manager. Rename the three flags and poles as shown in Figure 6.6.

Renaming the flags and poles is not required for animation or for applying the three flag materials. It is part of the best practices project organization to help make it clear exactly what function each item in the Objects Manager hierarchy plays. This is particularly useful if you must return to work on a project 6 months later or if you are working with a team of modelers and animators.

13. Now drag the material Flag 1 to the object Flag 1, the material Flag 2 to the object Flag 2, and the material Flag 3 to the object Flag 3. Also, drag the Flag Pole material to each of the three flagpoles. Render the perspective view to see an image similar to Figure 6.7.

FIGURE 6.6   The three flags and flagpoles are renamed in the Objects Manager.

 To see the applied material properly, deselect all objects or select the light object.

FIGURE 6.7   The three flags and poles now have their materials applied.

14. To bring the first flag to life, in the Objects Manager, right-click on Flag 1 and choose **Clothlide Tags/Cloth**. To see the result of adding the cloth tag to the flag, play the animation. The flag falls and bounces on the floor (shown in Figure 6.8).

FIGURE 6.8   The flag falls and bounces on the floor.

15. Earlier, in step 1, the default project (FlagDay-Start.c4d) loaded with the floor and wall already set up to interact with cloth objects. That's why the flag didn't just fall through the floor. To view this, in the Objects Manager, on the Floor object, the first tag is a Collider tag (orange ball pushing left into a blue cloth) (see Figure 6.9).

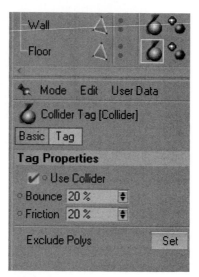

FIGURE 6.9   The floor already has a Collider tag.

16. For the simulation of the flags to realistically interact with the flagpoles, add a Collider tag to the flagpoles by right-clicking on each pole and choosing **Clothlide Tag/Collider**. With this tag applied, the flag will not go through the pole. At this point, the flag still falls to the floor if you play the animation because the flag isn't connected to the flagpole.

It's important to understand that when animating with dynamics (either soft body or rigid body), the hierarchical structure in the Objects Manager does not cause child objects to behave and move in sync with their parent objects. Instead, it is the physics interaction of the objects colliding, gravity pulling, and forces such as wind that determine motion. Additionally, key frames for the position, rotation, and scaling of an object with a cloth tag are ignored. Once a cloth tag is applied, all motion for that object is set in the cloth tag.

17. To connect the flag to the flagpole, start by first selecting the flag in the Objects Manager. In the front view, hit "**o**" to frame the flag. Switch to **Point** mode and use the **Live Selection** tool to select the leftmost row of points (shown in Figure 6.10).

FIGURE 6.10   Left row of points selected on the first flag.

18. While still in **Point** mode, select the **Cloth** tag in the Objects Manager. In the Attributes Manager, **Dresser** tab, click **Set** in the **Fix Points**. This locks the selected points in the flag to their location next to the pole. Play the animation to see that the flag no longer drops to the floor. Now it appears to be held by the flagpole (shown in Figure 6.11).

It is very important to note that Fix Points really does fix the cloth object's points to one location. If you wanted to create an animation in which the flagpole was moving around and the flag remained attached to it, you would need to employ the Belting method. More on this later.

FIGURE 6.11   The leftmost row of points in the Flag object are now fixed in their position relative to the flagpole. The flag now appears to hang from the pole and no longer falls to the floor.

19. To add the energy of wind blowing the flag, select the **Cloth** tag in the Attributes Manager, **Forces** tab, and set the **Wind Direction** to **X** = 2, **Y** = 0, and **Z** = 0. This determines what angle the wind will blow from. Set the **Wind Strength** to 5 so that the flag flies with visible force. Set the **Turbulence Strength** to 1 and **Turbulence Speed** to 1. Turbulence causes the disruption in the wind that produces the undulating variation found in real wind. Set the **Wind Lift** to 50 and check **Self Repulsion**. Wind lift is the amount of impact the wind will have on the surface of the flag and self-repulsion is used to cause the points in the flag to push away from each other when they are about to collide. This helps prevent the flag from appearing to fold through itself unnaturally. In the **Expert** tab, check **Self Collision** to additionally ensure the flag doesn't fold through itself.

If you sit in a room in front of a single-speed nonoscillating fan, you will experience the wind of the fan with very little turbulence. If you stand in a storm, the wind you will experience will be turbulent. Turbulence is the agitating interruption of the flow of the wind.

20. Now, to take a look at this simulation, rather than trying to play the animation and calculate each frame of the cloth, in the **Cache** tab, click **Calculate Cache**. This stores each frame of the simulation. Play the animation to see the flag fluidly flying in the wind. Render frame 148 to see an image similar to Figure 6.12.

 It is normal that playback of an uncached cloth simulation will be very slow. An enormous number of internal soft body calculations must be made. The more polygons in the cloth object, the slower the uncached simulation will play.

FIGURE 6.12   Rendered image of frame 148. The flag now flies in the wind without going through the flagpole.

21. Repeat steps 17 to 20 on the remaining two flags to make all three flags fly in the wind. Once completed, play the animation to see an image similar to Figure 6.13.

 Caching a cloth simulation in which there are several cloth objects (each having many polygons) can take several minutes to calculate. You can select all of the Cloth tags and then click Calculate Cache. Cinema 4D will calculate the cache for each cloth tag sequentially. When you come back to Cinema 4D, they will all be ready and you can simply play the animation. This can free you up to perform other non–Cinema 4D tasks during the caching process.

FIGURE 6.13   All three flags now fly in the wind.

Summary

The value of the illusion of wind can really bring an environment to life. The issues covered in this tutorial should prepare you to produce cloth- and wind-based animations. This method of fixing points to restrict movement of areas of a cloth object is a very powerful concept for animations where the fixed points won't need to move.

TUTORIAL 3   **DRAPES**

Covered in this tutorial:

- Mocca Cloth tags
- Mocca Collider tag
- Simulation caching
- Modeling the drapes
- Internal cloth-to-cloth simulation
- Material color channel mixing
- Sky plug-in
- Merging documents

FIGURE 6.14   Two layered drapes blow in the wind in this finished render.

In this tutorial, you will create an animation of two layers of drapes blowing in the wind. The challenge in this animation comes from the issues involving cloth-to-cloth simulation. If you were to simulate each layer of the drapes as a separate cloth object, the result would be very odd because Cinema 4D treats each cloth tag as a separate soft body simulation. Two cloth objects would pass through each other rather than collide with each other. Adding a collider tag to an object that already has a cloth tag makes for conflicting calculations in which neither the cloth nor the collider tags are effective. Still, it is useful to be able to create the illusion of multilayered cloth objects such as a character wearing a jacket over a shirt, a stack of napkins, or a two-layer set of drapes.

In this tutorial, you will create the illusion of two sets of two-layer drapes being blown inward from the wind coming through two open doors. Finished project files for four sections of this tutorial are included on the accompanying DVD-ROM in the tutorials folder. All of the images used in this tutorial are located in Tutorials/ProjectFiles/Chapter 06/Tutorial-03 on the Projects DVD-ROM.

ON THE DVD

1. Begin by loading the "**Tutorials/ProjectFiles/Chapter 06/Tutorial-03/Drapes-Start/Drapes-Start.c4d**" project from the DVD-ROM. This loads a scene of a room with two open doors, a ceiling and a tiled wood floor. A small exterior hill is in the scene as well. An interior light and an exterior light are already placed in the scene.

2. Start by creating a new material and naming it "**Walls**." In the **Color** channel, set the **Color** to 255, 242, 222. Uncheck the **Specular** channel. Check the **Bump** channel and in the **Texture**, browse to "**Tutorials/ProjectFiles/Chapter 06/Tutorial-03/Drapes-Start/ tex/**" and open "**cnc06.jpg**." Set the **Strength** to −34. Then apply the Walls material to the Walls object.

3. Create a new material and name it "**Floor**." In the **Color** channel **Texture**, browse to open "**Tutorials/ProjectFiles/Chapter 06/ Tutorial-03/Drapes-Start/tex/wood15M.jpg**." Check the **Diffusion** channel, set the **Texture** to wood15M.jpg. Be sure that both **Affect Specular** and **Affect Reflection** are checked. Check the **Reflection** channel and set its **Brightness** to 35.

 When Affect Reflection is first checked in the Diffuse channel, there is no apparent change. After setting the Reflection channel, toggle the Affect Reflection in the Diffuse channel to see the benefit of this feature being selected.

4. In the **Specular** channel, set the **Width** to 50 and the **Height** to 60 to keep the specular highlights small and crisp. In the **Specular Color**, set the **Texture** to wood15M.jpg to further control where the specular highlights occur. Apply the Floor material to the Floor object. In the Attribute Manager, set **Tiles X** to 20 and **Tiles Y** to 10 to create reasonably sized tiles on the floor.

5. Create a new material and name it "**DoorWood**." Set the **Color** channel **Texture** to "**Tutorials/ProjectFiles/Chapter 06/Tutorial-03/Drapes-Start/tex/wood15M.jpg**." Set the **Color** to 255, 75, 18. Up to this point, the color channel has either been used to set a color or to load an image as a texture. Now you will combine those functions in this material. Set the **Mix Strength** to 60. This material color mixing allows you to change only the color of the wood. This method allows you to more closely match a wood pattern with a known type of wood. Check the **Diffusion** channel and set the **Texture** to wood15M.jpg. To create the material for the glass inserts in the door, choose **File/ Shader/Banji** in the Material Manager.

6. Drag the DoorWood material to the Door object. The entire door appears to be made of wood. If you inspect the tags for this door in the Objects Manager, you will find a polygon selection tag named glass. Drag the Banji material to the Door object and drag the glass polygon selection to the **Selection** field of the Banji material to cause the inserts of the door to become glass.

7. Repeat step 6, applying the materials to the second door. Rendering the perspective will show an image similar to Figure 6.15.

Be sure to apply the door materials to the polygon object and not the null object parent. Otherwise the door will not be wooden with glass inserts.

FIGURE 6.15   The materials for the walls, floor, and first door are now applied.

8. Create a new material and name it "**Ground.**" In the **Color** channel **Texture**, browse to open "**Tutorials/ProjectFiles/Chapter 06/ Tutorial-03/Drapes-Start/tex/grnd01M.jpg.**" Set the **Color** to 255, 156, 55 and set the **Mix Strength** to 50. This adds some apparent saturation to the material. Check the **Diffusion** channel and set the **Texture** to grnd01M.jpg and set the **Mix Strength** to 40. Check the **Bump** channel and set the **Texture** to grnd01M.jpg and the **Strength** to −100. This makes the grit, dirt, and stone appear to have some elevation. To keep the ground from shining, uncheck the **Specular** channel. Drag the Ground material to the Ground object. In the Attributes Manager, set the **Tiles X** and **Tiles Y** to 5. This makes the ground and small hill outside appear like dirt (shown in Figure 6.16).

9. In previous tutorials, when creating a sky, you've used the Cinema 4D 9 method of adding a Sky object and then mapping an image onto the Sky object. Now you're going to create the sky using the Sky plug-in in Cinema 4D 9.5. In the **Main** menu, choose **Plugins/Sky/Create Sky**. If you look in the Objects Manager, you will see that an Environment object and a Sky volume material have been added. In the Materials Manager, double-click the **Sky Volume**. In the **Beginner** tab, change the **Time** to 16:0 30 June 2005. While making these adjustments, you may notice that both the material sample and the sky in the perspective view are changing in response to these settings.

FIGURE 6.16   The ground material is now applied.

 While you could simply click the Now button, this could produce undesirable results if you wish to see a bright sky and it is now nighttime at your location. This is because the Sky object gets its time from your system clock (shown in Figure 6.17).

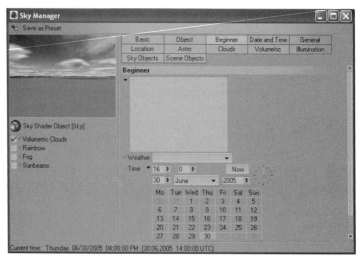

FIGURE 6.17   Current time on the system clock.

10. To adjust the clouds in the sky, click the **Clouds** tab and expand **Layer 2**. Set the **Noise** to Gasous, **Density** to 410, **Coverage** to 45, **Thickness** to 0 and **Scale N-S** and **E-W** to 20. Your Sky Manager should now look like Figure 6.18. Close the Sky Manager and render the perspective view to see an image similar to Figure 6.19.

A neat thing about these clouds is that they will automatically animate in the sky even if you don't instruct them to. This frees you up to do more challenging things.

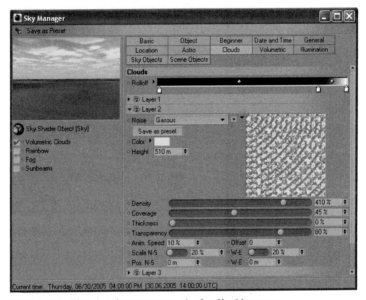

FIGURE 6.18   The clouds are now set in the Sky Manager.

11. The rods that appear to hold the drapes in place in front of the wall and above the doors have already been modeled and saved as a separate project. To combine them with the current project, in the **Main** menu, choose **File/Merge...** and in the "**Tutorials/ProjectFiles/Chapter 06/Tutorial-03/Drapes-02**" folder, open "**DrapesRods-01.c4d**." At the top of the Objects Manager, you now have a new object hierarchy with a null parent named Curtains. It contains a polygon object named CurtainRod-R and an instance object named CurtainRod-L. CurtainRod-L is an instance copy of CurtainRod-R.

12. Create a new material for these curtain rods and name it "**Rods**." In the **Color** channel, set the **Color** to 255, 202, 75. Check the **Environment** channel and in the **Texture** browse to open the "**Tutorials/**

FIGURE 6.19   The clouds are now rendering in the sky outside.

ProjectFiles/Chapter 06/Tutorial-03/Drapes-Start/tex/desert-1.jpg" image. Set the **Color** to 255, 197, 95. Set the **Brightness** to 59. Apply the Rods material to both CurtainRod-L and CurtainRod-R.

The colors set in the Color channel and Environment channel are very interactive and work together to determine the apparent color of this material. For a material like rich gold both sets of colors are required.

13. You will be creating two layers of drapes. Although the two layers will be in one polygon object, they will appear to be hanging from separate curtain rods. In the Objects Manager, select both curtain rods, then copy and paste them to create two more curtain rods. In the right view, position the new curtain rods as shown in Figure 6.20.
14. It's time to create the drapes. Start by choosing **File/New** in the **Main** menu to start a new project. As you may remember, starting a new project in Cinema 4D does not close your existing project, so don't worry. You haven't lost your work.

Even though Cinema 4D doesn't destroy the previous project with the room and the curtain rods, it's always a good idea to save your work periodically. It's also a good idea to save your work with version info such as Drapes-01, Drapes-02, Drapes-03, or some other identifier that lets you know where you were in the setup process.

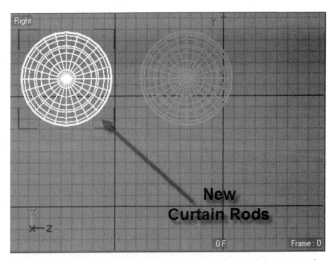

FIGURE 6.20   New curtain rods are moved in front of the original curtain rods in the right view.

15. To start spline modeling a cross section of the drapes, in the top view, add a **Formula Spline** (Figure 6.21). Set the **X** position to −365. In the Attributes Manager, **Object** tab, set the **Plane** to XZ, **Tmax** to 9 to add more cycles to the curve, **Samples** to 30, and **Intermediate Point**s to Uniform to help smooth the curves of the spline.

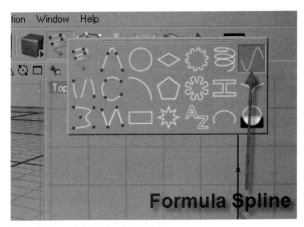

FIGURE 6.21   Add a Formula Spline.

16. Now with the parametric modeling of the spline completed, click the **Make Editable** icon to convert the spline into a simple curve and re-name the Formula object "**Profile**." In the Attributes Manager, change the **Type** from Linear to B-Spline to immediately see the curve become a smooth sine wave shape.

17. Switch to **Point** mode and use the **Live Selection** tool to select any point on the curve. Then type **Ctrl-A** to select all points on the curve. Use the **Scale** tool and hold the **Z** axis and scale to flatten the curve as shown in Figure 6.22.

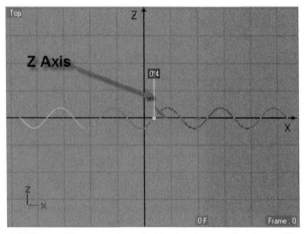

FIGURE 6.22   The curve is scaled in the Z axis only. The profile curve modeling is now completed.

18. With the profile curve still selected, hold the **Alt** key down and add an **Extrude NURBS** object. This makes the Extrude NURBS the parent of the profile curve. Select the Extrude NURBS. In the Attributes Manager, **Object** tab, set the **Movement** to 0, 1227, 0 for now. The final length will be set later when the drapes are copied and pasted into the project with the curtain rods and floor.

The main thing here is to have no movement in the X or Z axis.

19. If you look at the Extrude NURBS object in the front view, you will see that the geometry is very dense (shown in Figure 6.23). To re-duce the amount of detail in this object, select the profile curve and in the Attributes Manager, set the **Number** to 0. The geometry den-sity is greatly reduced while still maintaining the general shape of the drapes (shown in Figure 6.24).

All the white color in Figure 6.23 is the result of the high density of the drapes geometry so far.

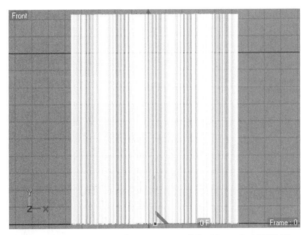

FIGURE 6.23   The original geometry of the Extrude NURBS is unnecessarily dense. This would lead to extraordinarily long cloth simulation processing times and long render times.

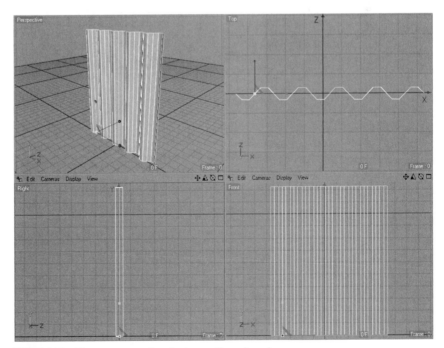

FIGURE 6.24   The geometry density is greatly reduced.

20. Now that the profile curve density is reduced, close inspection of the drapes will show that there are no subdivisions between the top and bottom. If this object were converted to a polygon object and given a cloth tag, it would respond poorly to wind. This is because it would be flexible horizontally, but not vertically, as there are no vertical subdivisions. So, select the Extrude NURBS and in the Attributes Manager, **Object** tab, set the **Subdivision** to 20. The drapes now have an appropriate amount of well-distributed geometry (shown in Figure 6.25).

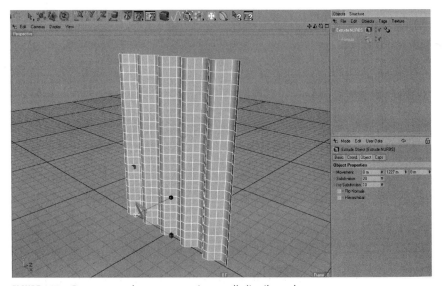

FIGURE 6.25   Drapes now have appropriate well-distributed geometry.

21. Make the Extrude NURBS editable and rename it "**Drapes**." Copy and paste to create a second drapes object and rename this new object "**Sheer**." In the top view, in **Model** mode, move the sheer object with the **Move** tool as shown in Figure 6.26.

22. In the Objects Manager, toggle the Drapes' **Editor Display Switch** off (red dot) so that only the Sheer object is visible in the viewports. Select the Sheer object and frame it in the front view. In the front view, using the **Rectangle Selection** tool, select the bottom nine horizontal rows of points and delete them. In the Objects Manager, toggle the Drapes' **Editor Display Switch** on (gray dot) so that both objects are once again visible.

23. To combine both objects into one object (as is needed for the cloth simulation), select both Drapes and Sheer and in the **Main** menu choose **Functions/Connect** to create a new object named "**Drapes.1**," which

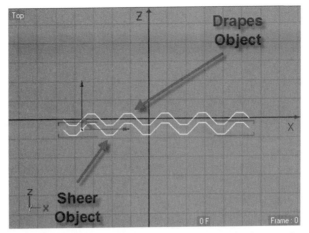

FIGURE 6.26   Sheer object moved into position in the top view.

contains both the Drapes and Sheer object. Then rename Drapes.1 **"Drapes"** and copy the Drapes object. Select the previous project from the bottom of the Windows menu and paste the Drapes into the original project.

24. With the Drapes selected, in the top view in **Model** mode, use the **Move** tool and the **Scale** tool to match the position and scale of the drapes to the curtain rods on the right side of the doors (shown in Figure 6.27).

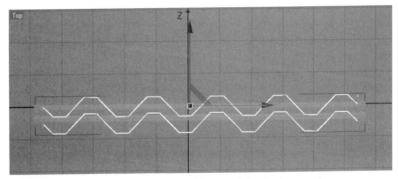

FIGURE 6.27   Drapes scaled and moved into position in the top view.

25. In the front view, move the drapes so that the top of the drapes touches the bottom of the curtain rods (shown in Figure 6.28). Switch to the **Use Axis** tool and use the **Move** tool to move the axis to the top of the Drapes.1 (shown in Figure 6.28) object. Switch to **Model** mode and

get the **Scale** tool. Mouse over the Y axis (green arrow) until it turns yellow, then drag it down until the bottom of the drapes is almost to the bottom of the door (shown in Figure 6.28).

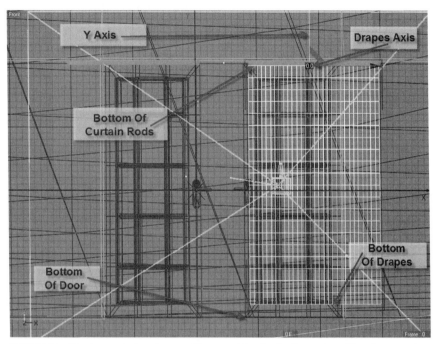

FIGURE 6.28   Drapes scaled and moved into position in the front view. The drapes axis is moved to the top. The drapes have been scaled into their final height.

26. To distinguish the Drapes from the Sheer, you will need to make a polygon selection. Working in the top view, turn off the **Editor Display Switch** for the Curtains hierarchy and select the Drapes object. Switch to **Polygon** mode and use the **Live Selection** tool (**Only Select Visible Elements** unchecked) to select the Sheer polygons. In the **Main** menu, choose **Selection/Set Selection**. In the Objects Manager, Drapes object, select the **Polygon Selection** tag (red triangle), and in the Attributes Manager, **Basic Properties**, set the Name to "**Sheer**."

27. Turn on the **Editor Display Switch** for the Curtains hierarchy. Copy and paste the Drapes object. Name the original drapes "**Drapes-R**" and name the new drapes "**Drapes-L**." In the Front view, using the **Move** tool, hold the Drapes-L object by the **X** axis (red arrow) and move it to be directly under the left curtain rods.

28. In the Materials Manager, create a new material and name it "**Drapes**." In the **Color** channel **Texture**, browse to open "**Tutorials/ProjectFiles/Chapter 06/Tutorial-03/Drapes-Start/tex/pattern12M.jpg**." Check the **Transparency** channel. Set the **Texture** to pattern12M.jpg. Set the **Brightness** to 50 and the **Mix Strength** to 66. There will be some transparency in the drapes. Uncheck the **Specular** channel. Check the **Bump** channel and set the **Texture** to pattern12M.jpg. Set the **Strength** to −100 to give the drapes a visual sense of texture. Apply the Drapes material to both Drapes-L and Drapes-R objects.

29. Create a new material and name it "**Sheer**." Right-click on the material sample and choose **Plane** so that the material sample will be flat and therefore more indicative of how this material will really look on the sheer drapes. In the **Color** channel **Texture**, choose Noise. To edit the Noise, click **Noise** and set **Color** 1 to 209, 243, 171. Check the **Bump** channel and in **Texture**, browse to open "**Tutorials/ProjectFiles/Chapter 06/Tutorial 03/Drapes-Start/tex/Drapes-01.png**." Set the **Strength** to 100. Check the **Alpha** channel and set the **Texture** to Drapes-01.png. Then uncheck the **Specular** channel.

30. Apply this Sheer material to the Drapes-R object and drag the sheer polygon selection into the **Selection** field in the Attributes Manager **Tag** tab. Repeat this for the Drapes-L object as well. Select the Sheer material tag for both Drapes-L and Drapes-R. In the Attributes Manager, **Tag** tab, set the **Tiles X** and **Tiles Y** to 15 to reduce the pattern of the Sheer material on the sheer part of the drapes. Render the perspective view to see an image similar to Figure 6.29.

FIGURE 6.29 Drapes and Sheer materials applied.

31. To create the illusion that the drapes are fastened to the curtain rods, select Drapes-L and switch to **Point** mode. In the front view, using the **Live Selection** tool (**Only Select Visible Elements** unchecked), select the top row of points. In the Objects Manager, right-click on the Drapes-L and choose **Clothlide/Cloth**. With the new cloth tag selected, in the Attributes Manager, in the **Dresser** tab, in the **Fix Points**, click **Set**. The fixed points turn purple. Now the top row of points for the left drapes and sheers are fixed in the initial position right below the curtain rods. Just like in Hollywood, we're focusing on the illusion, not on the reality.

32. Repeat step 31 for Drapes-R.

33. If you go to your perspective view and press the **Play** button on the Transport Control, the drapes will be active and respond to gravity, but since they have their top points fixed in place, they will not fall down.

34. Though the drapes are responding to the cloth tags, they are a bit boring right now. To add some life to this scene, select both cloth tags. In the Attributes Manager, **Tag** tab, set the **Stiffness** to 15 to allow the drapes to be very flexible. Set **Flexion** to 20 to cause the drapes minimal effort to return to their original shape, **Rubber** to 10 to stretch a little and the **Friction** to 5 so they don't get snagged on themselves.

35. In the **Forces** tab, set the **Global Drag** to 5, set the **Wind Direction** to **Z** = −2 so the drapes appear to be moving in wind coming through the doors from the outside. Set the **Wind Strength** to 1.4, **Turbulent Strength** to 5, and **Turbulent Speed** to 3. The turbulence controls how the wind is agitated. Set the **Wind Lift** to 20 to cause the wind to have great impact when hitting the surface of the drapes.

36. In the **Expert** tab, check **Self Collision** so the drapes and sheers don't pass through each other. Set the **Sub Sampling** to 10 to increase the accuracy of the simulation.

The Sub Sampling and Self Collision settings are set to ensure that the two layers of drapes don't pass through each other.

The Expert tab settings are most useful in solving accuracy errors when a cloth simulation seems to penetrate itself or collide with objects.

37. In the **Cache** tab, click **Calculate Cache** to cache the simulation. Cinema 4D caches one cloth simulation and then caches the other. After both cloth tags are cached, play the animation to see the drapes flying in the wind (shown in Figure 6.30).

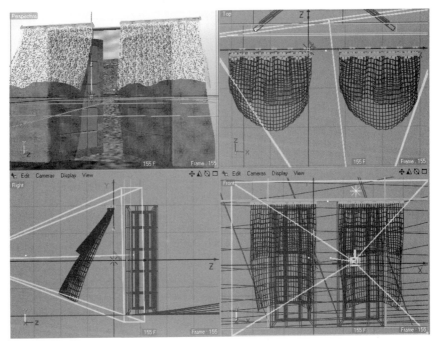

FIGURE 6.30   Drapes flying in the wind.

Summary

This tutorial opens up the possibilities of how some complex multilayered soft body animation might be accomplished. Again you saw in this tutorial the value of choosing the appropriate material to make the illusion a success. Real-world 3D animation production requires that you always think about all aspects of the illusion.

TUTORIAL 4	**TAILOR MADE**

Covered in this tutorial:

- Mocca Cloth tags
- Mocca Collider tag
- Belting
- Dress-O-Matic
- Stitch and Sew
- Clone

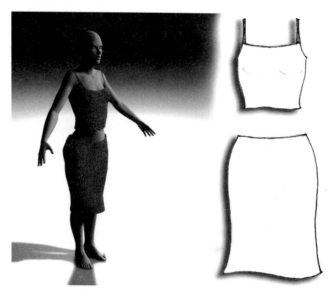

FIGURE 6.31   (Left) The finished render of the 3D modeled outfit.
(Right) The hand sketched drawing used as a modeling reference
to make the 3D outfit.

In this tutorial, you will create an outfit for a 3D female model. The outfit will be based on a hand-drawn sketch, which will be brought in as a reference. This tutorial combines polygon modeling and cloth simulation to create clothing that conforms to a 3D character. This clothing can be posed with the character and can be worn in full action scenes with the same limitations and restrictions as real-life clothing. Once you master this tutorial, you'll be ready to fashion 3D clothing for any character you create or add to Cinema 4D.

ON THE DVD

Finished project files for five sections of this tutorial are included on the accompanying DVD-ROM in the tutorials folder. All of the images used in this tutorial are located in Tutorials/ProjectFiles/Chapter 6/ Tutorial-04 on the Projects DVD-ROM.

1. Begin by adding the 3D female model to the scene. From the **Main** menu choose **Objects/Object Library/Human Meg**. This adds a HyperNURB 3D character named Meg to the scene (Figure 6.32). You will use Meg's default pose for designing and fitting the outfit.

2. To add the reference sketch of the outfit, first create a new material and name it "**Reference.**" In the **Color** channel **Texture**, browse to "**Tutorials/ProjectFiles/Chapter 06/Tutorial-04/TailorMade-01/tex**" and open "**Outfit-1.png.**" Check the **Alpha** channel and sit the **Texture** to "**Outfit-1.png.**" Uncheck the **Specular** channel and set the preview sample to **Plane** (shown in Figure 6.32).

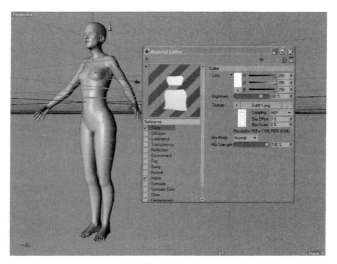

FIGURE 6.32 Meg and the reference material.

3. To add the sketch reference in 3D to the scene, add a **Plane** object and set its **Orientation** to –Z. Rename the plane "**Reference.**" To ensure that the sketch reference maintains its aspect ratio and is not squashed or stretched, set the initial **Width** to 56.5 and **Height** to 116.5. As you will not need any geometry detail in the reference, set the **Width Segments** and **Height Segments** to 1. Apply the Reference material to the Reference object.

The pixel resolution of the reference image (Outfit-1.png) is 565 × 1165, so by setting the reference object width to 56.5 and height to 116.5, the reference image is not distorted. Scaling the plane uniformly will then preserve the reference image's aspect ratio.

4. In the right view, position the reference object in front of Meg (shown in Figure 6.33).
5. In the front view, using the local menu, choose **Display/Gouraud Shading**. Use the **Scale** tool to uniformly scale the Reference object to match Meg's size and the **Move** tool to position the Reference object so that it appears as if Meg is wearing the sketched outfit (shown in Figure 6.34).
6. It will be easier to work with the Reference object and Meg if you create some difference in color between them, so in the Materials Manager, change the material (Meg's skin color) by changing the **Color** channel **Color** to 255, 180, 126.

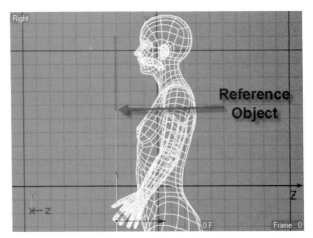

FIGURE 6.33   The Reference object is placed in front of Meg.

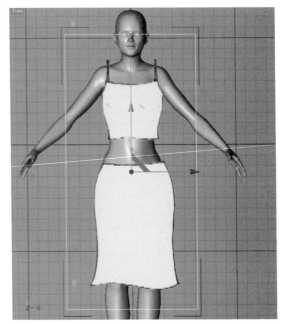

FIGURE 6.34   Front view of the Reference object in place with Meg.

7. To start creating the outfit's top, add a **Plane** object and set its **Orientation** to –Z. Set the **Width Segments** and **Height Segments** to 10 since this will be a cloth object. Use the plane's parametric handles (the two little orange dots on the edge of the plane) to be a little

larger than the Reference object. In the right view, move the plane in front of Meg (shown in Figure 6.35).

The plane object will be used to model the top of the outfit. Because this model will be formed using the cloth tag, it is important not to model the clothing for a precise fit. The Dress-O-Matic function in the cloth tag will need some room to conform the clothing to the character, so the reference sketch of the outfit gives general shape and style rather than being a strict modeling directive.

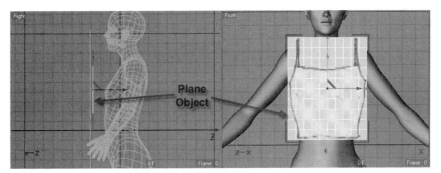

FIGURE 6.35   The outfit top plane is now in position.

8. Make the plane editable and check its **X-Ray** on in the Attributes Manager, **Basic** tab. Also check the **X-Ray** on for the Reference object. With the plane selected, in **Point** mode, select the five vertical rows of points on the right and delete them. The plane is now approximately half as wide as the Reference object (shown in Figure 6.36).

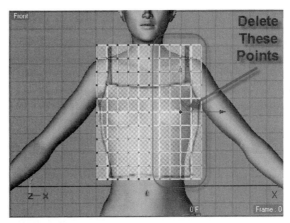

FIGURE 6.36   Delete the five vertical rows of points on the right of the plane.

9. With the plane still selected, add a **Symmetry** object with the **Alt** key held down. This makes the new symmetry object the plane's parent. The plane once again appears to be a little wider than the Reference object. Check the symmetry object's **X-Ray**.

 By deleting half of the plane's points vertically and then adding a symmetry object as the plane's parent, you will now be able to model the outfit top by only modeling the left half.

10. Select the plane and switch to **Polygon** mode. In the upper right corner of the plane, select the group of polygons shown in Figure 6.37 and delete them.

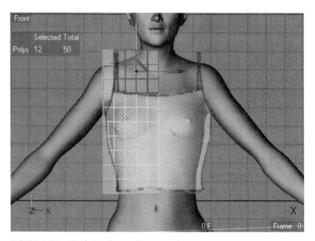

FIGURE 6.37 Delete the polygons shown.

11. Switch to **Point** mode. Right-click and choose **Optimize** and then **OK** to get rid of the orphaned points. Observe Figure 6.38 and use the **Move** tool in **Tweak** mode to move the plane's points to more closely match the Reference object.

 Be very careful not to move the rightmost points in the X axis. Moving these points can cause a tear in the center of the outfit.

12. Select the symmetry object and make it editable. This makes the virtual right side of the plane object become a real part of the plane object. Then remove the plane object from the symmetry object hierarchy and delete the symmetry object. Rename the plane "**Top**."

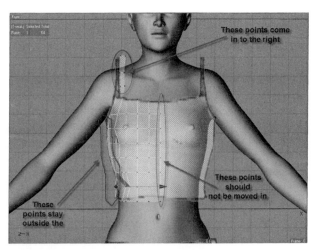

FIGURE 6.38   The plane's points moved into position.

13. In the right view and **Polygon** mode, switch back to **Default** mode. With the Top object selected, right-click and choose **Clone**. In the Attributes Manager, click **Apply**. Adjust the **Offset** in the **Z** axis to –125. Your front and right views should now look like Figure 6.39.

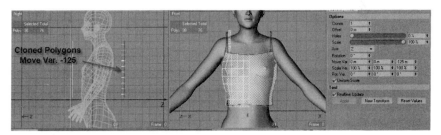

FIGURE 6.39   Cloned polygons are moved to –125 in the Z axis, which places them behind Meg's back.

14. Deselect all polygons, then right-click and choose **Subdivide** and then **OK**. This adds more geometry that will be useful when working with the Dress-O-Matic.

The number of width and height segments were initially reduced in the plane for easier control over the shaping of the outfit. In preparation for working with the top as an article of clothing, you now add more geometry with the subdivision because the placement of each point in the object will be controlled by the soft body deformation calculations of the cloth tag.

15. Switch to **Edge** mode and use the **Live Selection** tool (**Only Select Visible Elements** unchecked) to select the outer edges of the Top, which will form a clothing seam between the front and back of the Top, taking care not to select the edges indicated in Figure 6.40.

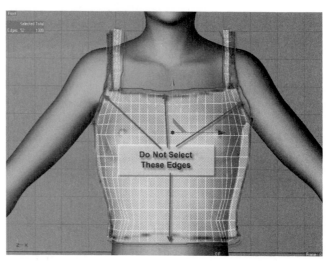

FIGURE 6.40 Select the edges along the sides and the tops of the shoulder straps, taking care not to select the outer edges indicated here.

16. In the perspective view, right-click and choose **Stitch and Sew** and with the **Shift** key held down, connect the front edges to the back edges as shown in Figure 6.41. Do this to each set of selected edges around the Top object.

Stitch and Sew works a lot like the Bridge tool except that entire groups of edges can be connected at once. Unlike the Bridge tool, Stitch and Sew will automatically and correctly connect the edges even if you accidentally cross the edges (for example at the top of the spaghetti straps) (Figure 6.42).

17. In the Objects Manager, in the HyperNURBS hierarchy, right-click on the Mesh polygon object and choose **Clothlide Tags/Collider** so that when the outfit is being fitted, it will not pass through Meg.

18. In **Polygon** mode, in the top view, with the **Live Selection** tool (**Only Select Visible Elements** unchecked), select the new polygons that connect the front polygons to the back polygons. In the Objects Manager, right-click on the Top object and choose **Clothlide Tags/Cloth** to make the Top into a cloth object.

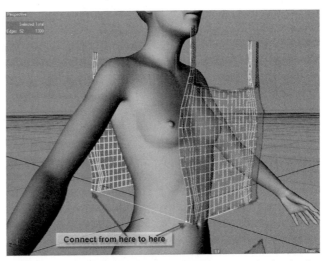

FIGURE 6.41   Stitch and Sew from the front edge to the back edge.

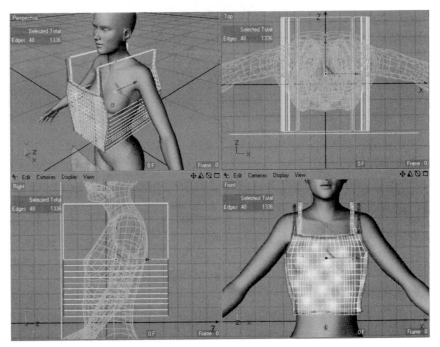

FIGURE 6.42   All selected edges connected with Stitch and Sew.

19. Select the Top object and the Cloth tag. Be sure that you are still in **Polygon** mode with the side polygons still selected. In the Attributes Manager, in the **Dresser** tab, in the **Seam Polys,** click the **Set** button.

This now identifies the side polygons as seams in the fabric of clothing and places an x in the center of each of the front unselected polygons. Set the Dress-O-Matic **Width** to 5 to make the seams pull tightly on the front and back of the Top object. Click the **Dress-O-Matic** button to cause the Top to fit Meg's upper body.

20. Toggle the Reference object's **Render Display Switch** off (red dot), and render the perspective view to see an image similar to Figure 6.43.

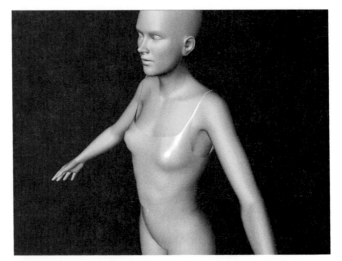

FIGURE 6.43   The outfit top fitted to Meg with Dress-O-Matic.

21. Click the **Relax** button to cause the outfit top to relax on Meg's upper body.

 This relaxing of the Top is determined by the Tag and Forces tabs of the cloth object.

 When trying to differentiate between different types of clothing such as silk, cotton, leather, and denim, the Stiffness, Flexion, and Rubber setting in the Tag tab are used to simulate the particular behavior of these different fabric types. To give the impression of weight, use the Mass setting in the Tag tab and the Gravity setting in the Forces tab.

22. With the Top still selected, select the Cloth tag. In the **Dresser** tab, in the **Init State**, click the **Set** button. This tells the Cloth tag that for all future simulation, this is the initial shape for this object. Flexion, Rubber, and Stiffness will all be applied with reference to this initial state.

Caution: Failure to set the Initial State will cause erratic behavior in simulation.

23. With the Top selected, hold the **Alt** key down and from the **Main** menu choose **Plugins/Clothlide/Cloth Nurbs** to add the Cloth Nurbs as the parent of the Top. With the **Cloth Nurbs** tag selected, in the Attributes Manager, **Object** tab, set the **Thickness** to 0.5 so that the fabric of the Top object is no longer paper-thin.

 The Cloth Nurbs causes the Top to render more smoothly by using a method similar to HyperNURBS, but it's more suited to creating the soft creases and wrinkles of a cloth surface. Additionally, the Cloth Nurbs tag can be used to give apparent thickness to the cloth object so that clothing is not paper-thin.

24. To create Meg's skirt, add a **Plane** object and set its **Orientation** to –Z. Then check the **X-Ray** and rename the Plane "**Skirt**." In the front view, use the skirt's parametric handles to shape it to be slightly larger than the skirt in the Reference object. In the right view, move the skirt to be in front of Meg but not in front of the Reference object. Set the **Width Segments** to 4 and the **Height Segments** to 10. Make the skirt editable.

25. Switch to **Point** mode and **Tweak** mode and use the **Move** tool to shape the skirt object to the reference of the skirt. Remember to keep the left and right points of the skirt outside Meg's body (shown in Figure 6.44).

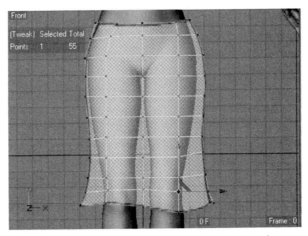

FIGURE 6.44   The skirt is now conformed to the basic shape of the Reference object skirt.

26. Switch to **Default** mode and **Polygon** mode. **Subdivide** the skirt. In the right view, right-click and select **Clone**. In the Attributes Manager, click **Apply**. The cloned skirt polygons appear behind Meg. The previous values used when creating the Top object are still present in the Clone Options.

27. In the front view, switch to **Edge** mode and select the left and right side edges only, leaving the top and bottom edges unselected. Then right click and choose the **Stitch and Sew**. With the **Shift** key held down, connect the front and back left edges and then the front and back right edges so that it looks like Meg is standing in a curved box (shown in Figure 6.45).

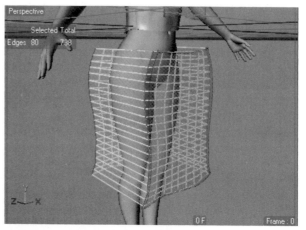

FIGURE 6.45   The front and back are now connected using Stitch and Sew.

28. Since the skirt will not have shoulders to hold it up, you will have to use a Belt tag to keep it in place. In preparation of adding the Belt tag, switch to **Point** mode and in the front view, select only the top row of points. These are the points that will be belted.

29. Switch to **Polygon** mode and select the side polygons created by the Stitch and Sew tool. Right-click on skirt in the Objects Manager and choose **Clothlide Tags/Cloth**. Select the **Cloth** tag. In the Attributes Manager, **Dresser** tab, in the **Seam Polys**, click the **Set** button. Set the **Width** to 2 and click the **Dress-O-Matic** button to fit the skirt to Meg. In **Init State**, click the **Set** button.

30. Switch to **Point** mode. In the Objects Manager, right-click on the skirt object and choose **Clothlide Tags/Belt**. With the **Belt** tag selected, select the object that the points will be belted to, so in the Hyper-

NURBS hierarchy, drag the Mesh polygon object into the **Belt On** field in the **Belt** tag, and in the **Points**, click the **Set** button.

In Cinema 4D 9, Belting is handled in the Cloth tag Dresser tab.

31. Let's go back to the outfit top for a moment and secure it so there are no "clothing malfunctions." In **Point** mode, select any point in the Top object, then type **Ctrl-A** to select all of the points in the object. In the Objects Manager, right-click on the Top object and choose **Clothlide Tags/Belt**. Drag the Mesh polygon object from the HyperNURBS hierarchy into the **Belt On** field. Then in the **Points**, click the **Set** button. Now Meg's top won't surprise her by falling off. Using the default Influence and Hover settings, the Top would be very rigid. Set the **Influence** and **Hover** to 50 to relax the belting of the outfit top.

When you're working with belted objects, each belted point is drawn in the viewport as a thick little yellow square. When you have many of them at once (as is the case with the outfit top), it can be difficult or even impossible to see other important aspects of some objects. With the Belt tag selected, in the tag properties, unchecking the Draw turns off the belting display while still keeping the belting functionality.

Though ultimately not as secure, you could use a very high value in the Stiffness setting in the Tag tab of the cloth object to cause the spaghetti straps (and the rest of the outfit top) to be more rigid and less likely to accidentally fall off.

32. Now, with the skirt selected, hold the **Alt** key down and from the **Main** menu choose **Plugins/Clothlide/Cloth Nurbs** to add the Cloth Nurbs as the parent of the skirt. With the **Cloth Nurbs** tag selected, in the Attributes Manager, **Object** tab, set the **Thickness** to 0.5.

33. In the Materials Manager, create a new material and name it "**Cloth**." In the **Color** channel **Texture**, browse to the "**Goodies/MarlinStudios/Seamless Textures 1—General Purpose Surfaces**" and open "**facr01L.jpg**." Check the **Bump** channel and set the **Texture** to fabr01L.jpg and the **Strength** to 80. Uncheck the **Specular** channel. Apply the Cloth material to the skirt and top objects.

34. Add a **Floor** object and move it to be just beneath Meg's feet. Add a **Light** and position it in the Coordinates Manager at **X** = 570, **Y** = 460, **Z** = −645. Add an **Instance** object of this light and position it at **X** = 570, **Y** = 460, **Z** = 645. With the original light selected, set the **Shadow** to Soft. In the **Shadow** tab, set the **Shadow Map** to be 1000 × 1000. Render the perspective view to see an image similar to Figure 6.46.

FIGURE 6.46   The finished scene of Meg wearing her new tailor-made outfit.

Summary

After going through this tutorial, you should have a real working sense of how to create clothing for any character. By combining creative modeling and the proper use of the cloth and belt tags, you can create all kinds of clothing including (but not limited to) scarves, hats, gloves, shoes, socks, robes, capes, and baseball gloves.

TUTORIAL 5   JELL-O®

Covered in this tutorial:

- Mocca Cloth tags
- Mocca Collider tag
- Subsurface scattering

In the past four tutorials, you have used the Mocca cloth to simulate a tablecloth, flags, drapes, and an outfit for Meg. These are all objects traditionally associated with fabric. In this tutorial, you're going to see a great example of how cloth can be used to simulate Jell-O. If you're having a hard time imagining how Cinema 4D's cloth can be used to simulate Jell-O, just remember that although it's called cloth, it's really a special

FIGURE 6.47   Jell-O cubes falling through an obstacle.

implementation of soft body dynamics with great support for simulating cloth. So, what this tutorial is really about is creating noncloth soft body dynamics simulation using Cinema 4D cloth. Don't worry. It gets less confusing as you begin to simulate your Jell-O.

Finished project files for four sections of this tutorial are included on the accompanying DVD-ROM in the tutorials folder. All of the images used in this tutorial are located in Tutorials/ProjectFiles/Chapter 6/Tutorial-05 on the Projects DVD-ROM.

ON THE DVD

1. Begin by loading the "**Tutorials/ProjectFiles/Chapter 06/Tutorial-05/Jello-Start/Jello-Start.c4d**" project from the DVD-ROM. This loads a scene of a transparent obstacle through which the Jell-O cubes will fall. Once through the obstacle, the Jell-O cubes will settle into a bowl on the floor. A light and two instances of that light are already placed in the scene. The camera and camera target have both been key framed as well.

This tutorial in not like the Driving tutorial, where you placed the camera target in the SUV so that where the SUV went, the camera's interest would follow. This highlights an important issue when simulating cloth objects. When cloth objects move via simulation, their object axis does not move, so making an object a child of a cloth object will not cause the child of the cloth object to move at all. The child object will in fact stay totally still.

2. To create the Jell-O cubes, begin by adding a **Cube** object. In the Attributes Manager set the **Segments X**, **Segments Y**, and **Segments Z** to 4 to give the cube detail for deformation by the Cloth tag. Position the cube at **X** = 385, **Y** = 2672, **Z** = −32.

If you want your Jell-O to have smoother deformation, increase the number of segments in X, Y, and Z. But note that this will slow down the simulation.

3. Make the cube editable and switch to **Polygon** mode. Right-click and choose **Clone**. In the Attributes Manager, set the **Clones** to 12 to create 12 more cubes of Jell-O. Set the **Axis** to Y so that the clones will be stacked upward. Set the **Offset** to 3825 to create enough space between the cubes of Jell-O so they do not intersect each other. Set the **Move Var** to 122, 0, and 128 to create some staggering between the Jell-O cubes in the X and Z axis. The Clone tool is still active, so any adjustments to its options will be updated instantly in the viewports. To commit the Clone settings, choose another tool such as the **Move** tool.

If you can't see clone as an option when you right-click, make sure that you are in Polygon mode and Default mode.

Another approach is to create as many cubes as you wish, and then connect them into one object.

4. In the Objects Manager add a **Cloth** tag to the cube. Rename the Cube **"Jello." Play** the simulation to see the Jell-O responding to gravity from the Cloth tag. The Jell-O cubes fall, but they don't interact with anything yet.

Until the simulation is cached, pressing the Play button on the Transport Control plays the simulation. Once the simulation is cached, pressing Play plays the animation. In simulation, each frame is based on what happened in the previous frame as well as all properties in the cloth tag. In animation, each frame's movement has been previously determined and therefore requires less processing power to play back and plays more quickly.

5. Set the Transport Control back to frame 0. In the Objects Manager, in the **Obstacle** object, select all four walls and cubes. In the **Hyper-NURBS** object select the bowl. Right-click and choose **Clothlide Tags/Collider** so that the Jell-O cubes can collide with the elements of the obstacle and the bowl.

6. If you play the simulation now, you will notice that it moves very slowly. This is because of all the collisions that must be calculated. To get a real sense of what's happening, with the **Cloth** tag selected, in the Attributes Manager, **Cache** tab, click **Calculate Cache**. This will record every frame of the simulation. It will take a few minutes to be completed. Once completed, play the animation to see a result similar to Figure 6.48.

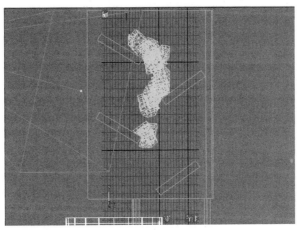

FIGURE 6.48   Jell-O cubes colliding as they travel through the obstacle object.

7. As you can see, the Jell-O cubes are squashing too much. To make them retain their original shape better, with the **Cloth** tag selected, in the Attributes Manager, **Tag** tab, set the **Stiffness** to 25 to make the Jell-O more firm. Set the **Flexion** to 40 to cause the Jell-O cubes to try to get back to their original shape. Set the **Rubber** to 40 to allow them to stretch their volume some and set the **Friction** to 0 so they will be slippery. In the **Forces** tab, check **Self Repulsion** to aid the cubes in not penetrating each other. In the **Expert** tab, check **Self Collision** so the Jell-O cubes will collide with each other. Next, set the **Point EPS**, **Edge EPS**, and **Poly EPS** values to 3 to increase the distance at which a collision is calculated. This reduces the chance that a Jell-O cube will stick through a collision object such as the bowl. Now **Cache** the simulation and play the animation (shown in Figure 6.49).

 Real Jell-O cubes don't repel each other. However when simulating reality, you must sometimes take these extra steps.

FIGURE 6.49   Much firmer Jell-O cubes colliding as they travel through the obstacle object and collect in the bowl.

8. To make the Jell-O cubes look like Jell-O, in the Materials Manager, create a new material and name it "**Jello.**" In the **Color** channel, set the **Color** to 0, 255, and 15. Set the **Brightness** to 45. Check the **Transparency** channel and set the **Color** to 172, 255, and 137. Set the **Brightness** to 90. Set the index of **Refraction** to 1.05. In the **Texture** choose Effects/Subsurface Scattering. Click on the **Subsurface Scattering** to enter its settings. With the **Ctrl** key held down, click and drag the first Knot to the right. This adds a second knot. Double-click the second knot and choose black as the color. This creates a gradient that defines how the material's thickness will be colored. Set the **Strength** to 75 to cause the Subsurface Scattering effect to be bright. Set the **Filter Length** to 85 to cause the Subsurface effect to travel deep into the jello material. Set the **Absorption** to 250 to set how far the light must pass through each Jell-O cube before the Jell-O absorbs it. Set the **Samples** to 12 to get rid of the dithering effect. Set the **Minimum Thickness** to 1 to determine the thinnest penetrated surface that will have the Subsurface Scattering effect. Set the **Scattering Length** to 250 to define how deep into the Jell-O light can go. Change the material sample to a Cube (shown in Figure 6.50).
9. Set the **Specular** channel **Width** to 42 and **Height** to 67 so the Jell-O's specular highlights are well defined visually. Now apply the Jello material to the Jello object. With the Jello object selected, add a Cloth Nurbs object as the parent and render a frame to see an image similar to Figure 6.51.

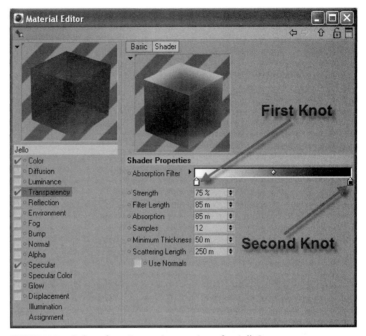

FIGURE 6.50   Subsurface Scattering settings for Jell-O.

FIGURE 6.51   Final rendered image of the Jell-O with the final material settings.

Summary

After creating Jell-O with the Cloth tag and polygon cubes, you should be starting to look at various animation challenges with a perspective on possible solution methods. This tutorial gives the direct basis for creating such advanced animation as soft bouncing text and soft furniture. Remember, "out of the box" thinking really pays off when producing real-world 3D animation in Cinema 4D!

DYNAMICS SIMULATION

In This Chapter

- Tutorial 1: Bowling
- Tutorial 2: Dynamics Driving

 Software used: Cinema 4D 9.5 Studio

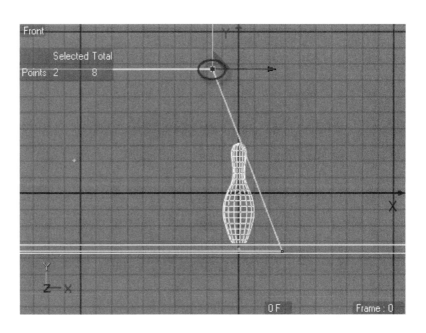

Before starting to model for an animation, you would of course first decide how you are going to animate the scene. Some animation challenges may at first seem possible to complete using simple methods such as keyframing and paths. But if you take the case of a bowling ball traveling down a bowling lane and crashing into bowling pins, you could waste days trying to get everything keyframed just right, only to step back and look at it again and find that some of the pins aren't bouncing quite right. Even worse, after a week of setting up this tedious animation with the nightmarish number of key frames, the client wants to have only nine pins. So you have to start over from the beginning. Pure madness? Yes.

Such an animation project requires a more procedural approach to creating the interactions between bowling ball, bowling lane, and bowling pins. In Cinema 4D, that method is the dynamics module (found in Cinema 4D 9.5 Studio). Dynamics allows you to create simulations based on Newtonian law (physics) so that you act less like an animator and more like a technical director, making decisions such as the ones listed below:

- How heavy is the object?
- When an object hits the floor, does it bounce like a golf ball or act like a sand bag?
- When an object at rest is hit by other objects, does it move from its location easily or does it resist and try to stay put?
- Do you really need so many polygons in that object for simulation, or can you use a low polygon stand-in proxy object instead?
- Will your colliding objects be moving quickly or slowly?
- Is the object like a wall or should other objects be able to move it?
- Does the object need to be self-motivated with a motor?
- Where is the object's center of gravity?
- What modeling consideration should be considered prior to simulation?

These questions and more are the kinds of issues to be resolved when animating with dynamics. Dynamics is a bit like playing with particles in Cinema 4D, in that it's mesmerizing and a bit addictive once you get the hang of it.

 Any object that will interact in a dynamics simulation must first be a polygon or spline curve object.

In Cinema 4D, simulation and animation are related but are not the same thing. Simulation uses physics to recreate an event possible in physical space. In Cinema 4D, animation is the playback of simulation that has been converted to key frame animation and no longer responds to physics rules such as gravity and collision.

This chapter presents two dynamics simulation tutorials. In Tutorial 1 (Bowling), you will learn the basics of dynamics simulation by first modeling all the elements in a bowling simulation and then simulating them with dynamics. Because modeling is the start of preparations for dynamics simulation, all models for this tutorial will be built and not loaded. In Tutorial 2 (Dynamics Driving), you will load the SUV from Chapter 4, model dynamics proxy objects for the SUV, create very uneven terrain, and drive the SUV along the terrain strictly using dynamics components. You'll then drop boulders from the sky and watch the SUV interact with the falling rolling boulders. Wow! All dynamically interacting objects will be built, and the loaded SUV will then be animated by dynamically driven objects.

ON THE DVD

These tutorials are also on the accompanying DVD-ROM as video tutorials, along with the tutorial project files.

Remember, as you make progress in each tutorial, to save your Cinema 4D projects.

TUTORIAL 1   **BOWLING**

FIGURE 7.1   Gravity and collision allow the bowling ball to crash into the once upright pins.

Covered in this tutorial:

- Modeling for dynamics simulation
- Rigid body dynamics
- Calculating an object's mass center
- Stabilizing a simulation
- Baking a solver
- Creating a sky

ON THE DVD
Finished project files for six sections of this tutorial are included on the accompanying DVD-ROM in the tutorials folder. All of the images used in this tutorial are located in Tutorials/ProjectFiles/Chapter 07/Tutorial-01 on the Projects DVD-ROM.

The words "spline" and "curve" are used interchangeably.

1. Begin by modeling a bowling pin. In the front view local menu, choose **Edit/Configure**. In the Attributes Manager, in the **Back** tab, browse the DVD-ROM to "**Tutorials/ProjectFiles/Chapter 07/Tutorial-01**" to open the "**BowlingPin-1.png**" image file. This places a blue-green reference silhouette of a bowling pin in the front viewport.

If you have difficulty seeing the reference image once it is opened, go to Cinema 4D's Preferences and make sure you are using Open GL and not Software mode in the Viewport page.

2. To create the bowling pin, you will first create a profile curve of half of the pin in the reference image. From the **Main** menu choose **Objects/ Create Spline/B-Spline** or choose **Draw B-Spline** from the splines in the top tool bar. When creating B-Splines, you click points to create the outline of a shape, so click along the left half of the bowling pin in the reference image. Create a few points. Since you're performing a spline modeling function, let the curve work for you. Creating just a few points that can later be positioned well goes a long way in spline modeling. Additionally, this bowling pin is being modeled for dynamics simulation and will be converted to polygons before the simulation process can begin. A well-shaped object with fewer well-positioned polygons is easier to control than one with many polygons. Don't worry about making the B-Spline follow the shape of the reference image perfectly when you first create the spline.

Just as in the modeling chapters, because the reference image is from a photograph, you won't match the profile curve exactly to the bottom of the reference image.

If the object axis gets in the way when adding the points at the bottom of the profile curve, simply add points outside the reference image. You can easily move them into place very soon.

3. Switch to **Point** mode and use the **Live Selection** tool to select the start and end points. This profile curve will be revolved to form the 3D bowling pin. To ensure that there is no modeling defect at the top or bottom of the revolved bowling pin, the start and end points of the curve need to be set to 0 on the X axis, so from the **Main** menu, choose **Structure/Set Point Value**. In the **Options**, set **X** to Set and **Val.** to 0 (shown in Figure 7.2). Then click **Apply** to move the selected points to be centered at 0 on the X axis.

 If Set Point Value is grayed out (inaccessible), be sure that you are in Default mode and not Tweak mode.

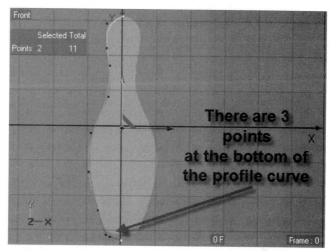

FIGURE 7.2   Set Point Value to center the start and end points of the profile curve. You should have three points at the bottom of the curve.

4. Switch to **Tweak** mode and select the **Move** tool. Drag the points of the profile curve to match the shape of the left half of the bowling pin reference image. Be very careful not to move the start and end points in the X axis.

As you may know, when editing a spline, simply using the Move tool to click and then move the points works. This is two motions (click and then drag). The reason to use Tweak mode is because you select and move the points in one motion. Tweak mode lets you operate more like an artist.

5. Select the end point at the bottom of the curve. Holding only the **Y** axis, move this point to the very bottom of the reference image. Move the two points to the left of the end point to approximately the same position in the Y axis. Switch to **Default** mode and select all three bottom points and use **Set Point Value**. In **Options**, set only **Y** to Center and then click **Apply** (shown in Figure 7.3). This ensures that the bottom of the bowling pin will be flat.

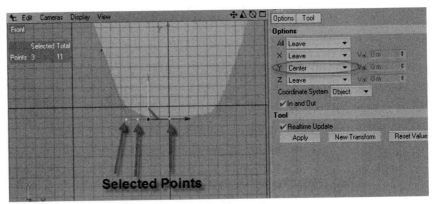

FIGURE 7.3   Set Point Value to center the bottom three points of the profile curve vertically.

6. Now use the **Move** tool in **Tweak** mode and finish positioning the rest of the profile curve to match the reference image (shown in Figure 7.4).
7. In the front view local menu, choose **Edit/Configure** and in the **Back** tab, uncheck **Show Picture**. The reference image is no longer needed. To revolve the profile curve, hold the **Alt** key down and choose **Add Lathe NURBS** from the NURBS tools. This makes the profile curve a child of the Lathe NURBS and automatically revolves the curve to build the bowling pin.
8. In the front view local menu, choose **Display/Wireframe**. The default setting of Isoparms gives a clean low detail view of NURBS objects. Usually, that's what you want when working with NURBS. However, when working with NURBS as a starting point for creating polygon objects for dynamics simulation, it is more important to clearly see the projection of where and how many polygons will be created when you eventually make the NURBS object editable.

COLOR PATE 1 Cell phone from Chapter 3.

COLOR PATE 2 SUV in action from Drive Tutorial in Chapter 5.

COLOR PATE 3 Wood chipper from Chapter 5.

COLOR PATE 4 Results of the Burn Tutorial in Chapter 5.

COLOR PATE 5 Tablecloth from Chapter 6.

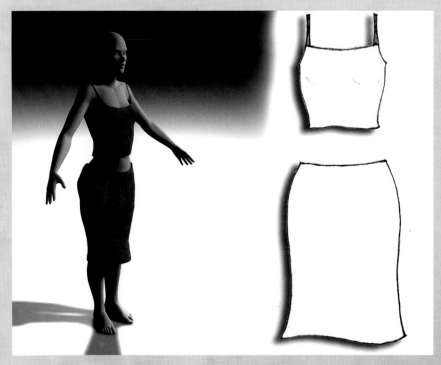

COLOR PATE 6 An outfit for a 3D model from Chapter 6.

COLOR PATE 7 Strike! From the Bowling Tutorial in Chapter 7.

COLOR PATE 8 The SUV takes on a boulder field from Dynamic Driving Tutorial in Chapter 7.

COLOR PATE 9 James walks in Chapter 8.

COLOR PATE 10 Jessi dances in Chapter 8.

COLOR PATE 11   RPC content from Chapter 8.

COLOR PATE 12   iDrive video game ready to go.

COLOR PATE 13   The meatball particle fountain from Chapter 3.

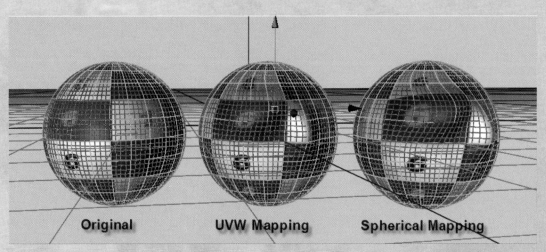

Original   UVW Mapping   Spherical Mapping

COLOR PATE 14   Three types of texture mapping discussed in Chapter 4.

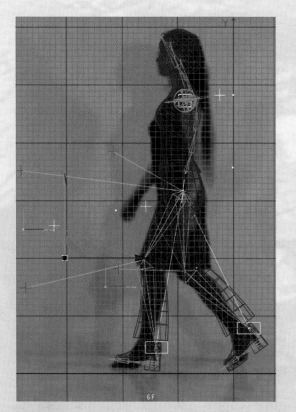
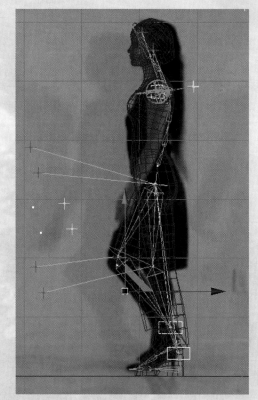

COLOR PATE 15   Setting the second and third key frames for the Lady Walk tutorial in Chapter 8.

COLOR PATE 16   Jessi on the Ultra 2 Oriental virtual set.

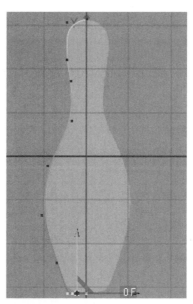

FIGURE 7.4   Profile curve now matches the reference image.

9. Now that the front view is in Wireframe mode, the pin geometry shows more detail. The detail would be great if you were simply modeling a bowling pin for a still image or for non-dynamics animation. Reducing the amount of detail in the model without compromising the basic shape will give you a faster frame rate when you start to run the dynamics simulation, so with the **Lathe NURBS** selected, in the Attributes Manager, **Object** tab, set the **Subdivision** to 10. This will immediately reduce the level of geometry detail in the model while maintaining the basic shape.

When the dynamics simulation is run, every polygon in each of the 10 bowling pins must be tested for collision with every other dynamics object in the solver object. Efficient modeling from the start is very important. Truthfully, you could dynamically simulate an object with 65,000 polygons or more. The problem is that because of such a high polygon count, you could have to wait 100 times longer than with a lower resolution model. In real-world production, time is money. Really! In addition to that, the less time the simulation takes, the more opportunity you will have to make adjustments and improvements.

10. To further edit the detail of the bowling pin, with the spline selected, in the Attributes Manager, **Object** tab, set **Intermediate Points** to

Uniform to uniformly distribute the points along the profile curve and set **Number** to 1 to reduce the geometry density. By doing this, you avoid creating a model with high polygon density at the top of the pin. This higher density of polygons at the top would not have helped the dynamics simulation. Make the Lath NURBS editable and rename it "**Pin-01**." Your perspective view should now look like Figure 7.5. A render of the bowling pin won't look attractive yet. We'll deal with that later.

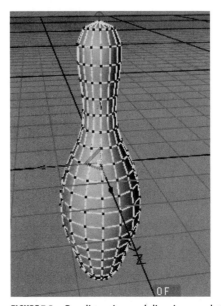

FIGURE 7.5   Bowling pin modeling is complete.

11. To create the bowling lane, add a **Cube** object and rename it "**Lane**." In the Attributes Manager, **Object** tab, set the **Size X** to 11050, **Size Y** to 50, and **Size Z** to 1890. In the Coordinates Manager, set **Y** to −342 and **X** to 3400 to place the lane at the base of the bowling pin. Make the lane editable.

12. To create the gutters for the lane, add a **Tube** object and rename it "**Gutter**." In the Attributes Manager, **Object** tab, set the **Inner Radius** to 161, **Outer Radius** to 200, **Rotation Segments** to 36, **Cap Segments** to 1, **Height** to 8800, **Height Segments** to 1, and **Orientation** to +X. In the **Slice** tab, set **From** to −90 and **To** to 90. In the Coordinates Manager, set the **Position** at X = 4513, Y = −318 and **Z** = −1140. Add an **Instance** copy of the gutter and position it on the other side of the lane. Group the gutter and the instance copy,

and name the group "**Gutters**." The gutters won't be dynamically simulated.

13. Add a **Floor** object and set its Position in the **Y** axis to −506.

14. To create the bowling ball, add a **Sphere** object and rename it "**BowlingBall**." In the Attributes Manager, in the **Object** tab, set the **Radius** to 250. In the Coordinates Manager, set **Position X** to 8565 and **Position Y** to 700.

Because the collision method to be used on the bowling ball will be Ellipsoid, the bowling ball's level of geometry detail will not be considered since dynamics considers only the collision of a bounding ellipsoid shape around the bowling ball, and not the bowling ball's actual polygons. Ellipsoid is a spherical shape that stretches to encompass all polygons of an object.

15. To place 10 pins in the proper bowling arrangement, you will add a pin placement guide. In the Materials Manager, create a new material and name it "**Pins Placement**." In the **Color** channel **Texture**, browse to "**Tutorials/ProjectFiles/Chapter 07/Tutorial-01**" and open "**PinsPlacement-01.png**." Check the **Alpha** channel and use the same image here as well. Set the material preview to **Plane**.

This image was prepared in Photoshop CS2 by saving the 10 circles in a layer with the background layer turned off.

16. Add a **Plane** object for the pins placement and set its **Width** to 1398 and **Height** to 1195, as these are factors of the dimensions of the pixel resolution of PinsPlacement-01.png. This preserves the original aspect ratio. Position the plane at **X** = −504, **Y** = −311, and **Z** = 5.5. Rename the plane "**Pins Placement**" and apply the Pins Placement material to the Pins Placement object.

17. In the top view local menu, choose **Display/Gouraud Shading** to see the pins placement guide. Rotate the pin placement object 90 degrees (**H**) so the orientation of the reference image will be correct.

18. To create an enclosure to keep the ball and pins from scattering too far, add a **Cube** object, rename it "**LeftSide**," and shape and position it as shown in Figure 7.6.

19. Make the cube editable and switch to **Point** mode. In the front view, with the **Live Selection** tool (**Only Select Visible Elements** unchecked), select the points in the top right corner and move them back as shown in Figure 7.7.

20. Switch to **Model** mode. Make a copy of the cube, rename it "**RightSide**," and drag it to the other side of the lane. Make a copy of RightSide and rename it "**Back**." Rotate its heading (**H**) 90 degrees and

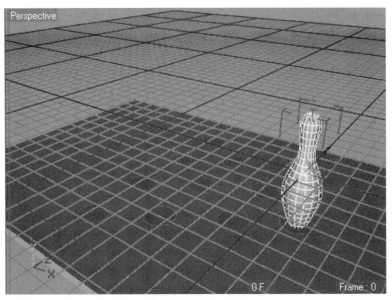

FIGURE 7.6 Left side of the enclosure in its initial shape.

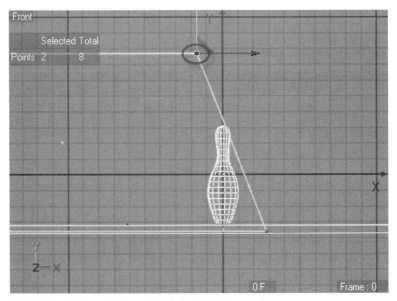

FIGURE 7.7 Final modeling of the left side of the enclosure.

move it to the back of the lane so that it connects the left and right sides of the enclosure. Switch to **Point** mode. In the right view, with the **Live Selection** tool, select the right most points (shown in Figure 7.8) and straighten that edge by using **Set Point Value**. Set **X** to Center (**Y** and **Z** to Leave) and then click **Apply**. Then use the **Move** tool to shape this back cube to fit between the left and right sides of the enclosure.

In dynamics simulations, you never want to have objects that must be moved by forces such as gravity intersecting other objects. However, objects that are fixed in place such as walls and floors can intersect each other as long as none of them will be moved by dynamics forces. This is true even if other objects affected by forces will collide with these stationary objects.

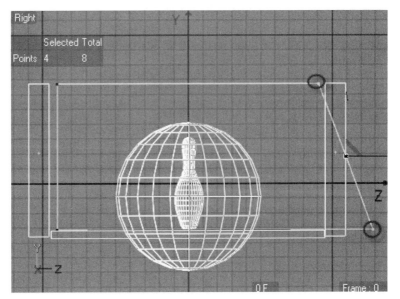

FIGURE 7.8 The back of the enclosure modeling is complete.

21. Switch to **Model** mode and make a copy of the Back object and name it "**Top**" and rotate it 90 degrees in the pitch (**P**). In the front view, move the Top object into position to form the top of the enclosure. Line up the left side of the Top object with the back of the enclosure. Switch to **Point** mode and in the Top object, move the front-most points to match Figure 7.9. Select all four pieces of the enclosure and group them (**Alt-g**). Rename the group "**Enclosure**." This completes the modeling of the enclosure.

22. To create the other nine bowling pins and position them on the pin placement reference, in the top view, set the display to **Gouraud Shading** if it is not already set. Make nine copies of the bowling pin. With the **Move** tool in **Model** mode, position all ten pins on the pin placement

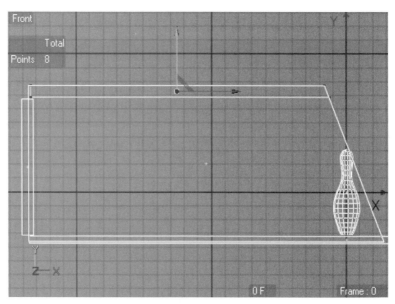

FIGURE 7.9 The enclosure modeling is complete.

reference. Select all ten pins and group them (**Alt-g**). Rename the group "**Pins**."

 Just like in real life, the placement of the pins at this point in the project will directly affect how the bowling simulation plays. A poorly placed pin could cheat you out of a strike and bless you with a spare.

23. With all the modeling completed, you're now at the point where you start to add the dynamics elements to the scene. From the **Main** menu, choose **Plugins/Dynamics/Solver Object**. The solver object is like a dynamics simulation container, meaning only polygon and spline objects within a solver object are calculated by the Cinema 4D Dynamics module. Choose **Plugins/Dynamics/Gravity**.

 By default, the gravity object is axial (applies its force in a single defined axis, namely the −Y axis) and has the same effect as gravity on Earth, in that it pulls objects down to the ground. In Cinema 4D Dynamics, however, this is controllable so that gravity can be adjusted to pull objects in any direction. A chair could fall up toward the ceiling, for example. Additionally, the gravity can be set to have a shape (including shapes such as cubes, spheres, and cones) rather than use an axis to define its force. Place the gravity in the solver object so that objects placed in the solver object will be affected by gravity.

24. Place the Enclosure, Pins, BowlingBall, and Lane into the solver object. In the Objects Manager, select all polygon objects. Right-click on one of the polygon objects and choose **Dynamics Tags/Rigid Body Dynamic** to add a rigid body dynamics tag to each of the selected polygon objects.

25. Now select only the rigid body tags for the 10 pins (shown in Figure 7.10). In the Attributes Manager, **Collision** tab, set **Collision Detection** to Full. Now every polygon in each pin will be able to collide with other objects (such as other pins, the enclosure, ball, and lane). Set the **Static** friction to 20 to help the pins stay in position and wait for the bowling ball to collide with them.

In Cinema 4D, multiple objects or tags of the same type can be edited simultaneously. This is helpful for cases like dynamics where you cannot use instance copies of object. If some parameters in the Attributes Manager had been set differently for some of the pins, those parameters would have been unavailable for input while editing the multiselected rigid body tags.

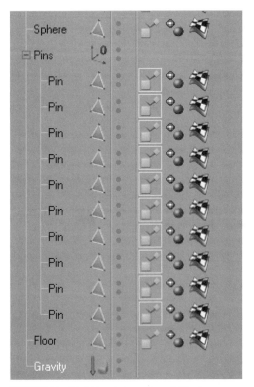

FIGURE 7.10   Rigid body tags for all 10 pins are selected and edited together.

26. Select the rigid body tags for the four enclosure objects and the lane object. In the Attributes Manager, **Mass** tab, set the **Mass** to 0. This will prevent these objects from responding to gravity, so they will not fall. Imagine what it would be like for gravity to pull the floor down. No matter which objects collide with a zero mass object, the zero mass object will not move. Set the enclosure LeftSide and RightSide objects **Collision** to Full since they are not really cubic in shape. Set the enclosure Top and Back and the Lane objects **Collision** to Cube.

27. Select the bowling ball's rigid body tag and set its **Collision** to Ellipsoid so that an internal and efficient collision calculation model is used. Set its Mass to 10. This makes the bowling ball behave like an object 10 times heavier than each bowling pin.

28. Set the solver object **Integration Method** to Midpoint for fast accurate collision detection. In the **Main** menu, choose **Edit/Project Settings** and set the **Maximum** to 300 frames. This makes the animation 10 seconds long. In the solver object Attributes Manager, **Main** tab, set the **Stop** to 300 so that the simulation will also be calculated over 300 frames.

The choice of integration methods is based on what kind of objects and complexity is involved in the simulation. The fastest and least accurate is Euler. The slowest and most accurate is Runge-Kutta.

Not extending the Stop to 300 would cause the simulation to end at frame 90, so from frame 91 to 300, there would be no movement. Be careful to always set the solver object Stop value to the proper number of frames, as setting the Maximum frames in the project setting does not automatically update the solver object Stop value.

29. On the Transport Control, click the **Play** button to get a first look at the simulation. The bowling ball slowly drops to the lane and bounces back up. The bowling pins seem to have some slight motion to them as well.

30. To send the bowling ball down the lane to crash into the pins, the ball will need to travel in the −X axis. In the Attributes Manager, **Start** tab, set **v.X** to −10868. **Play** the simulation to see the bowling ball flying down the lane and crashing into the pins.

If you need to reposition objects in a solver hierarchy, and if those objects' mass is greater than 0, first turn the solver off by clicking the green check. This will become a red X. (Failure to turn off the solver will cause the objects to be unmovable.) Then move the objects as desired. From the main menu, choose Plugins/Dynamics/Initialize All Objects to set the new start positions for the moved objects. Failure to initialize the objects will result in them jumping back to their original start positions.

Objects with a 0 mass can be moved freely whether or not the solver is active and do not require Initialize All Objects.

31. The ball seems to sail through the air effortlessly. This takes away from the illusion of bowling. To improve this, select the gravity object in the Objects Manager. In the Attributes Manager, **Field** tab, set the **Strength** to 2. This doubles the force of **Gravity** in the simulation. Play the simulation again to see the bowling ball bounce on the lane once before hitting the pins. Notice that the pins are leaning toward the ball (shown in Figure 7.11). That's unnatural and will have to be addressed. The pins' behavior indicates that this simulation needs to be more stable.

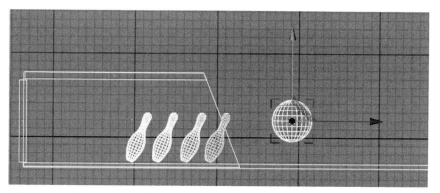

FIGURE 7.11   The bowling ball hits the lane once before crashing into the pins, but the pins are leaning toward the bowling ball.

32. Improving the collision calculation accuracy will improve the stability of the simulation. To do this, select the solver. In the Attributes Manager, **Main** tab, set the **Over Sampling** to 16. This makes the simulation four times more accurate. Doing this also slows down the simulation playback, as Cinema 4D must perform more collision detection calculations per frame.

The time required to calculate a simulation is separate from the time required to render an animation. If you set up a simulation that requires 30 minutes to go from the start to the end, and if the render time of the animation is 30 minutes, it will take at least 1 hour for the simulation to be rendered.

33. In the **Details** tab, set the **Collision Eps** (Eps = Epsilon) to 6. Check the **Collision Use Rest Speed** and set **Collision Rest Speed** to 20.

This helps objects whose mass is greater than 0 but are standing still to not drift. When you play the simulation again, it now advances through the frames more slowly, and the pins no longer drift (shown in Figure 7.12).

In a dynamics simulation the collision epsilon is the space between colliding objects. For example, if the collision epsilon was set to 100 and a ball was supposed to bounce on the floor, the ball would fall but would bounce before even coming close to the floor. It would look very unnatural. On the other hand, if the collision epsilon was set to 0.1 and the ball was falling very quickly to the floor and the subsampling was set to 1, if the ball was supposed to collide with the floor at frame 10 (for example), the ball might fall straight through the floor without ever colliding. Thus, subsampling and collision epsilon work together as the solver simulation stabilization parameters.

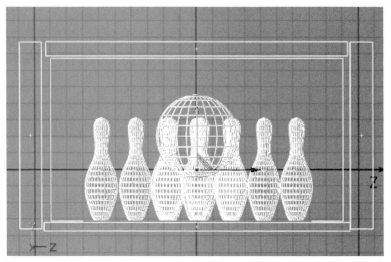

FIGURE 7.12   Simulation stabilized.

34. To add some rotation to the bowling ball so it spins like when a pro bowler is bowling, you wouldn't use the rotate tool. Because this is dynamics, select the bowling ball rigid body tag. In the Attributes Manager, **Start** tab, set the **w.H** to 1200 and the **w.B** to 90. These values set the initial rotation of the bowling ball, so after the bowling ball collides with the pins and loses its momentum, it will lose its ability to spin. Because the bowling ball is a sphere, it may be a little difficult to see it rotate during the simulation, so first select the bowling ball object and

then play the simulation. This way, the bowling ball's axis and red out-line bounding box will rotate to clearly show how the ball is spinning.

 When selecting a tag in Cinema 4D, it is not necessary to first select the object and then select its tag. For example, you could have a pin polygon object selected and then select the rigid body tag for the bowling ball. The Attributes Manager shows the properties for the last object or tag to be selected.

35. Add a **Light** object and set its **Position** to **X** = 4260, **Y** = 5840, and **Z** = −1845. In the Attributes Manager, **General** tab, set the **Shadow** to Shadow Maps (Soft) and **Brightness** to 50. In the **Shadow** tab, set the **Shadow Map** to 1000 × 1000. Add an **Instance** of the light. Position the instance at **X** = −7030, **Y** = 5840 and **Z** = 6111. Render the perspective view to see an image similar to Figure 7.13.

FIGURE 7.13   Scene modeling is complete. No materials are applied to the objects yet.

36. To fill in the rest of the scene's environment, from the **Main** menu, choose **Plugins/Sky/Create Sky**. In the Materials Manager, double-click the **Sky Volume**. In the Sky Manager, in the **Beginner** tab, set the **Time** to 16:00, 13 July 2005. Doing this ensures you will get a bright sky.

Not setting the time as shown in the above step, or clicking the Now button could result in a nighttime scene.

To access all of the Sky Manager tabs, go to the Object page and set Mode to Advanced.

37. In the **Clouds** tab, expand **Layer 1** and **Layer 2** and set **Scale N-S** and **Scale W-E** to 50 in both layers. This makes the clouds half as large so that you can see more cloud detail in the sky. Little steps like this help sell the illusion of the whole scene. Render the perspective view to see an image similar to Figure 7.14.

To see all changes in the Sky Manager instantly update in the viewport, check Update Editor in the Object tab.

In the Sky Manager preview, drag with the right button to look all around the sky environment.

FIGURE 7.14 The lighting is currently too bright.

38. Notice that even though the lighting was a bit low before, the lighting now appears to be too bright. This is because the sky casts environmental lighting and also adds shadows. This adds to the previously added lights. Select the light object and set its **Brightness** down to 30. Render the perspective view to see a scene with more balanced lighting (shown in Figure 7.15).

FIGURE 7.15   The lighting is now more balanced.

39. In the Materials Manager, create a material and name it "**Enclosure**." In the **Color** channel set the **Color** to 180, 255, and 180. Set the **Brightness** to 57. Check the **Transparency** channel and set the **Color** to 192, 255, and 192. Set the **Brightness** to 80. Apply the Enclosure material to the Enclosure group.
40. Create a material and name it "**Pins**." In the **Color** Channel, set the **Color** to 255, 207, and 111. Check the **Reflection** channel and set the **Color** to 16, 123, and 75. Set the **Brightness** to 80. In the **Specular** channel, set the **Width** to 30 and the **Height** to 35. Apply the Pins material to the Pins group.

To easily create a new material, double-click in the Materials Manager.

41. Create a new material and name it "**Bowling Ball.**" In the **Color** channel, set the **Brightness** to 10. Check the **Luminance** channel and set the **Texture** to Tiles. Set the **Grout Width** to 60. In the **Specular** channel, set the **Width** to 43 and **Height** to 60. This material is for a black shiny bowling ball with a couple spots of color that will show the bowling ball's rotation. Apply the Bowling Ball material to the BowlingBall object.

One way to apply a material to several objects is to click Assignment in the Material Editor and drag objects from the Objects Manager into the large empty Assignment space.

42. With the Bowling Ball material tag selected, in the Attributes Manager, **Tag** tab, set the **Projection** to Spherical and **Tiles X** and **Tiles Y** to 0.2. This stretches out the color of the material to create only a couple spots of color.
43. A close-up render of the bowling ball shows some polygon faceting. With the BowlingBall selected, hold the **Alt** key down and add a HyperNURBS object to smooth the bowling ball polygons. Do this to the Pins group as well. In the perspective view, frame the Pins group and render to see an image similar to Figure 7.16.

FIGURE 7.16 Bowling pins with their material and HyperNURBS.

Although adding the HyperNURBS to the bowling ball and bowling pins causes the ball and pins to effectively render as higher polygon resolution objects, only the polygons in the bowling ball object are considered during simulation.

44. Create a new material and name it "**Lane.**" In the **Color** channel, set the **Brightness** to 50. Check the **Reflection** channel and set the **Brightness** to 43. Apply this material to the lane and gutters.
45. From the **Main** menu, choose **Edit/Project Settings** and set **Frame Rate** to 120 and **Maximum** to 600. This will make the resulting animation play back four times slower. The main benefit of doing this is that the simulation is also now four times more accurate.

 This frame rate is independent of the rendering frame rate. So you can still render the finished animation at 30 frames per second. Although it is possible to get the same increase in accuracy by changing the subsampling from 16 to 64, this method has the added benefit of allowing very smooth slow motion playback.

46. To bake the simulation from dynamics to key frames, from the main menu, choose **Plugins/Dynamics/Bake All Solvers.** This is similar to the result of caching a cloth simulation. It converts the dynamics simulation to an animation by creating a key on every frame for each object in the solver hierarchy, so the dynamics features such as gravity and collision will no longer be calculated once the solver is baked.

 Notice that the baked solver no longer has a green check. It now has a red X.

If you do not wish to wait for the baking process to be completed, you may load the Bowling-05 project for ProjectFiles/Chapter 07/Tutorial-01 on the DVD-ROM.

ON THE DVD

47. To view the baked key frames, in the **Main** menu, choose **Window/ Timeline (Shift-F3).** Once in the Timeline, expand the solver object to find each of the polygon objects now having a key frame created for every frame of the animation (Figure 7.17).

 The timeline is where you can view and edit key frames for all objects and all tags in a project.

48. Play the animation back to see the ball crashing into the pins. As for creating the simulation and converting it to an animation, this is great, but to sell it to a customer, you still need some camera work, so add a **Target Camera.** In the perspective view local menu, choose **Cameras/Scene Cameras/Camera** to make the perspective view

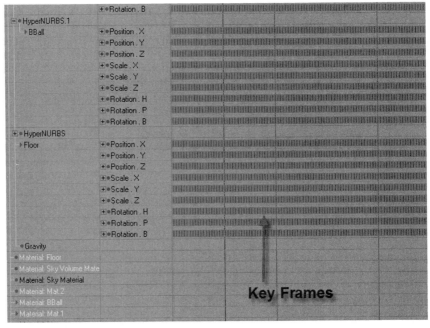

FIGURE 7.17 Within the Timeline, in the solver object, all polygon objects now have a key frame for every frame of the animation.

look through the target camera. Make sure that in the Attributes Manager, **Object** tab, the **Projection** is set to Perspective.

49. Select the Camera Target. Set the following key frames for the camera target's position:

Frame 1: **X** = 8570, **Y** = 217, **Z** = −24
Frame 36: **X** = −783, **Y** = 217, **Z** = −72

50. Select the Camera. Set the following key frames for the camera's position:

Frame 1: **X** = 6476, **Y** = 793, **Z** = −2821
Frame 54: **X** = 3660, **Y** = 912, **Z** = −330
Frame 249: **X** = 1832, **Y** = 912, **Z** = 630

You may notice that the target wasn't placed in the subject (bowling ball) as was done in previous tutorials. That's because the kind of motion the bowling ball has when it collides with the pins would make the camera view look very jumpy.

Summary

Dynamics can provide very elegant solutions to some of the most daunting challenges in 3D animation production such as:

- A brick wall being broken by a crashing car
- The contents of a box being emptied onto the floor
- A thousand beads filling a jar

In preparation for dynamics simulation, modeling efficiently will determine if your collisions can look natural and whether your solver baking time is as short as possible. While Cinema 4D makes dynamics simulation accessible, closer review of the solver object and rigid body tags will prepare you more for handling real-world production crises only solved through the use of dynamics.

TUTORIAL 2   **DYNAMICS DRIVING**

FIGURE 7.18   Using only dynamics simulation, the SUV drives itself into and out of a difficult situation.

Covered in this tutorial:

- Modeling for dynamics simulation
- Rigid body dynamics
- Motor constraint
- Proxy objects modeling

- Randomize (Functions menu)
- Subdivide (HyperNURBS Subdivide)
- Convert Selection
- Baking a solver
- Creating a sky
- House cleaning the Materials Manager

Once you have completed this tutorial, you will be able to make any vehicle drive realistically on any terrain.

Finished project files for six sections of this tutorial are included on the accompanying DVD-ROM in the tutorials folder. The front wheels and the front axle will be one object and the rear wheels and the rear axle will be another object, so this will not be a simulation of four independent wheels. All of the images used in this tutorial are located in Tutorials/ProjectFiles/Chapter 07/Tutorial-02 on the Projects DVD-ROM.

ON THE DVD

The words "spline" and "curve" are used interchangeably.

ON THE DVD

1. Begin by loading the **"Tutorials/ProjectFiles/Chapter 04/Tutorial-01/SUV-GlassDone/SUV-GlassDone.c4d"** from the DVD-ROM. This loads the SUV that will ultimately be driving through the terrain. When the loaded SUV-GlassDone project loads, you will notice that it's still in BodyPaint mode. Just click the **Move** tool to exit that mode. In the Objects Manager, rename CBRed **"SUV Body."** Right-click on the **SUV Body** icon and choose **Cinema 4D Tags/Display,** and select the **Display** tag. In the Attributes Manager, **Tag** tab, check **Use** and set **Shading Mode** to Lines. This allows you to see through the SUV and will be very helpful when modeling the proxy object. Delete the Sky, Camera, Camera Target, and Floor. From the **Main** menu, choose **Edit/Project Settings** and set **Maximum** to 300 so this project will be 10 seconds long.

The display tag overrides the viewports display settings for an object with a display tag.

The vehicle that will drive through this simulation will be a proxy object. In Cinema 4D Dynamics, proxy objects are the low polygon objects. They are used because they simulate faster and can be more easily edited to alter the response of a simulation. For example, to extend the front of a vehicle's proxy object, only four points must be moved. Moving the front of the original high polygon object could involve thousands of points and may look unnatural.

2. To create the proxy object, start by adding a **Cube** object and check **X-Ray**. Shape and position the cube to match the lower section of the SUV as shown in Figure 7.19.

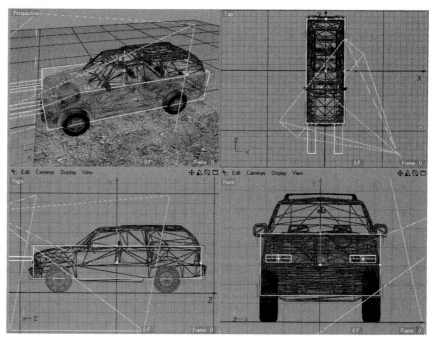

FIGURE 7.19   The proxy object cube is shaped and positioned to match the lower section of the SUV Body object.

3. With the cube selected, in the Attributes Manager, set the **Segments Z** to 3. Working in the right view, the proxy object still appears to have only one Z segment. In the local menu, choose **Display/Wireframe** to see the detail added by setting the **Segments Z** to 3. Make shaping and position adjustments to the proxy object and make it editable (shown in Figure 7.20).

4. Switch to **Point** mode and use the **Live Selection** tool (**Only Select Visible Elements** unchecked) to select points and move them into position (shown in Figure 7.21).

 By using the Live Selection tool with Only Select Visible Elements unchecked and selecting a point in the right view, you can manipulate point pairs for the left and right side of the proxy objects.

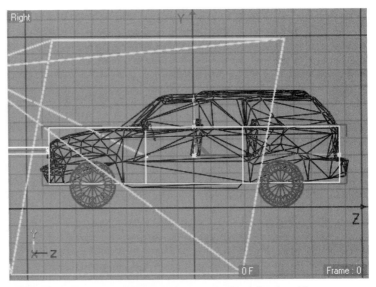

FIGURE 7.20   The proxy details can be seen in the right view. The proxy object shape and position matches the SUV-Body more closely now.

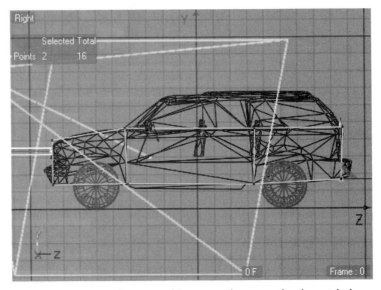

FIGURE 7.21   Points in the proxy object moved to more closely match the approximate shape of the SUV-Body.

5. In the right view, choose the **Knife** tool. In the knife options, uncheck **Restrict To Selection** and **Visible**. Make a vertical cut at the rear of the front wheels (shown in Figure 7.22).

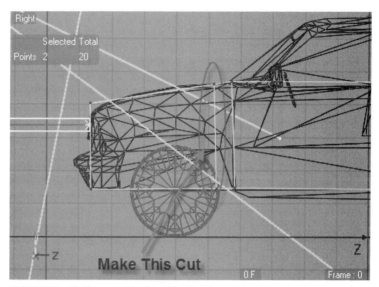

FIGURE 7.22   Knife cut adds detail for the front wheel area polygons to be further edited.

6. Switch to **Point** mode and select the front four sets of points. In the perspective view, use the **Scale** tool and scale on the **X** axis only, as shown in Figure 7.23. This is done so that when the wheels proxy object is rotating, it won't be touching the SUV proxy object.

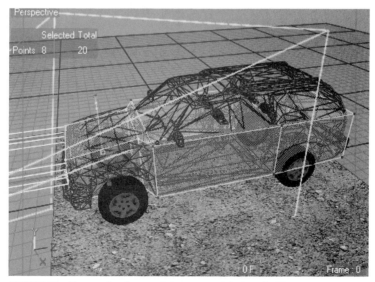

FIGURE 7.23   Front wheel area of the proxy object scaled in.

With a dynamics simulation started with objects that each have a mass greater than 0, their intersecting each other can cause accurate collisions or complete collision detection failure.

7. To further protect the SUV proxy object front rubbing or hitting the wheels proxy object, select the two sets of points created by the cut and move them back (shown in Figure 7.24).

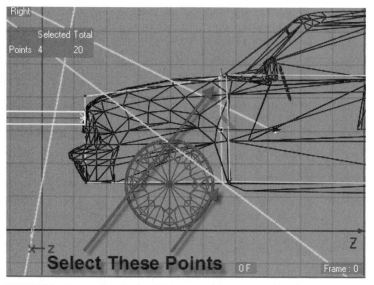

FIGURE 7.24   Two points in the SUV proxy object created by the cut, moved back to create better clearance for the rotation of the front wheel proxy object.

8. In the right view in **Polygon** mode, make two cuts a little wider than the wheel axle would be. Switch to **Point** mode and from those two cuts, select the two bottom sets of points and move them up (shown in Figure 7.25). These points are moved up to make room for the tube objects, which will hold the wheel axle in place.
9. Make these same types of cuts and point edits in the rear of the SUV.
10. To start adding the objects that hold the wheel axles in place, add a **Tube** object and name it "**Axle-Support-Rear**." Set the **Orientation** to –X. Place the Axle-Support-Rear over the rear wheel and frame it ("**o**"). Set the **Inner Radius** to 35, **Outer Radius** to 50, and **Rotation Segments** to 20.
11. In the front view, move the Axle-Support-Rear in the **X** axis only to align the Axle-Support-Rear with the side of the proxy object. To make seeing the Axle-Support-Rear easier, toggle the **Editor Display Switch**

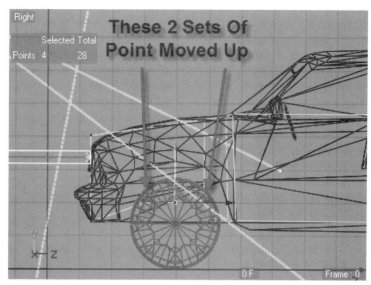

FIGURE 7.25   Front wheel area of the SUV proxy object with two knife cuts. Two sets of points at the bottom of the cuts are moved up to make room for the objects that will hold the wheel axle in place.

off (red dot) for the SUV-Body object in the Objects Manager. Your front view should now look like Figure 7.26.

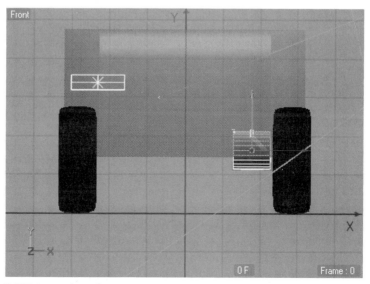

FIGURE 7.26   The Axle-Support-Rear is moved into its final position aligned with the rear of the SUV proxy object.

12. In the front view, and with the Axle-Support-Rear still selected, add a **Symmetry** object. Drag the Axle-Support-Rear into the symmetry object to create the Axle-Support-Rear on the other side of the SUV Proxy object. Make the symmetry object editable and drag the Axle-Support-Rear out of the symmetry hierarchy. Then delete the symmetry object.

 Making the symmetry object editable converts the symmetry object into a null object.

13. Make a copy of the Axle-Support-Rear object and rename it "**Axle-Support-Front**." In the right view, drag the Axle-Support-Front using only the **Z** axis and position it at the front of the SUV Proxy, centered with the tires object. Select the Axle-Support-Front, Axle-Support-Rear, and SUV Proxy and from the **Main** menu, choose **Functions/Connect**. Rename the new object "**SUV Proxy**" and delete the original Axle-Support-Front, Axle-Support-Rear, and SUV Proxy objects (shown in Figure 7.27). Next, drag the Headlight and Instance.1 objects into the SUV proxy object hierarchy.

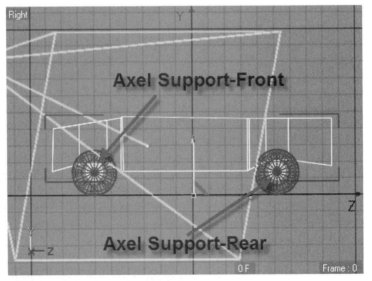

FIGURE 7.27 Axle-Support-Front in position.

14. In the perspective view local menu, choose **Cameras/Editor Camera** to free the perspective view from the constraint of the loaded scene camera. Render the perspective view to see an image similar to Figure 7.28.
15. To create the upper section of the SUV Proxy object, first toggle the **Editor Display Switch** of the SUV-Body object so the Wireframe of

FIGURE 7.28   Axle-Support-Front in position.

the SUV-Body can be seen with the SUV Proxy object. In the perspective view, switch to **Polygon** mode and choose the **Live Selection** tool (**Only Select Visible Elements** checked) and select the polygons on the top of the SUV Proxy object as shown in Figure 7.29.

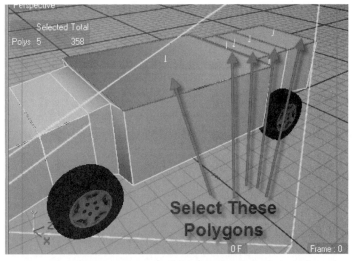

FIGURE 7.29   Polygons at the top of the SUV Proxy object are selected.

16. In the right view, **Extrude** the selected polygons to reach the top of the SUV-Body object. Use the **Scale** tool and scale the extruded polygons to match the basic shape of the top of the SUV-Body. Be careful to scale in only the X or Z axis at any time.

17. In the right view, switch to **Point** mode and with the **Live Selection** tool (**Only Select Visible Elements** unchecked), select the points circled in Figure 7.30.

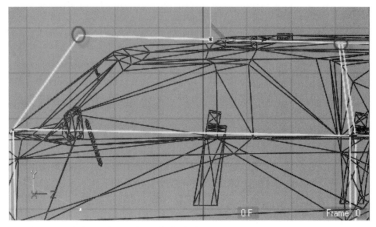

FIGURE 7.30   Select the points circled above.

18. In the front view, scale the selected points in the X axis to match the width of the top of the SUV-Body object. In the right view, move the points indicated in Figure 7.31 to match the SUV-Body object.

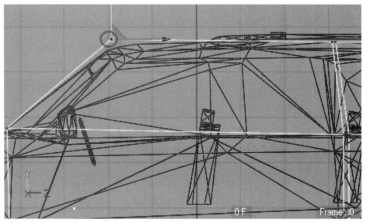

FIGURE 7.31   The points circled above are moved to match the SUV-Body object.

19. In the rear of the SUV Proxy object, the top three polygons will need to be extruded, but first, you will need to clean up the point centering. So toggle the **Editor Display Switch** for the Tires and the SUV-Body to hide them in the viewports. In the perspective view, working on only the driver's side of the SUV, select the 12 points circled in Figure 7.32.

FIGURE 7.32   Select the 12 points circled above.

20. The selected points do not currently form a flat surface, so extruding polygons in this area would produce undesirable results. To correct this, right-click and choose **Set Point Value**. In the **Options**, set **X** to Center (**Y** and **Z** to Leave) and then click **Apply** to flatten the surface defined by those 12 points. Choose the **Live Selection** tool again and select the corresponding 12 points on the rear of the passenger side of the SUV. Then use Set Point Value to flatten them as well.

 If you try to select 12 points from both the driver and passenger side of the SUV at the same time, they will collapse into each other and create an object that is unusable as a dynamics proxy.

21. In the front view, with the **Live Selection** tool, select the two sets of points circled in Figure 7.33. Use **Set Point Value** and set **X** to Leave, **Y** to Center, and **Z** to Leave.

22. Switch to **Polygon** mode. In the right view, use the **Live Selection** tool (**Only Select Visible Elements** unchecked) to select the three sets of polygons (shown in Figure 7.34) on both sides of the vehicle.

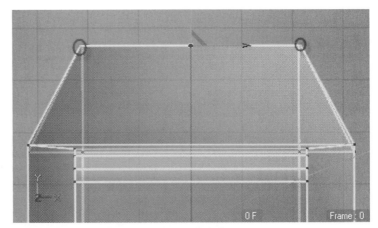

FIGURE 7.33 Select the two points circled above.

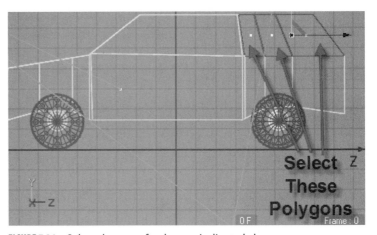

FIGURE 7.34 Select the sets of polygons indicated above.

23. In the top view, **Extrude** the selected polygons as indicated in Figure 7.35.
24. Now the bottom points of the extruded polygons are well positioned, but the top points are out too far. To easily select the points, in the **Main** menu, choose **Selection/Convert Selection**. On the left, choose **Polygons**. On the right, choose **Points**. Then click **Convert**. Now the eight points (four upper and four lower) on the driver and passenger side are selected and the polygons are deselected. Use the **Live Selection** tool and hold the **Ctrl** key down and deselect the bottom sets of selected points.

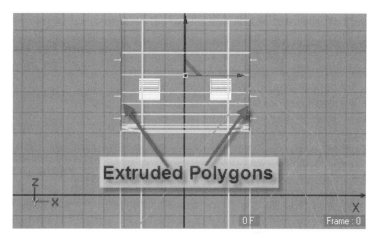

FIGURE 7.35   Extrude three sets of selected polygons as indicated above.

25. In the front view, use the **Scale** tool and scale the top points in to match the other points at the top of the SUV Proxy object, using only the **X** axis. Set the SUV Proxy phong tag **Phong Angle** to 40 and render the perspective view to see an image similar to Figure 7.36.

FIGURE 7.36   SUV Proxy object modeling is complete.

26. It's time to create the tire proxy objects. Be sure to toggle the **Editor Display Switch** and the **Renderer Display Switch** off (red dot) for the Tires object. This makes it easy to position the tire proxy objects accurately. Add a **Cylinder** object and rename it "**WheelsFront.**" Set its **Radius** to 138, **Height** to 650, **Height Segments** to 3, **Rotation Segments** to 20, **Orientation** to +X, and **Caps** to 2. Set the **Position** to **X** = 0, **Y** = 144, and **Z** = −605 and make it editable.

27. In the top view, in **Point** mode, select the two inner rows of points and **Scale** them out so that they are outside of the SUV Proxy object, to form the thickness of the tires (shown in Figure 7.37).

The distance of the scaled points from the SUV Proxy object is very important for dynamics collision detection calculations. It is safer to be too far away from the SUV Proxy object than too close to it. This distance will be a factor later when setting the Collision Eps.

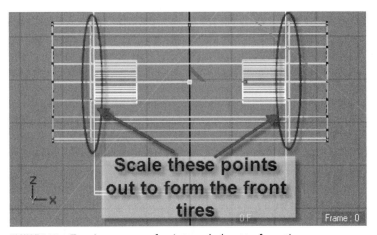

FIGURE 7.37   Two inner rows of points scaled out to form tires.

28. In **Polygon** mode, select the polygons still within the SUV Proxy object. In the right view, **Extrude** them in to be within the axle support portion of the SUV Proxy object. In the **Options**, the **Offset** should be −109.

29. In the Objects Manager make a copy of WheelsFront and rename it "**WheelsRear.**" In the right view, center the WheelsRear object on the rear axle support. Its **Position** should be **X** = 0, **Y** = 144, and **Z** = 516. All proxy object modeling is now complete. You should of course be saving periodically to protect from loss of data. To see how you've

done so far, open "**Tutorials/ProjectFiles/Chapter 07/Tutorial-02/DynamicsDriving-02/ DynamicsDriving-02.c4d**" for a reference of the current setup.

30. As mentioned earlier, it is the proxy objects that will be moving in the simulation, not the original SUV object. In order to see the original SUV object driving once the dynamics simulation is completed, you will now need to move the SUV into the proxy object hierarchy. In the Objects Manager, drag the SUV-Body into the SUV Proxy. For now, keep both the **Editor Display Switch** and the **Renderer Display Switch** off so that it's easy to clearly see what's happening.

If you wait to move the SUV into the proxy object until after the dynamics simulation is complete, you may find that the SUV and the proxy object no longer share the same orientation and position.

31. The Tires object currently has all four tires modeled in one object (Tires). As the tires need to rotate to drive the SUV, a single object made of four tires will rotate badly, so you need to delete the rear tires. In **Point** mode, top view, with the Tires object selected, use the **Rectangle Selection** tool (**Only Select Visible Elements** unchecked) to select the points in the rear tires (shown in Figure 7.38) and delete them.

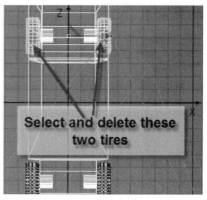

FIGURE 7.38   Select the points of the rear tires and delete them.

32. Still in the top view, switch to the **Use Axis** mode and use the **Move** tool to move the object axis. Move it by holding only the **Z** axis and center it on the front tires/axle. In the right view, complete the centering of the axis. This time use only the **Y** axis to move it into position. When completed, the axis should be perfectly centered as shown in Figure 7.39.

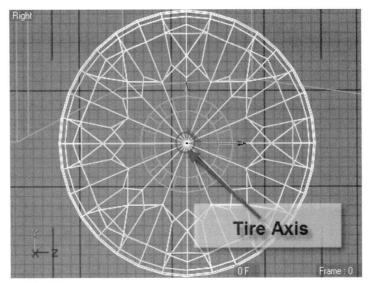

FIGURE 7.39   Front tires' axis perfectly centered.

33. Rename the Tires "**TiresFront**." Make a copy of TiresFront and rename it "**TiresRear**." In the right view, position TiresRear to be centered on WheelsRear. In the Objects Manager, place TiresFront within the WheelsFront hierarchy. Now when WheelsFront moves and rotates in the dynamics simulation, TireFront will be moved and rotated. Place TiresRear within the WheelsRear hierarchy. To make working in the dynamics simulation easier, toggle the **Editor Display Switch** and the **Renderer Display Switch** off so that only the WheelsFront and WheelsRear can be seen and rendered.

34. Sometimes, the oversimplified proxy objects' movement and rotation can be difficult to see. Creating and applying some simple materials can be very helpful. Create a new material and name it "**SUV-Proxy**." In the **Color** channel, set the **Color** to 173, 255, and 255. Then apply the SUV-Proxy material to the SUV Proxy object.

35. Now, create a new material and name it "**Wheels**." In the **Color** channel, set the **Texture** to Checkerboard. Click **Checkerboard** and change **Color** 2 to 0, 128, and 128. Apply the Wheels material to the WheelsFront and WheelsRear objects.

36. For the ground, add a **Plane** object and name it "**Ground**." Set the **Width** and **Height** to 20,000. Set the **Width Segments** and **Height Segments** to 40 and make the ground editable. To allow the simulation to settle in the beginning, set the **Position** of the ground to −50 in the **Y** axis. This means the SUV Proxy and its wheels will first fall to the ground. Also set the ground **Position** to −7170 in the **Z** axis to

follow the movie-making principle of building what is seen and not wasting unnecessary effort on elements that are off camera.

The Floor object from the Objects/Scene menu cannot be used. A dynamically interactive ground through which objects cannot fall must be polygonal.

37. It's time to make the ground interesting! First, toggle the SUV Proxy's **Editor Display Switch** off. Then switch to **Point** mode and right-click to choose **Magnet**. In the **Options**, set the **Radius** to 2500. In the perspective view, use the magnet to make the terrain uneven with hills and depressions. *Making the terrain too challenging may cause your SUV to get stuck or meet with disaster while interacting with the falling boulders, which you will create later.* Your terrain should look similar to Figure 7.40 in the perspective view. Switch to **Model** mode and choose the **Move** tool to get rid of the Magnet tool. All modeling is now complete. If you wish to check your work so far or use the terrain provided for this tutorial, open the "**Tutorials/ProjectFiles/Chapter 07/Tutorial-02/DynamicsDriving-03/DynamicsDriving-03.c4d**" on the DVD-ROM.

ON THE DVD

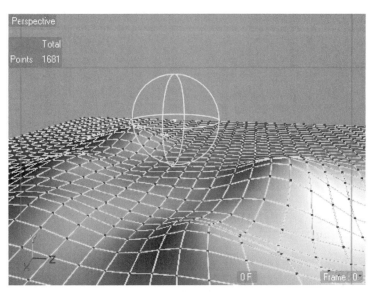

FIGURE 7.40   The Magnet tool has been used to make the ground more challenging for the SUV to drive through the falling boulders.

38. In the **Main** menu, choose **Plugins/Dynamics/Solver Object** and then choose **Plugins/Dynamics/Gravity**. Place the Gravity, Ground,

WheelsRear, WheelsFront, and SUV Proxy into the solver object hierarchy so that they can all be part of the dynamics simulation.

39. With the solver selected, in the Attributes Manager, **Main** tab, set the **Integration Method** to Midpoint and **Oversampling** to 16. To set the duration of the dynamics simulation to match the current project length, set **Stop** to 300. In the **Details** tab, set the **Collision Eps** to 6. Check **Collision Use Rest Speed** and set **Collision Rest Speed** to 20. These two rest speed settings are for stabilizing the boulders when they are coming to rest so they don't continue to try to collide with the ground.

The choice of a Collision Eps of 6 is based on the space between the wheels and the SUV Proxy object.

While creating simple bouncing ball dynamics simulations may be very easy, the challenge comes in creating accurate interconnecting objects within object collisions. Six factors contribute to the stability and accuracy of collision detection:

> **The project frame rate:**   A higher project frame rate provides more frames to detect a collision and therefore increases the accuracy of the collisions.
>
> **The initial space between objects that are positioned with other dynamics objects:**   The smaller the initial gap between such interacting colliding objects, the greater the effort needed in setting the other five factors to ensure accurate collisions.
>
> **The solver integration method:**   Some integration methods work faster but create less accurate collisions.
>
> **The speed at which the objects will move or rotate relative to each other:**   Fast-moving objects require greater effort in setting the other five factors to ensure accurate collisions.
>
> **The Collision Eps Value:**   Setting the value too high can make collision detection unstable. Setting the value too low can make collision detection inaccurate.
>
> **Oversampling/Subsampling:**   The higher the oversampling and subsampling values, the higher the collision accuracy as well as the time needed to calculate the dynamics simulation.

These are the areas to check when troubleshooting collision detection problems

40. Select the Ground, WheelsFront, WheelsRear, and SUV Proxy polygon objects in the Solver hierarchy and right-click to choose **Dynamics Tags/Rigid Body Dynamic**. Select the rigid body tag for the Ground object. In the **Mass** tab, set the **Total Mass** to 0 to prevent the ground from being pulled down by gravity. In the **Collision** tab,

set the **Collision Detection** to Full, **Elasticity** to 5, **Static** (friction) to 40 and **Dynamic** (friction) to 35 so objects hitting the ground will not rebound like a golf ball on concrete, and they will have traction.

The ground's dynamic friction value is important in getting the wheels to have enough traction to pull the SUV forward.

41. On the SUV Proxy rigid body tag, in the **Mass** tab, set the **Total Mass** to 11 to project the behavior that the body of the SUV is weighing down on the wheels. In the **Collision** tab, set the **Collision Detection** to Full, **Elasticity** to 0, **Static** (friction) to 0, and **Dynamic** (friction) to 0. These settings result in stable interaction with the wheels.

42. Select the rigid body tags for both sets of wheels. In the **Collision** tab, set the **Collision Detection** to Full, **Elasticity** to 10, **Static** (friction) to 25, and **Dynamic** (friction) to 20. As the wheels are between the SUV Proxy and the ground, these settings are made to ensure a stable simulation.

43. So far, the dynamics setup has only been for creating stable collisions and traction. To cause the SUV to actually drive, in the Objects Manager, select the WheelsFront and WheelsBack objects. Right-click on one of them and choose **Dynamics Tags/Constraints**. In the Attributes Manager, **Tag** tab, set **Type** to Motor.

This is what gives the wheels the rotational energy that will drive the SUV. Motor is a constant rotation no matter what obstacle is encountered, much like if a car is facing and pressing against a solid steel wall, if you mash the accelerator down, the tires will rotate even if the car cannot go through the steel wall.

44. If you play the simulation in the right view, you will notice that the wheels are turning clockwise very slowly and that the SUV would reverse. Set the **Angle** to −429 to reverse the rotation (counterclockwise) and increase the speed.

To further control the wheel rotation, turn the solver off and Ctrl-click the keyframing circle immediately preceding Angle. Go to another frame, change the value set in Angle, and set another key frame. Doing this on several different frames can cause the SUV to speed up, slow down, and even reverse.

45. To test the dynamics simulation, in the Objects Manager, select the solver object. From the **Main** menu, choose **Plugins/Dynamics/Bake Solver**. If you don't wish to wait for the dynamics simulation to be baked, open the "**Tutorials/ProjectFiles/Chapter 07/Tutorial-02/DynamicsDriving-04/DynamicsDriving-04.c4d**" on the DVD-ROM.

ON THE DVD

The dynamics simulation takes a few minutes to bake. You can also simply hit the Play button on the transport control, but doing so may play back too slowly for you to analyze how the simulation is working. Also, a baked solver replaces the green check mark with a red X.

46. Play the animation from various viewports to observe how the current settings affect the SUV's driving ability.

47. To create the first of the falling boulders, add a **Sphere** object. Set the **Radius** to 300 and set the **Position** to **X** = 0, **Y** = −3767, and **Z** = −5230. Make the sphere editable. Switch to **Point** mode and choose the **Magnet** tool. In the **Options**, set the **Radius** to 250. Frame the sphere in the perspective view and use the magnet to deform the sphere into a boulder (shown in Figure 7.41).

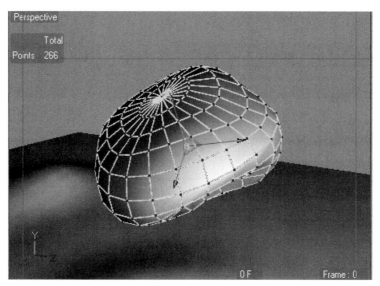

FIGURE 7.41   The Magnet tool has been used to make the sphere into the first of the falling boulders.

48. In the Objects Manager, Copy (**Ctrl-c**) the sphere and Paste (**Ctrl-v**) 11 times to have a total of 12 spheres. Select them all and from the **Main** menu, choose **Functions/Randomize**. In the **Tool** tab, click **Apply**. In the **Options** tab, set the **Move** to 2273, 1391, and 2250. Set the **Scale** to 168, 135, and 153; the **Rotation** to 25, 11, and 26; and the **Speed** to 21. All this scatters and randomly modifies the shapes of the 12 boulders (shown in Figure 7.42).

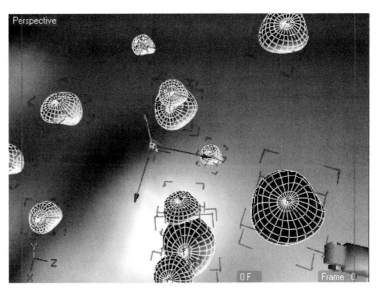

FIGURE 7.42   Twelve randomized boulders.

49. With the 12 spheres still selected, right-click one of them and choose **Dynamics Tags/Rigid Body Dynamics**. In the Attributes Manager, **Collision** tab, set **Collision Detection** to Full, **Elasticity** to 50, **Static** (friction) to 6, and **Dynamic** (friction) to 7. Then group the sphere objects (**Alt-g**) and rename the group "**Boulders**." Place the Boulders group into the solver object hierarchy.

50. To see how the falling boulders interact with the driving SUV, from the **Main** menu, choose **Plugins/Dynamics/Clear All Solvers** to clear any previously baked data. Because the solver was baked, it will now have a red "X." Click the red X to change it into a green check mark. Then choose **Plugins/Dynamics/Bake All Solvers** to bake the simulation with the boulders added. If you don't wish to wait for the dynamics simulation to be baked, open the DynamicsDriving-05 project from Chapter 07/Tutorial-02 on the DVD-ROM.

ON THE DVD

Failure to check the solver's red X will result in no simulation baking. A solver must be active in order to be baked.

51. Play the animation to see the SUV driving and colliding with the falling boulders. It would be even more interesting to see the SUV have to make more of an effort to get through, so select the ground's rigid body tag and in the Attributes Manager, **Collision** tag, set the **Static** (friction) to 20 and the **Dynamic** (friction) to 15. These changes will require the SUV to work harder to get through the boulders.

52. Because the SUV will have to work harder to get through the boulders, the simulation and animation need to be longer. In the **Main** menu, choose **Edit/Project Settings** and set **Maximum** to 450. In the solver object, Attributes Manager, **Main** tab, set the **Stop** to 450. Now the simulation and animation are both set to be 15 seconds long.

53. To see the result of changing the ground's friction, from the **Main** menu, choose **Plugins/Dynamics/Clear All Solvers** to clear any previously baked data. Click the red X next to the solver to enable it. The green check appears. Then choose **Plugins/Dynamics/Bake All Solvers** to bake the simulation with the new ground friction values. If you don't wish to wait for the dynamics simulation to be baked, open the "**Tutorials/ProjectFiles/Chapter 07/Tutorial-02/Dynamics-Driving-06/DynamicsDriving-06.c4d**" on the DVD-ROM.

ON THE DVD

54. Play the animation to see the change in behavior of the boulders and the SUV. The SUV now struggles to get through the boulders and has even altered its path. What a difference, just from changing the friction of the ground!

55. Now all the dynamics simulation is complete. It's time to make this animation look great. Set the **Editor Display Switch** and the **Renderer Display Switch** for the SUV Proxy, WheelsFront, and WheelsRear to be off (red dots). Set the **Editor Display Switch** and the **Renderer Display Switch** for the SUV Body (in the SUV Proxy hierarchy), TiresFront (in the WheelsFront hierarchy), and TiresRear (in the WheelsRear hierarchy) to be on (green dots) so that the fully textured models are displayed and the proxy objects are no longer displayed.

56. Select the **Display** tag from the SUV Body and uncheck **Use** so the SUV Body is no longer displayed as a Wireframe object in the perspective view.

57. In the SUV Body hierarchy, on the Headlight and Instance.1 objects, set the **Editor Display Switch** and the **Renderer Display Switch** to default (gray dots) so that they are visible in the editor and will be rendered. Deselect all objects and play the animation to see the SUV driving (powered by the baked dynamics simulation of the proxy objects) and hitting boulders (shown in Figure 7.43).

58. Drag the Rock material and apply it to the first sphere in the Boulders hierarchy. Then, with the **Ctrl** key held down, select the sphere's rock material tag and drag a copy to each of the remaining 11 sphere objects, as well as to the Ground object. Select the rock material tags for the ground. In the Attributes Manager, **Tag** tab, set the **Tiles X** and **Tiles Y** to 5 to scale the material properly. Render frame 35 in the perspective view to see that the geometry of the ground needs some smoothing (shown in Figure 7.44).

FIGURE 7.43   The SUV is now powered by the baked dynamics simulation of the proxy objects.

FIGURE 7.44   The ground geometry needs some smoothing.

59. Because the ground is part of a baked dynamics simulation, you won't be able to use a HyperNURBS object to smooth the ground object. Switch to **Polygon** mode and select the ground object. Right-click and choose **Subdivide**. Check **HyperNURBS Subdivide** and **OK** to arrange the original polygons and the polygons added by subdividing using the HyperNURBS algorithm.

60. Later, you will add a sky with the Sky plug-in. This will add light to the scene. There is currently a light and an instance of that light in the scene. These lights will be in addition to the light from the sky. So, to light the scene well, select the light object and in the Attributes Manager, **General** tab, set its **Brightness** to 70. In the **Shadow** tab, set the **Shadow Map** to 750 × 750 to make the shadow map more accurate. Set the **Sample Radius** to 6 to soften the edge of the shadow. Rendered now, the perspective view will look a little dark. That's OK.

61. Because the Ground object is finite and the view to the horizon is infinite, add a Floor object to create the illusion that the Ground object extends to the horizon. In order for the floor not to cut through the Ground object, in the Coordinates Manager, set the floor's **Y Position** to −880. Apply the Rock material to the Floor object.

62. To create the sky, from the **Main** menu, choose **Plugins/Sky/Create Sky**. Render frame 149 in the perspective view to see an image similar to Figure 7.45.

FIGURE 7.45 The sky and floor are added to the scene.

63. When working from previous projects or merged projects, there are sometimes unused or duplicate materials. To take care of a little house cleaning, in the Materials Manager menu, choose Function/ Remove Unused Materials and then choose Functions/Remove Duplicate Materials.

Before rendering the final animation is always a great time to save your project.

64. Add a Target Camera and place the camera target in the SUV Body hierarchy. Center the camera target in the SUV Body in the front and top views. This way, as the SUV drives, it will always appear to be the camera's subject of interest.

65. In the perspective view local menu, choose **Cameras/Scene Cameras/Camera**. In the Objects Manager, select the camera and set its Position to **X** = 1430, **Y** = 713, and **Z** = –2263. Then click the **Record Key Frame** button (red ball) on the Transport Control (shown in Figure 7.46) to set a key frame for the camera's position.

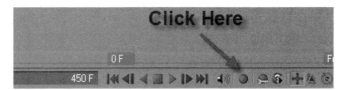

FIGURE 7.46   Click to add a key frame for the camera.

66. Go to the last frame (450) and set the camera's **Position** to **X** = 4990, **Y** = 713, and **Z** = –11,262 and set another key frame. In the Transport Control, double-click the Play Head (gray box displaying the current frame) and set it to 225. Then set the camera's **Position** to **X** = 4716, **Y** = 713, and **Z** = –6151 and set another key frame. Play the animation to see that the camera now keeps up with the animation.

67. To set up the final render, click the **Render Settings** icon. In the **Output** page, set the **Resolution** to 640 × 480 (or whatever resolution you like). Set **Frame** to All Frames so the entire animation will be rendered. In the **Save** page, set the **Format** to AVI Movie (for example). Click **Options** to choose the Intel Indeo 4.5 codec (on the Mac you could choose Quicktime Sorensen 3). Uncheck **Data Rate** and set the **Compression Quality** to 100 to ensure high quality and click OK. Click **Path** to name the animation video file and choose where you will save it.

Depending on the file formats and codecs installed on your system, you may have to choose a codec other than Intel Indeo 4.5. Be aware that different codecs have different color and pixel resolution options.

68. Close the Render Settings window and click the **Render In Picture Viewer** icon to start the rendering process and see the final animation render start by rendering an image similar to Figure 7.47.

FIGURE 7.47   The final animation rendering the first frames.

SUMMARY

While dynamics simulation often provides a more effective solution to some production challenges, it opens up a new set of challenges as well. These issues will seem a bit less challenging once you get familiar with the interactions and dependencies within dynamics simulation. Exploring the application of dynamics to many production challenges such as spinning a top, breaking a drinking glass, and billiards can arm you with the confidence to know when and how Cinema 4D Dynamics should be employed as the solution of choice.

CHARACTER ANIMATION

In This Chapter

- Tutorial 1: Arm Rig
- Tutorial 2: Lady Walk
- Tutorial 3: James Walk
- Tutorial 4: Jessi Dance
- Tutorial 5: RPC

 Software used: Cinema 4D 9.5 Studio, Poser 6, BodyStudio 2.6, RPC, Zygote Humans

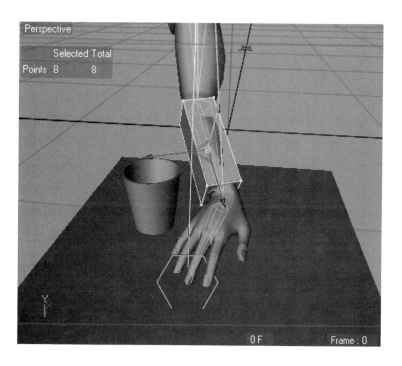

In this chapter, we'll look at a few character animation methods used in different 3D animation production situations. The idea here is to show how to produce basic character animation using only Cinema 4D and how to produce character animation by integrating Cinema 4D with other support products (programs, plug-ins, and 3D content).

Traditionally, 3D character animation is taught and discussed as an intricate and laborious interdependent symbiosis of principles, processes, and technical setups. This chapter will focus on creating 3D character animation from a less technical and a more visual perspective that allows you to spend more of your time on the storytelling and less time on the technical details.

Once the principles taught in these tutorials are understood, you will be able to produce 3D character animation in a variety of ways with maximum output for minimum effort and do so in the shortest amount of time. Additionally, you will be able to produce 3D character animation using reference video as a motion guide, providing a simple but effective low-cost motion capture solution.

In Tutorial 1 (Arm Rig), you will learn the basics of rigging a human arm for character animation using the character animation tools provided in Cinema 4D's Mocca module. This Mocca rigged arm will then be animated to search around and accidentally knock a coffee cup (from Chapter 2) off the table by using XPresso and Dynamics.

 This Mocca tutorial is a basic introduction to using some of the Mocca elements. For a more thorough tutorial of really putting Mocca to use, see Chapter 8 of "The Cinema 4D 9/9.1 Handbook" by Adam Watkins and Anson Call, also published by Charles River Media.

In Tutorial 2, you will load a video clip of a lady walking across the screen as a reference for character animation of a fully rigged female character for the Zygote collection. Here you'll learn about the issues of animating 3D characters rigged with Mocca and experience the benefits and limitations of reference video in an orthogonal viewport. After completing this tutorial, you'll probably look at your camcorder and your friends and family in a new character animation light.

In Tutorial 3, you will start by easily creating a great 3D character in Poser 6 and then make the character walk using the "Walk Designer," which allows you to visually adjust a fluidly walking character style in real-time by simply dragging walk parameter sliders. This walking character will then be brought into Cinema 4D 9 via BodyStudio 2.6 and merged with the Flag Day project from Chapter 6. You will experience character animation *made painless*.

In Tutorial 4, you will again begin in Poser 6 and create a 3D character. This time the character will be animated to perform an expressive dance, using a BVH motion capture file. The character will then be merged with a stage performance environment in Cinema 4D 9 via BodyStudio 2.6.

Tutorial 5 covers a different character animation objective by using RPC content from Archvision (*http://www.archvision.com*) to add photo-realistic people to a Cinema 4D scene. While some of these people will be perfectly cut-out video clips, others will be amazing photographs that allow you to view the person from any camera angle. This method will be particularly helpful for finishing an architectural previsualization project that must blow away the client.

ON THE DVD
These tutorials are also on the accompanying DVD-ROM as video tutorials, along with the tutorial project files.

Remember, as you make progress in each tutorial, to save your Cinema 4D projects.

 **TUTORIAL 1**   **ARM RIG**

FIGURE 8.1   A Mocca rigged arm will collide with the coffee cup.

Covered in this tutorial:

- Applying bones
- Using the Claude Bonet tool
- Forward Kinematics (FK)
- Mocca's Setup IK Chain
- Inverse Kinematics (IK)
- Up Vector
- XPresso
- Rigid Body Dynamics

In Cinema 4D (like all programs dedicated to general 3D animation), after modeling a character, the character must be rigged (prepared) for animation. This tutorial begins with the Mocca rigging of an arm. The concepts of Bones, Claude Bonet painting, and IK Setup will be made simple and clear. The upper arm, lower arm, and hand will be rigged. After completing this tutorial, you will have an understanding of how to rig the fingers as well.

After rigging the arm, the arm will be key frame animated to search for something on a tabletop. The arm will search blindly next to a coffee cup (from Chapter 2) sitting on the tabletop. Through the aide of both XPresso and Dynamics, the arm will "accidentally" knock over a cup on the tabletop. Finished project files for six sections of this tutorial are included on the accompanying DVD-ROM in the tutorials folder. All of the images used in this tutorial are located in Tutorials/ProjectFiles/Chapter 08/Tutorial-01 on the Projects DVD-ROM.

ON THE DVD

The words "spline" and "curve" are used interchangeably.

1. Begin by loading "**ArmRig-01.c4d**" from the "**Tutorials/Project-Files/Chapter 08/Tutorial-01**" folder on the accompanying DVD-ROM. This loads the arm, which is a single polygon mesh object that you will rig and animate in this tutorial. In the Objects Manager, turn off the HyperNURBS so that only the editable polygons are visible.

ON THE DVD

2. Using the **Mode Selector** (shown in Figure 8.2), switch the Cinema 4D interface to the **Mocca** layout. To increase the work area, in the lower left corner, in the **Timeline**, click the blue thumbtack (shown in Figure 8.3) and choose **Close**. Also close the **F-Curve** window to increase the work area.

FIGURE 8.2   Mode Selector being switched to Mocca.

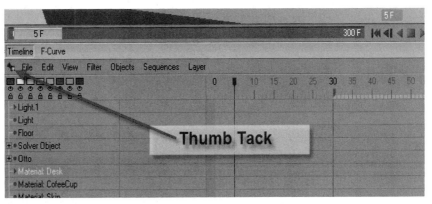

FIGURE 8.3   Closing the Timeline window.

 When working in screen resolutions of 1280 × 1024 and above, it may not be necessary to close windows such as the Timeline.

    3. Select the **Bone** tool (shown in Figure 8.4). In the Attributes Manager, click **Add Bone** and rename the bone "**Bone1**." Working in the top, front, and right views, move the Bone Root and Bone Tip (shown in Figure 8.5) into position in the upper arm (shown in Figure 8.6). In the Attributes Manager, **Object** tab, check **Absolute Vertex Map** to have better polygon deformation between the bones. Later in this tutorial, when you paint with Claude Bonet, having Absolute Vertex Map checked will prevent a bone from affecting areas of the mesh not associated with the bone through Claude Bonet paint.

 It is crucial to check the bone placement in all three orthogonal views to ensure proper bone placement.

 As the mouse moves over the bone root and tip, the moveable control points highlight, indicating that they can be moved. This is Cinema 4D's very helpful hinting at work.

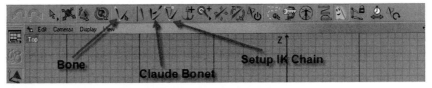

FIGURE 8.4   The Bone tool indicated from the Mocca tool palette.

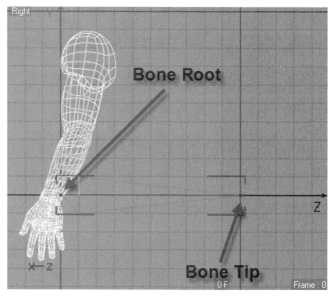

FIGURE 8.5   The Bone Root and Bone Tip identified.

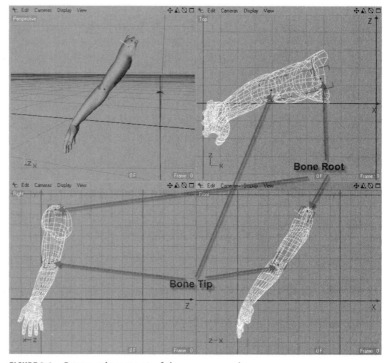

FIGURE 8.6   Proper placement of the upper arm bone.

4. With the upper arm bone still selected, in the Attributes Manager, click **Add Child Bone** to create the bone for the forearm. Rename the bone "**Bone2**." This new forearm bone has its root connected to the upper arm bone's tip. Where these two bones connect is called a joint, so moving this joint affects the placement of both bones. Position the new forearm bone as shown in Figure 8.7.

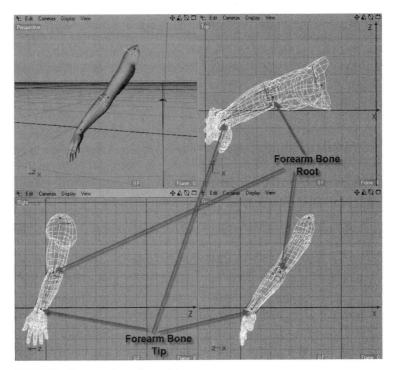

FIGURE 8.7   Forearm bone in position.

5. To create the final bone for this arm rig, click **Add Child Bone** again to create a bone for the hand. Rename this bone "**Bone3**." Position the hand bone as shown in Figure 8.8.

6. In the Objects Manager, drag the bone hierarchy into the Mesh polygon object (the arm) as shown in Figure 8.9.

7. In order to define what area of the arm is controlled by movement of each bone, with Bone1 selected in the Objects Manager, choose the **Claude Bonet** tool from the Mocca tool palette (shown in Figure 8.4). This will allow you to paint the arm's polygons to associate each bone with the area of the arm it will control. In the Attributes Manager, uncheck **Only Modify Visible Elements**, check **Paint Absolute**, set

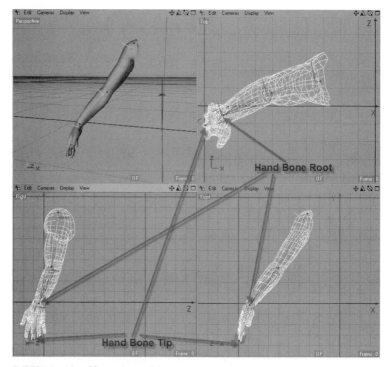

FIGURE 8.8   Hand bone in position.

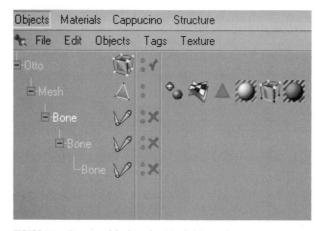

FIGURE 8.9   Bones added to the Mesh hierarchy.

Strength to 100 and set **Radius** to 20 to make controlled painting more manageable.

8. With Bone1 still selected in the Objects Manager, in the front and right views, paint the polygons of the upper arm so that Bone1 will affect only those polygons and not try to pull polygons in the forearm and hand. Claude Bonet turns the upper arm area green so that you can clearly see where you have painted.

If you accidentally paint over an area, hold the Ctrl key and paint over the area again to remove the paint.

It's very important to be very sure that every polygon has received paint for its associated bone. Failure to do this will result in the unpainted polygons staying behind when the rest of the object moves. It won't be a pretty sight.

9. Select Bone2 and paint the forearm area, checking your work in the front and right views. Now the forearm area is green and the upper arm area is red, so you can clearly see which polygons of the arm each bone now controls.

After selecting a new bone to be painted, to ensure that you don't accidentally start painting in the wrong area, place the mouse just outside the polygons to be painted and press the left mouse button down and drag it into the polygon area. This displays the Claude Bonet paint brush circular cursor, showing you exactly where it will be painted. This is particularly helpful when performing detailed Claude Bonet work.

10. Select Bone3 and paint the hand polygons, again checking your work in the front and right views. Looking at your work in all four views, you should see a result similar to Figure 8.10. The hand area is green, the forearm area is blue, and the upper arm area is red.
11. Now to activate the bones so they can move the polygon mesh, select Bone1 in the Objects Manager. In the Attributes Manager, **Fixation** tab, choose **Fix With Children** to activate the bone chain. In the Objects Manager, the bones now have a green check indicating they are active (shown in Figure 8.11).

Once the bones are active, with Bone2 selected, you could use the Rotate tool to swing the forearm. Setting key frames for the forearm bone at different frames in the timeline would allow you to animate the arm using Forward Kinematics (FK) animation. This method has the benefit of allowing precise positioning of all segments of a character and has the drawback of requiring you to position each segment manually.

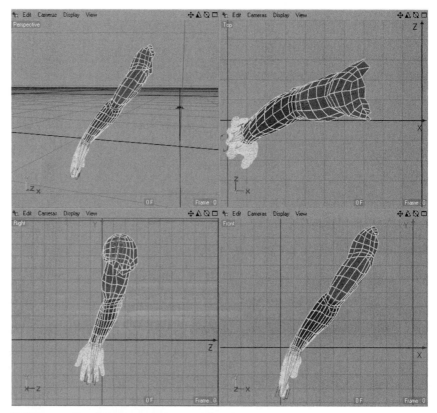

FIGURE 8.10   Claude Bonet painting completed.

FIGURE 8.11   Bones are now active.

12. With Bone1 selected, from the Mocca tool palette, choose **Setup IK Chain** (shown in Figure 8.4). This adds the Bone3.Tip Goal and Bone3.Tip Effector Goal to the bone chain in the Objects Manager. In

the Objects Manager, select the Bone3.Tip Goal and move it out of the bone chain to become the first child of the polygon mesh object (shown in Figure 8.12). Now, by simply moving the Bone3.Tip Goal in the viewports, the entire arm can be posed. Because of the way that the child bone affects the parent bone, this type of animation is called "Inverse Kinematics" (IK) animation.

When moving the Bone3.Tip Goal out of the bone chain, be very careful that the Bone3.Tip Goal is absolutely the only object selected, or you may get unexpected results.

The Bone3.Tip Goal is seen in the viewports as a sky blue wireframed cube at the middle finger of the hand object.

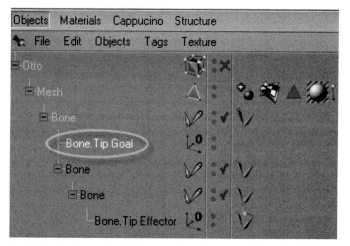

FIGURE 8.12   Bone3.Tip Goal moved to the proper hierarchical position.

13. As you move the Bone3.Tip Goal around the viewports, you will notice that the orientation of the hand is uncontrollable. So, select Bone3 and from the **Main** menu, choose **Plugins/Mocca/Add Up Vector**. This adds a Bone3.Up null object to the bone chain. By changing the position of this up vector for Bone3, you can rotate the hand to be palm up or palm down. This increases the control, predictability, and stability of the arm rig. Rigging of the arm is now complete.

The Up Vector controls a bone's Y axis orientation.

14. To begin animating the arm, from the **Main** menu, load the "**Tutorials/ProjectFiles/Chapter 08/Tutorial 01/ArmRig-03.c4d**" project. This includes the rigged arm, a cube named Desk, and a coffee cup (modeled in Chapter 2) sitting on the desktop. In **Model** mode, select the Bone3.Tip Goal and the **Move** tool. At frame 0, create a key frame to store the starting position and pose of the arm.

15. On frame 90, move the Hand.Tip Goal to **X** = –58, **Y** = –79, and **Z** = –76 and create another key frame.

 While it may seem OK to simply enter the positional coordinates in the Coordinates Manager, when working with IK animation, it is best to drag the Bone3.Tip Goal into the correct position so that the IK solver can produce the expected result. Otherwise, the results could be very different than expected.

16. At frame 120, position the Bone3.Tip Goal position at **X** = –102, **Y** = –74, and **Z** = –58 and record a key frame.

17. At frame 180, position the Bone3.Tip Goal position at **X** = –99, **Y** = –80, and **Z** = –25 and record a key frame.

18. At frame 240, position the Bone3.Tip Goal position at **X** = –82, **Y** = –80, and **Z** = –42 and record a key frame.

19. At frame 300, position the Bone3.Tip Goal position at **X** = –116, **Y** = –80, and **Z** = –6.5 and record a key frame. This completes the IK animation of the arm searching blindly on the desk top. Working in the perspective view only, play the animation to see the arm searching blindly around the desk top. Toward the end of the animation, you'll see the arm going through the coffee cup. You'll need to add some XPresso and Dynamics to complete the illusion that the arm is hitting the coffee cup.

20. Now you will add XPresso and Dynamics simulation to the scene so the arm can knock the cup. Load "**Tutorials/ProjectFiles/Chapter 08/Tutorial-01/ArmRig-05.c4d**" to see a polygon object named Collider added to the scene and positioned along the forearm.

21. Right-click the Collider polygon object and choose **Cinema 4D Tags/XPresso**. Drag the Collider polygon object and Bone2 into the XPresso Editor window.

22. In the XPresso Editor, Bone2 node **Output Menu** (pink upper right corner), choose **Coordinates/Global Rotation/Global Rotation**. This means the rotation of Bone2 will be used to control something. On the Collider node **Input Menu** (blue upper left corner), choose **Coordinates/Global Rotation/Global Rotation**. This means the rotation of Collider will be controlled by something. Drag a wire from the Bone2 **Global Rotation** output to the Collider **Global Rotation** input. The Collider polygon object will now assume the rotation of the forearm's Bone2.

23. On the Bone2 node, create a new output of **Coordinates/Global Position/Global Position**. This means the position of Bone2 will be used to control something. On the Collider node Input Menu (blue upper left corner), choose **Coordinates/Global Position/Global Position**. This means the position of Collider will be controlled by something. Drag a wire from the Bone2 **Global Position** output to the Collider **Global Position** input. The XPresso Editor should now look like Figure 8.13. Close the XPresso Editor window. The Collider polygon object will now assume the position of the forearm's Bone2. In short, the Collider's rotation and position are now parented to Bone2 via XPresso.

In previous chapters, such parenting relationships were defined by simply dragging one object into another. In this case, though, rather than having the collider as part of the bone chain hierarchy, the collider will need to be part of a dynamics simulation hierarchy. XPresso is used to have the collider in the dynamics hierarchy assume the position and rotation of Bone2 in the bone chain hierarchy. This method can be used to create movement relationships between hierarchies. While there are other ways of ultimately achieving the same end result of parenting, learning this method will enable you to easily apply XPresso to otherwise nearly impossible animation production challenges.

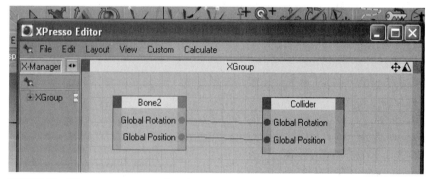

FIGURE 8.13   XPresso setup completed.

24. Moving the Bone3.Tip Goal in the viewports shows that the Collider moves and rotates along with Bone2. However, the Collider object has been offset along its Z axis. To correct this offset, select the Collider object and switch to **Point** mode and press **Ctrl-A** to select all points in that polygon object. Then drag the Collider by its **Z** axis (blue arrow) to move it into position along the forearm (shown in

Figure 8.14). Switch to **Model** mode and move the Bone3.Tip Goal in the viewports to see the Collider staying with the forearm.

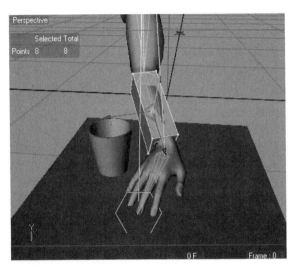

FIGURE 8.14   Bone3.Tip Goal moved to the proper hierarchical position.

So, it's really the Collider that will crash into the cup and not the polygons of the arm. This is because bone-deformed objects cannot collide with other objects in a dynamics simulation.

25. To add the dynamics simulation that will allow the collider to hit the cup when the arm sweeps into the cup, from the **Main** menu, choose **Plugins/Dynamics/Solver** and **Plugins/Dynamics/Gravity**. In the Objects Manager, drag the Gravity, Desk, HyperNURBS (cylinder.1), and Collider into the solver object (shown in Figure 8.15).

26. In the solver object hierarchy, select the Collider, Cylinder.1, and Desk and right-click in the Objects Manager (on the name or icon of one of the selected objects) and choose **Dynamics Tags/Rigid Body Dynamics**. With just the rigid body tags for the Collider and Desk selected, in the Attributes Manager, **Mass** tab, set the **Total Mass** to 0 to prevent gravity from pulling them down. In the **Collision** tab, set **Collision Detection** to Box.

27. With just the rigid body tag for the Cylinder.1 selected, in the Attributes Manager, **Mass** tab, leave the **Total Mass** to 1 to allow gravity to pull it down. In the **Collision** tab, set **Collision Detection** to Full.

28. Play the dynamics simulation to see that the collision between the collider and the cup will need further work: "**Tutorials/Project-**

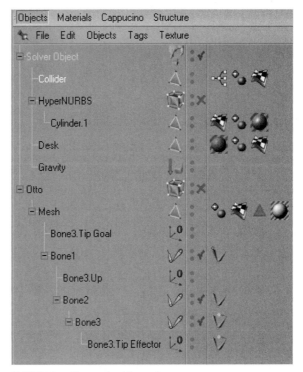

FIGURE 8.15   Dynamics hierarchy setup.

Files/Chapter 08/Tutorial-01/Load ArmRig-06.c4d." A cylinder object has been added to the collider hierarchy. This is because collisions between objects with XPresso tags can be erratic. The rigid body tag for this cylinder object has a mass of 0 so that gravity will have no effect on it and its collision detection type is set to full so that every polygon is checked for collision with the cup. By setting the **Editor** and **Render Display Switches** for the Collider object off (red) and setting only the **Editor Display Switch** for the Cylinder on (green) (shown in Figure 8.16), you will see the Cylinder playback in the viewport, but it will not be rendered in the final animation.

Additionally the rigid body tag for the Desk and cylinder objects have their Static and Dynamic friction set to 50 to help stabilize the simulation.

29. Select the solver object and in the Attributes Manager, **Main** tab, set the **Integration Method** to Midpoint and **Over Sampling** to 16. In the **Details** tab, set the **Collision Eps** to 3, check **Collision Use Rest Speed**, and set the **Collision Rest Speed** to 20 to keep the initial stationary cup from bouncing in place.

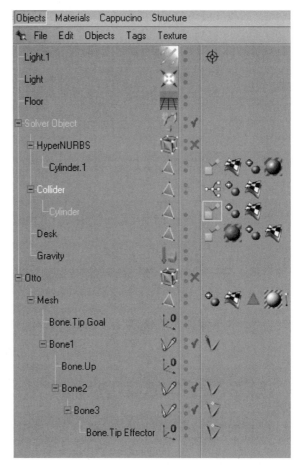

FIGURE 8.16 Display switches for the collider and cylinder are setup.

30. Now that the dynamics simulation setup is completed, from the **Main** menu, choose **Plugins/Dynamics/Bake All Solvers** to bake the dynamics simulation into animation key frames.

 If your scene contains a previously baked solver, you must first choose Plugins/Dynamics/Clear All Solvers to delete previously baked frames.

 Once the simulation is baked, as you play back the animation, you will notice that when you press the Go To Start Of Animation button, the posing of the arm may be incorrect. This is due to the interaction between the dynamics-controlled Bone3.Tip Goal. Playing a few frames, stopping, and then pressing the Go To Start Of Animation button will set the arm in the proper initial pose.

Summary

We hope this tutorial has demystified the basics of character rigging for character animation. Using Mocca to set up character animation with the visually intuitive tools such as Bones and Claude Bonet painting brings a real sense of control and creativity to the character rigging process. The integration of Mocca, XPresso, and Dynamics can lead to excellent problem solving during challenging real-world 3D animation productions.

TUTORIAL 2   **LADY WALK**

FIGURE 8.17   A 3D lady walks based on the video reference of a real lady walking.

Covered in this tutorial:

- Reference video in viewport
- Mocca rigged Zygote character
- IK Character animation

This fully Mocca rigged character will be animated to match the motion from a reference video placed in the right viewport. The reference video is of a lady walking across the screen from right to left. This reference video was shot with a typical household camcorder to emphasize the versatility of this method of character animation.

In Chapter 2, when you modeled objects to photo references, you saw that the photo (having real-world perspective distortion) didn't line up precisely with the orthogonal-view 3D model. This difference between photography and the orthogonal 3D world will be something to keep an eye on in this tutorial as well. As the lady walks across the screen, her perspective angle will change. Additionally, as this reference video clip is seen from one stationary point, her right arm is often obscured.

The fact that you will animate a 3D character to a reference video with such limitations and still get great results will help you discover a whole new world of possibilities just using your household camcorder, your friends, and your family to turn acting into animation. The objective of this method of character animation isn't to create a perfect likeness of the actor motion, but rather to use the actor motion as a position and timing guide. To create a perfect likeness of the actor motion, you would use a process known as "motion capture." First you will animate the body and legs walking forward; then you'll animate the arms swinging.

ON THE DVD

Finished project files for two sections of this tutorial are included on the accompanying DVD-ROM in the tutorials folder. All of the images used in this tutorial are located in Tutorials/Chapter 08/Tutorial-02 on the Projects DVD-ROM.

The words "spline" and "curve" are used interchangeably.

ON THE DVD

1. Begin by loading "**Goodies/Zygote/Women/Casual/Woman 1/ w1casual_rigged.c4d**" from the accompanying DVD-ROM. This loads the Mocca rigged lady from the Zygote collection "Humans To Go."

ON THE DVD

2. You will animate the body moving right to left and the legs walking in the right view. Once that's all done, you'll animate the arms as well. Working in just the right view, in the local menu, choose **Edit/Configure**. In the Attributes Manager, **Back** tab and browse to open "**Tutorials/ProjectFiles/Chapter 08/Tutorial-02**" from the DVD-ROM. This displays the reference video in the right view. Set the **Offset X** to –540, **Offset Y** to 317, **Size X** to 1224, and **Size Y** to 816. Now the 3D character and the lady in the reference video are the same size (shown in Figure 8.18). If you drag the viewport around now, the 3D character and the reference video will stay together.

In addition to the quality of the acquired video file, the quality of the reference video is affected by whether you are using Open GL or Software mode. This is set by going to the Main menu and choosing Edit/Preferences and then going to the Viewport page. Additionally, the capabilities of your video card are a factor in both the quality of the video reference image and the speed with which you can move between frames.

FIGURE 8.18   3D character and lady in reference video are matched in size.

3. In the Objects Manager, look within the Woman World hierarchy to find the control objects that will be moved and key framed to make the character walk according the reference video. The first control object is the full mesh object named woman1_casual (wcas1). This is the polygon object that will be rendered. In previous tutorials, moving an object would simply change its position. That is not the case here. When working with IK (e.g., pull the finger and the hand will follow) rigged characters, moving parts of a character results in very interactive behavior. To see just what this means, select the woman1_casual (wcas1) and use the **Move** tool in **Model** mode to move the character's body around in the perspective view. You'll notice that the arms and legs try to stay in place. This means that when you animate the character, moving the woman1_casual (wcas1) object will give you more of a sense that you are posing a body than simply moving an object. Before moving the body, check to make sure all three **Axis Locks** (shown in Figure 8.19) are turned off.

Be sure to undo the movement of the character to its initial state.

FIGURE 8.19 Axis Locks.

4. The R Leg Goals and L Leg Goals hierarchies are used to move the feet into position. Because the character is IK rigged, this means the legs will be posed by moving the feet. The R Leg UpV and L Leg UpV (Up Vectors) hierarchies are used to control the twisting of the legs (Figure 8.20). Without these up vectors, animating the legs would be a nightmare.

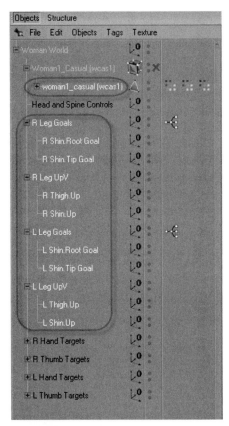

FIGURE 8.20 Character animation controls for the body and legs identified in text.

body and then positioning the left leg is important because by positioning the body first, the left leg will more easily bend naturally when placed into position to match the reference video of the lady's left foot planted on the floor. In the Objects Manager, select the right leg control objects and position the right foot to match the reference video lady's right foot. Because the floor in the right view is defined as the blue line on which the character is placed, and because the reference video color has perspective scaling, position the right foot with the toe touching the blue line (floor). Your right view should now match Figure 8.26.

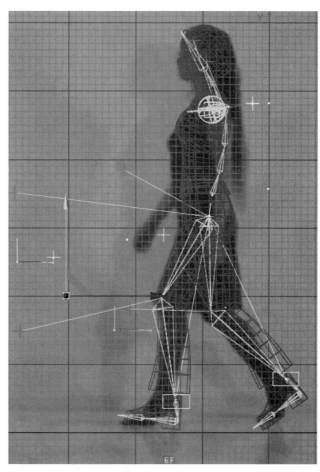

FIGURE 8.26   Second key frame for the body and legs.

11. Go to frame 12, where the reference video lady's weight is centered and completely on her left leg. Move the character's body and then the right leg to match the reference video. On this frame, the left leg will not be moved. It still needs to receive a key frame so that it doesn't slide between the previous and next key frame positions, so in the Objects Manager, select the left leg control objects and press the Record button to manually create a key for the left leg. Your right view should now match Figure 8.27.

 "Move the character's body" will mean "position the character's chin to match the video reference lady's chin" from this point forward.

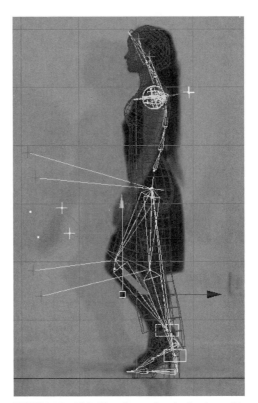

FIGURE 8.27 Third key frame for the body and legs.

12. Go to frame 22, where the reference video shows the lady's right foot planted on the floor. Move the body into position. Place the right foot into position. Adjust the left foot so that it matches the left heel in the reference video and the left leg has a natural bend (like the reference video left leg) as shown in Figure 8.28.

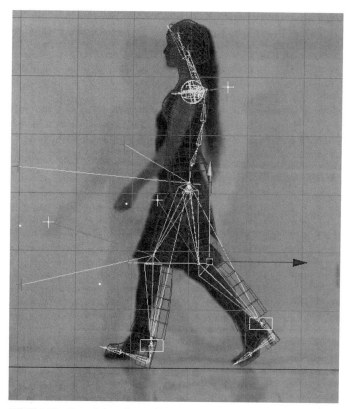

FIGURE 8.28   Fourth key frame for the body and legs.

13. Continue matching the body and leg positions to the rest of the refer-
    ence video footage, being careful to apply the rules established in step 6.

 *While moving the legs into position, you may at times see some extreme twisting of
the geometry. As long as the leg is not twisted when you finally place it into position, the twisting in between (while the leg is being placed) can be ignored.*

 *Remember, if you move the left leg on a frame and the right leg doesn't need to move,
you must manually create a key frame for the right leg to prevent it from sliding.*

 *While animating a walking character in the right view, if you feel confused about
which leg is really in front, take a look in the perspective view. You will immediately regain your perspective on which leg needs to be moved. On dual display systems, it's helpful to keep the perspective view on one display while working on the
other display in the right view to animate the character.*

14. Once these initial key frames are set, orient the perspective view as shown in Figure 8.29 and play the animation to see the character walking with the arms stretched out. The walk animation is still crude. The leg motion doesn't have the swing that reflects the biomechanics of a walking human. Also, the rotation of the feet and the bending of the toes have not been set yet, so the feet appear to be wooden.

FIGURE 8.29 Perspective view of the 3D character with all initial body and leg key frames set.

15. Go back to frame 0. Working in just the right view, zoom in on the character's feet. In the Objects Manager, select the L Leg Goals. In the Attributes Manager, **User Data** tab, with the **Ctrl** key held down, click the **Key Frame** dots (Figure 8.30) for **Heel Adjust P** and **Toe Adjust**. Drag the Heel Adjust P slider so that the left foot is flat on the floor. With the R Leg Goals selected in the Objects Manager, and with the **Ctrl** key held down, click the **Key Frame** dots (shown in Figure 8.30) for **Heel Adjust P** and **Toe Adjust** and adjust the Heel Adjust P for the right foot to be flat on the floor as well.

Clicking with the Ctrl key held down is known as Ctrl-clicking.

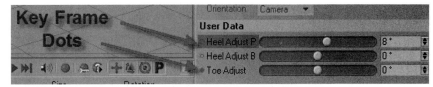

FIGURE 8.30   Key Frame dots for Heel Adjust P and Toe Adjust.

16. Select the L Leg Goals and press **Ctrl-G** to go to the next L Leg Goals key frame. **Ctrl-click** a key frame for the Heel Adjust P and the Toe Adjust. As you then drag the play head on the Transport Control forward, look for where the left shoe rotates through the floor most (frame 17) and position the left shoe heel to be centered with the reference video left shoe heel. Then drag the Heel Adjust P slider to flatten the shoe on the floor.

Remember, as long as you move an object or adjust a slider (Heel Adjust P or Toe Adjust), you are creating a key frame because you are working in Automatic Keyframing mode.

17. Because by default, Cinema 4D key frames together create a curve motion path, the key frame just created for the Heel Adjust P on frame 17 and the initial key frame for the Heel Adjust P at frame 0 have caused a curve in the Heel Adjust P at frame 10. Go to frame 10 to see the shoe rotating slightly into the floor. Use the Heel Adjust P to correct this so the left shoe is flat on the floor.

18. On frames 16 and 17, with the L Leg Goals selected, center the left shoe heel with the reference video heel to keep the foot from slipping.

19. As you slowly drag the play head forward, in the reference video, you will start to see the toe of the left shoe bending, so go to frame 16 and **Ctrl-click** a key frame for the Toe Adjust. This key frame is set because the toe is about to bend. At frame 21 drag the Toe Adjust slider to bend the toe of the shoe to match the left shoe toe bend in the reference video. At this point you also need to use the Heel Adjust P to rotate the shoe to touch the floor. It is also necessary to move the L Leg Goals to center the heel of the shoe with the left shoe heel in the reference video.

20. As you drag the play head forward, you will notice that the left shoe position will not match the reference video. This is because by default, key frame animation distributes changes in position smoothly

without accounting for biomechanical movement in the human body as we balance and shift our weight while walking. To reconcile the difference between the natural motion of the body and the default operation of keyframing, look for the point at which the left shoe has deviated most from the reference video (frame 25, shown in Figure 8.31) and move the L Leg Goals to center the heel of the shoe on the reference video heel. Also use the Heel Adjust P and the Toe Adjust to rotate the shoe and the toe of the shoe to match the reference video left shoe (shown in Figure 8.31).

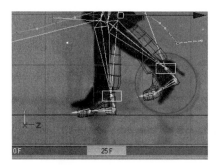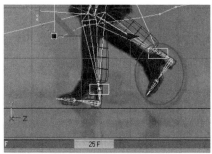

Before Adjustment   **After Adjustment**

FIGURE 8.31   The left shoe before and after correction on frame 25.

21. Go through the remaining frames (up to frame 90) and correct the Heel Adjust P, Toe Adjust, and L Leg Goals using the techniques from steps 15–19.

 The process of setting key frames for the L Leg Goals and adjusting the heel Adjust P and Toe Adjust is very interactive. It is normal that even though the L Leg Goals is positioned well, after adjusting the Heel Adjust P and Toe Adjust, it may be necessary to once again make a fine positional adjustment to the L Leg Goals.

 Ctrl-F goes to the previous key frame for the selected object, and Ctrl-G goes to the next key frame for the selected object.

 This process requires patience and focus. While this is not complex, it will require that you stay attentive to what is connected to each other.

22. Once the left leg key frames are complete, use the same techniques to complete the key frames of the right leg. Setting the key frames for the right leg is a little different, only in that in the reference video,

the right leg is sometimes partly obscured by the left leg, so it is helpful to view the reference video through the Cinema 4D Browser. In Cinema 4D 9, in the **Browser** tab menu (to the right of the Objects Manager tab), choose **File/Import File** (**Ctrl-Shift-O**) (shown in Figure 8.32) and browse to "**Tutorials/ProjectFiles/Chapter 08/ Tutorial 02**" on the DVD-ROM accompanying this book and open "**LadyWalk-1.mov**." The icon for the reference video will now be in the Browser (shown in Figure 8.32). Double-click the reference video icon to play it.

ON THE DVD

*You need the QuickTime player (*http://www.apple.com*) installed to play Quick-Time video files. For the purposes of this tutorial, the free version of the QuickTime player will be OK.*

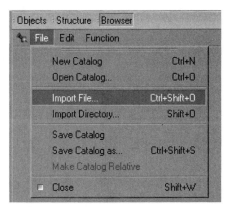
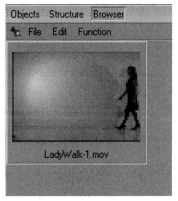

FIGURE 8.32   The reference video in the Cinema 4D 9 Browser.

In Cinema 4D 9.5, in the **Main** menu, choose **Window/Content Browser** (**Shift-F8**) and in the upper left pane of the Content Browser, browse to "**Tutorials/ProjectFiles/Chapter 08/Tutorial-02**" on the DVD-ROM accompanying this book. The reference video "**LadyWalk-1.mov**" will be displayed on the right (shown in Figure 8.33). Double-click the reference video icon to play it.

23. Once you have completed the right leg key frames, in the right view local menu, choose **Edit/Configure**. In the Attributes Manager, **Back** tab, uncheck **Show Picture** to allow for smoother playback of the animation in the right view. Because you will now see the wire-frame of the character more clearly, you may see that you need to make some fine adjustments to the L Leg Goals and the R Leg Goals (shown in Figure 8.34).

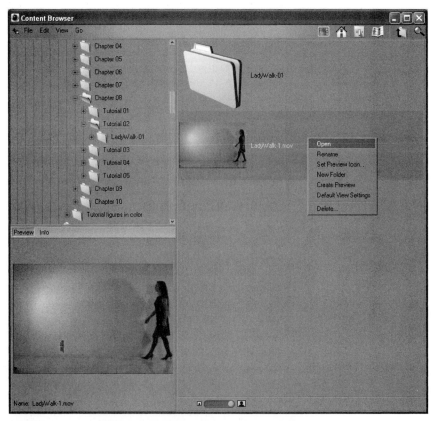

FIGURE 8.33 The reference video in the Cinema 4D 9.5 Content Browser.

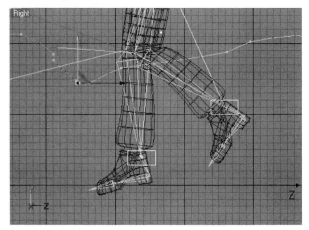

FIGURE 8.34 A Wireframe view of the character with no reference video shows a little tweaking of key frames needs to be done.

24. After making these final tweaks to the legs, play the animation in the perspective view to see the improvement in the way the character now walks. If you wish to compare your work so far to the project file, load the **"Tutorials/ProjectFiles/Chapter 08/Tutorial-02/ LadyWalk-01/LadyWalk-01.c4d"** file from the Tutorials folder on the DVD-ROM accompanying this book.

ON THE DVD

25. To animate the arms, you will work with the R Arm Goals, R Arm UpV and L Arm Goals, and L Arm UpV (shown in Figure 8.35).

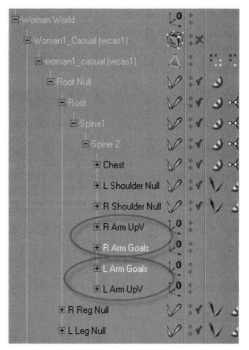

FIGURE 8.35   Arm control objects.

26. To further position the arms, in the L Arm Goals hierarchy, select the L Elbow Tip Goal and bring the left arm up a little (Figure 8.36). This will cause the arm to unnaturally turn in toward the body. In the L Arm Goals hierarchy, select the L Elbow Root Goal, and in the top view swing the elbow out to create a more natural pose of the left arm (Figure 8.37).

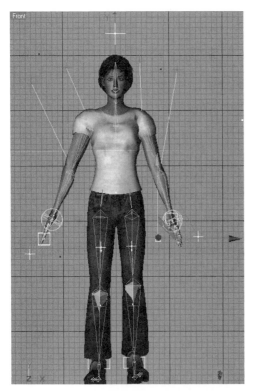

FIGURE 8.36 L Elbow Tip Goal is used to pull the left hand and arm up. This results in the elbow turning in toward the body.

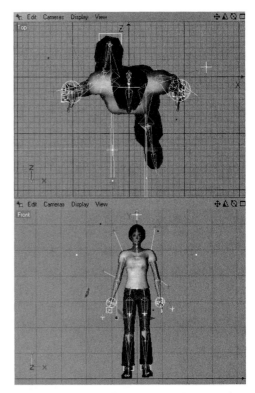

FIGURE 8.37 The L Elbow Root Goal is moved in the top view to create a more natural pose.

27. In the L Arm UpV hierarchy, select the L Elbow Up. In the right view, drag (in the empty layout space) to adjust the position of the up vector (L Elbow Up) so that your perspective view looks like the "after" image in Figure 8.38.
28. Repeating steps 26 and 27, use the right arm controls to pose the right arm.

Check the perspective view closely to look for any unwanted distortion or deformation in the arms. Move the up vector for the appropriate arm to remove any such problems.

29. With both arms posed well, work in the right view and be sure that the reference video is visible. Since in the beginning of the reference

FIGURE 8.38   Up vector L Elbow Up positioned to pose the left arm as shown in the "after" picture above.

video the right arm is out front, from the R Arm Goals hierarchy, select the R Elbow Tip Goal and from the R Arm UpV hierarchy, select R Elbow Up. With those two control objects selected, position the right hand to match the reference video (shown in Figure 8.39). From the L Arm Goals hierarchy, select the L Elbow Tip Goal and from the L Arm UpV hierarchy, select L Elbow Up. With those two control objects selected, position the left hand to match the reference video (shown in Figure 8.39).

If the up vector (R Elbow Up) is not selected and moved with the R Elbow Tip Goal, the right arm will be deformed.

30. Drag the play head forward and look for where the hands in the reference video exchange positions (frame 18). Then use the L Elbow Tip Goal and L Elbow Up to position the left arm to swing forward to match the reference video, and use the R Elbow Tip Goal and R Elbow Up to position the right arm so the right elbow is slightly behind to match the reference video.

31. Repeat step 30, dragging the remaining frames, setting the keys for the left and right arms.

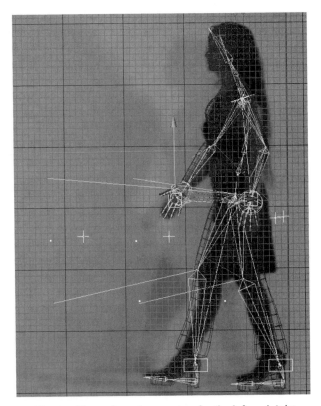

FIGURE 8.39 Tip goals and up vectors for the left and right arms used to set the initial pose of the arms on frame 0.

 Be very careful not to accidentally select the Bicep Up or Elbow Root Goal objects during this process.

 Because in the reference video, as the lady approaches the extreme left of the screen, the perspective angle becomes more pronounced, it is important to review earlier key frames of the placement of the arms and maintain that same kind of positioning. This is one of those differences between the real-world perspective view and the 3D orthogonal view. As long as you are aware of this issue, you will create great character animation with this process.

32. Position the character in the perspective view and play the animation to see the character's arms now animated (shown in Figure 8.40).

FIGURE 8.40   The arms are animated now.

ON THE DVD

33. Add a floor and light to the scene or load "**Tutorials/ProjectFiles/ Chapter 08/Tutorial-02/LadyWalk-01/LadyWalk-02.c4d**" file from the Tutorials folder on the DVD-ROM accompanying this book. In your Render Settings, you can now choose your Antialiasing, Resolution, file Path, and file Format and render the finished animation. You can also view the rendered animation by going to "/html/ dvideo.html" in the accompanying DVD-ROM.

Summary

This method of character animation can be applied to many real-world production situations that require you to make a character move like an actor on video. Though motion capture equipment may be technically more accurate, such equipment is expensive and won't help at all if you need to animate a character based on a video reference.

Proper planning of how you will compensate and adjust for the difference between the real-world perspective video reference and the orthogonal view used to animate the 3D character will have a serious impact on how quickly you can work and how beautiful the end result will be.

TUTORIAL 3   **JAMES WALK**

FIGURE 8.41   James (a cool character from Poser 6) walks past three flags.

Covered in this tutorial:

- Poser 6 Character setup
- Poser 6 Walk Designer
- Bringing Poser 6 characters into Cinema 4D with BodyStudio 2.6
- Merging Cinema 4D projects

In this tutorial you will create character animation by first designing a 3D character in Poser 6, use the Walk Designer to make the character walk, and then import the walking character into Cinema 4D 9. Once in Cinema 4D 9, you will merge a project from an earlier chapter so that the Poser animated character can be part of a complete visual scene.

Poser 6 is a program dedicated to the creation, posing, and animation of 3D characters. Poser is used in the development of 3D characters for application in video games, television commercials, music videos, and movies. You can see the Poser 6 interface in Figure 8.42.

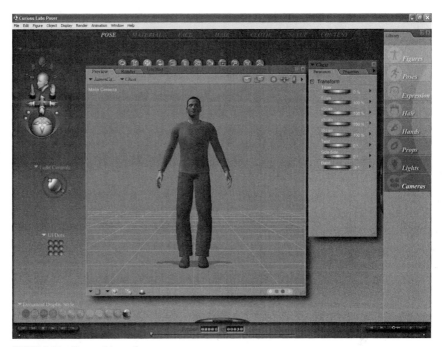

FIGURE 8.42   Poser 6 interface.

The BodyStudio 2.6 plug-in is used for Poser 6 characters, their textures, and animation to be brought into the world of Cinema 4D 9. In Cinema 4D, the BodyStudio plug-in adds a Poser object (a special case object) to the Objects Manager from which you will load Poser scenes and set their parameters. The integrative work flow of Poser, BodyStudio, and Cinema 4D make for a very fun-filled highly productive experience for both the animator and the client.

Three Cinema 4D files and two Poser 6 files of this tutorial are included on the accompanying DVD in the tutorials folder.

As of this writing, the BodyStudio plug-in from Reiss Studios (http://www.reiss-studio.com/) *is compatible with Cinema 4D up to version 9, but not 9.5.*

ON THE DVD

All of the images used in this tutorial are located in Tutorials/Chapter 08/Tutorial-03 on the Projects DVD-ROM.

1. Begin by opening Poser 6. James (in casual wear) is the default character. On the very right of the screen, in the Library, choose **Figures**. A few headshots for variations of the James character appear. Choose the first character named **James** (shown in Figure 8.43). At the very bottom of the library are four icons (1 check, 2 checks, plus, and minus). Choose the **Change Figure** button (1 check) to replace the default James in casual wear with a James character with no clothing. Two requesters pop up. Simply click **OK** on each of these requesters. Don't worry about your temporarily naked synthetic James. You'll give him some clothes.

FIGURE 8.43 Choose the first James headshot.

Poser 6 defaults to the James figures when you click Figures in the Library palette. If you're working on another scene on another character and the James headshot icons don't appear in the figures library, go to the top of the library and just below the word "Figures," click the arrow pointing down and choose Figures/James/ James (shown in Figure 8.44).

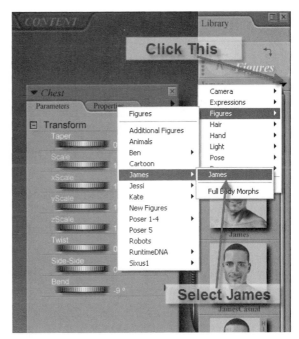

FIGURE 8.44   Using the Library menu to choose the James figures.

To see a textured shaded document view in Poser, use the keyboard shortcut Ctrl-9.

2. In the Library, this time go to the **Props**. Props are where you get clothing and accessories. Scroll down and choose the **Shorts Dark** and click the **Apply Library Preset** button (checkmark at bottom of library) to give James his shorts. Also give James the **Watch Sports** and the **Tshirt Green**. When the Tshirt Green is added, you will notice that the Tshirt does not automatically conform to James' body, so in the **Main** menu, choose **Figure/Conform To...** and then choose **JamesCasual**. The Tshirt now fits James well (shown in Figure 8.45).

In Poser 6, props are the items that can be added to a character.

You can also make props in Cinema 4D and bring them into Poser 6 for use with your characters.

3. Add the **Shoe Athletic L** and **Shoe Athletic R** as well. As you add each shoe, in the **Main** menu choose **Figure/Conform To...** and then choose **JamesCasual**.

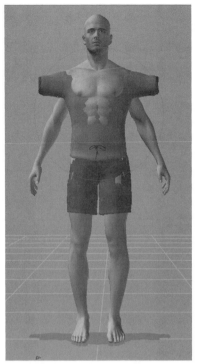
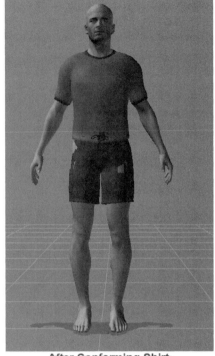

Before Conforming Shirt   **After Conforming Shirt**

FIGURE 8.45 Before and after the Tshirt is conformed to James.

4. Before you make James walk, you will define where he will walk by creating a "walk path." In the Preview window, right-click on **Main Camera** and choose **Top Camera**. Use the camera controls (shown in Figure 8.46) to pan and zoom the view to arrange the preview to look like Figure 8.47.

The windows in Poser 6 can be freely moved by dragging the top dark gray area. Palettes can be dragged by their names. Windows are sized with the sizing gadget in their lower right corner.

5. From the **Main** menu, choose **Figure/Create Walk Path**. The walk path control points can be dragged to shape the path. Drag the points to form a straight line.

Holding down the Alt key allows you to delete points in the walk path. Clicking between the points in the walk path adds control points.

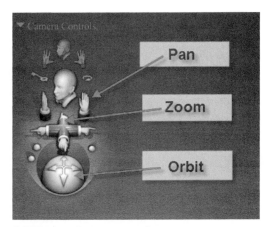

FIGURE 8.46   Camera controls.

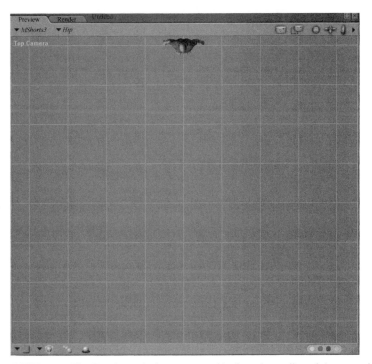

FIGURE 8.47   The Preview window arranged before the walk path is created.

6. With the walk path created, in the **Main** menu, choose **Window/ Walk Designer** (**Shift-Ctrl-S**) to work in the Walk Designer (shown in Figure 8.48). Click the **Walk** button to see the outlined character

walk continuously. Dragging the **Blend Styles** and **Tweaks** sliders adjusts the character's walk instantly. If you've adjusted the sliders, click the Defaults button to put all sliders back to their initial values. In the **Blend Styles**, scroll down to **Power Walk** and set its value to 90. Click **Apply** and choose **Follow Path** and click **OK**. The default number of frames in a Poser project is 30. Poser determines how many frames (e.g., 120) of animation are required for James to walk in the style defined by the Walk Designer to complete the walk path and changes the project to now be 120 frames long. Close the Walk Designer.

While you can use any values you wish, it's important to know that very high or very low values can result in troublesome animation requiring manual cleanup. For example, changing the Power Walk value from 90 to 130 will give a more dramatic walk, but it will also cause some steps to bend the legs in an unnatural way. It's very important to keep a close eye on the Walk Designer character's legs when designing a walk style to ensure that you are not causing the legs to bend erratically or otherwise unnaturally, unless of course you're intentionally making a creatively bizarre character.

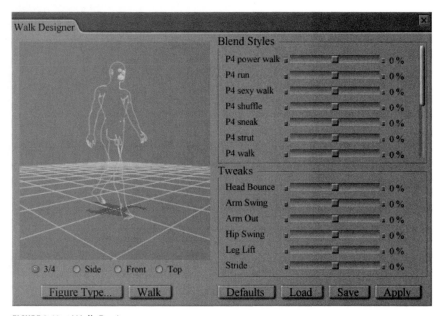

FIGURE 8.48 Walk Designer.

7. From the **Main** menu, choose **Display/Camera View/Posing Camera**. Then use the Camera Controls to arrange the Preview window to see James walk on the walk path. You can see that James (amazingly) walks right out of his pants, as in Figure 8.49. This is because his pants were positioned where he initially stood, but his pants weren't conformed to him. In the Preview window, click the down arrow currently selecting JamesCasual and choose **MShorts3**. In the main menu, choose **Figure/Conform To...** and choose **JamesCasual**. Now when James walks, his pants move with him naturally.

FIGURE 8.49   The pants have not yet been conformed to James.

8. As you play the animation, you may see a few frames where his legs may kick or jump a little. To correct this, in the **Main** menu, choose **Animation/Resample Key Frames...** and accept the default values by clicking **OK**. The Walk Designer creates a key frame for every frame of animation. By resampling the keys, erratic keys are smoothed away.
9. Before saving this animated character for use in Cinema 4D, in the Preview window second drop-down menu, choose **Ground** (shown in Figure 8.50). In the **Main** menu, choose **Object/Properties** (if the Properties palette is not already open) and uncheck **Visible** and **Visible In Raytracing** so the saved scene file will not contain a ground object.

This is important because Poser scenes brought into Cinema 4D are a special object class. If an animated scene is brought in with a ground, the ground cannot be separated from the animation.

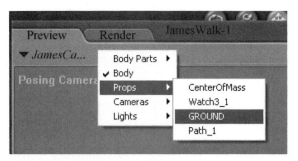

FIGURE 8.50   Choosing the ground object.

10. In order to use the character animation in Cinema 4D, in the **Main** menu, choose **File/Save As** and name the file "**JamesWalk-1.pz3**." This is a standard Poser 6 project file that can be reloaded and edited in Poser 6.

11. For the Poser scene file to be brought into Cinema 4D, the Reiss Studios plug-in BodyStudio must first be installed. With BodyStudio installed, launch Cinema 4D. In the **Main** menu, choose **Plugins/ Poser Object**. In the Attributes Manager, **Object** tab, click **Browse** (to the left of the Reload button) to load JamesWalk-1.pz3, which was saved in step 10 (or load "**Tutorials/ProjectFiles/Chapter 08/Tutorial-03/JamesWalk-1B.pz3**" from the DVD-ROM).

ON THE DVD

 Loading the Poser scene into Cinema 4D via BodyStudio may take a minute or two. Wait until the character appears before taking any further actions in Cinema 4D.

12. In the Attributes Manager, **Object** tab, click the **Create Materials** button for BodyStudio to create and properly apply all materials required by the Poser object.

 Be sure to wait until the last Poser material has been completely created before taking further action in Cinema 4D. Failure to wait could result in an incompletely textured Poser character.

13. In the perspective view, frame the Poser object and render to see James in Cinema 4D (shown in Figure 8.51).

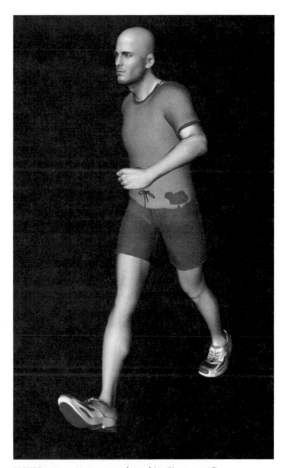

FIGURE 8.51   James rendered in Cinema 4D.

14. In Figure 8.51, you may notice James' thighs poking through his pants and his pants poking through his Tshirt. To correct this, go back to Poser and load the **"Tutorials/ProjectFiles/Chapter 08/Tutorial-03/JamesWalk-1B.pz3"** project.

15. In the **Main** menu, make sure you are working in the posing camera (Display/Camera View/Posing Camera). Use the Camera Controls to orient your view similarly to Figure 8.52.

16. As you move your mouse over the left thigh, the left thigh of the pants is outlined in red, indicating that if you click, it will be selected. Select the pant's **left thigh**. In the object **Properties** palette (**Object/Properties...** or **Ctrl-I**), in the **Parameters** page, set the **xScale** and **zScale** to 105 so that they are large enough to stop his thighs from peeking through. Click the lowest area of the Tshirt (Hips) and

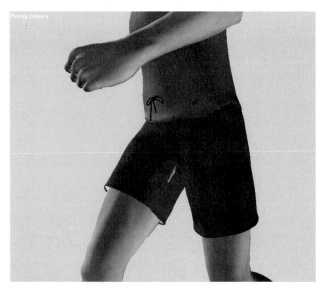

FIGURE 8.52   Poser Posing Camera view closeup to inspect James' thighs poking through his pants and his pants poking through his Tshirt.

set its **xScale** and **zScale** to 110 to keep the pants from peeking through.

17. Since you're back in Poser now, in the **Library**, **Props**, add the **Glasses Wire** prop to James to give him a little style. Save this Poser project as "**Tutorials/ProjectFiles/Chapter 08/Tutorial-03/ JamesWalk-1noPeeking.pz3**."

18. Switch back to Cinema 4D and select the **Poser** object. In the Attributes Manager, **Object** tab, **Browse** to load the "**Tutorials/Project-Files/Chapter 08/Tutorial-03/JamesWalk-1noPeeking.pz3**" object. Click the **Create materials** button to update the Poser textures. Now, the James character has no more peeking problems and he's sporting his cool new glasses.

19. To quickly give James a world to walk in, in the **Main** menu, choose **File/Merge** and open "**Tutorials/ProjectFiles/Chapter 08/Tutorial-03/FlagDay-Short/FlagDay-Short.c4d**." This scene adds a shortened version of the three flags blowing in the wind and includes a camera (cam1) and lights.

20. To scale James to his new world, select the Poser object and switch to the **Use Object** tool. In the drop-down menu below Size in the Coordinates Manager, choose **Scale**. Set the **X**, **Y**, and **Z** values to 1.5 to make James 50% larger and click the **Apply** button (or press Enter on the keyboard).

21. Set the Rotation **H** to −90 in the Coordinates Manager and the Position to **X** = 2183, **Y** = 0, and **Z** = −443.4.
22. Since the Poser project goes from frame 0 to 120, set the Cinema 4D **Maximum Frames (Edit/Project Settings)** to 120.
23. Select Cam1 in the Objects Manager and set its **Position** in the Coordinates Manager to **X** = −726, **Y** = 479, and **Z** = −1390. Switch to the perspective view in single view and play the animation to see James walking next to the three flags blowing in the wind (shown in Figure 8.53).

FIGURE 8.53   James walking next to the three flags blowing in the wind.

ON THE DVD

24. In your Render Settings, you can now choose your Antialiasing, Resolution, file Path, and file Format and render the finished animation. You can also view the rendered animation by going to "/html/dvideo. html" on the accompanying DVD-ROM.

Summary

The powerful combination of Cinema 4D and Poser 6 connected via BodyStudio gives you an incredible 3D character animation facility to face incredible character animation challenges allowing you to produce more high-quality character animation faster. The ability to go back and forth between Poser and Cinema 4D via BodyStudio also allows for small studios to have one 3D artist focused on character development in Poser and another 3D artist focused on putting it all together in Cinema 4D.

TUTORIAL 4   **JESSI DANCE**

FIGURE 8.54   Jessi dances on stage.

Covered in this tutorial:

- Poser 6 Character setup
- Motion capture data
- Bringing Poser 6 characters into Cinema 4D with BodyStudio 2.6
- Merging Cinema 4D projects

In this tutorial you will create character animation by first designing a 3D character in Poser 6. Rather than create the animation with the Walk Designer, you will import motion capture data to animate the character to dance and then import the dancing character into Cinema 4D 9. Once in Cinema 4D 9, you will merge a project with the dancing character so that the Poser-animated character can be on a glittering performance stage. You can see the Poser 6 interface in Figure 8.42.

The BodyStudio 2.6 plug-in is used for Poser 6 characters, their textures, and animation to be brought into the world of Cinema 4D 9. Three Cinema 4D files and two Poser 6 files of this tutorial are included on the accompanying DVD-ROM in the "Tutorials/ProjectFiles/Chapter 08/ Tutorial-04" folder.

As of this writing, the BodyStudio plug-in from Reiss Studios (http://www. reiss-studio.com/) *is compatable with Cinema 4D up to version 9, but not 9.5.*

ON THE DVD

All of the images used in this tutorial are located in "Tutorials/ ProjectFiles/Chapter 08/Tutorial-04" on the Projects DVD-ROM.

1. Begin by opening Poser 6. James (in casual wear) is the default character. In this tutorial, you will work with a female character named Jessi, so in the **Main** menu, choose **Figure/Delete Figure** (so that you won't have to go through the mental acrobatics of calling cute Jessi, James). At the moment, the Poser scene has no character. At the bottom of the palette, click the double checkmarks (Create New Figure) to add Jessi to the scene.
2. In the Library, **Figures** page, choose the first Jessi headshot (shown in Figure 8.55).

FIGURE 8.55 Choose the first Jessi headshot.

3. In the Library, **Props** page, choose Jessi Clothing.

When you click Props in the Library palette, the Jessi Clothing doesn't automatically appear. Go to the top of the library and just below the word "Props," click the arrow pointing down and choose Props/Jessi Clothing (shown in Figure 8.56).

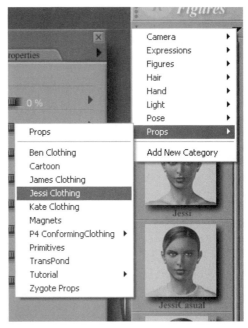

FIGURE 8.56   Using the Library menu to choose the Jessi props.

4. Apply the following clothing props to Jessi and conform (Figure/Conform To) each one to Jessica:
   - Polo Sleeveless
   - Jeans Capri
   - Shoe Flat L
   - Shoe Flat R
5. Apply the following clothing props to Jessi:
   - Watch Round
   - Sunglasses Wide
   - Earring Pearl L
   - Earring Pearl R
6. In the Preview window, in the first drop-down menu, choose **Jessica**. In the second drop-down menu, choose **Props/GROUND**. In

the **Main** menu, choose **Object/Properties** (if the Properties palette isn't already open) and uncheck **Visible** and **Visible In Raytracing**, so that when you save Jessi, the ground object won't be saved with her. Save the Poser scene as "**JessiDance-A.pz3**."

The purpose of saving this particular file is so that if you wish to apply a different motion capture file to this same character later, you won't have to redesign Jessi with props again.

You may load the "Tutorials/ProjectFiles/Chapter 08/Tutorial-04/JessiDance-A.pz3" Poser project to see the previous steps already completed.

7. To add the motion capture file, from the **Main** menu, choose **File/Import/BVH** Motion and navigate to "**/Goodies/Mocapdata/joke-shee-yokoyama.bvh**" on the DVD-ROM accompanying this book. Click **Along X** axis and then click **Scale Automatically** to apply the motion capture data to Jessi.

ON THE DVD

This motion capture file is from a free categorized library available from the creative group at http://www.mocapdata.com/. *There are a few sample motion capture files in the Goodies folder that you can apply to Jessi and other Poser characters.*

8. There is a difference between Jessi's original Y position and the Y position of the motion capture data. No problem. Just use Poser's Camera Controls to position Jessi as shown in Figure 8.57.

Frame 26   Frame 187   Frame 481

FIGURE 8.57   Jessi's Y position before and after motion capture data is applied.

9. Save the Poser scene as "**JessiDance-B.pz3**." This is the file you will load into Cinema 4D 9 via BodyStudio.

 You save the A and B version of Jessi so that if you wish to apply a different motion capture file or use the Walk Designer to make Jessi walk for a different kind of Cinema 4D animation project, you will load the JessiDance-A.pz3 Poser project file, which has no animation applied, and animate it.

10. In Cinema 4D, from the **Main** menu, choose **Plugins/Poser Object**. In the Attributes Manager, **Object** tab, browse to open "**Tutorials/ ProjectFiles/Chapter 08/Tutorial 04/JessiDance-B.pz3**." Click the **Create Materials** button for BodyStudio to set up all the required Jessi textures.
11. To add Jessi's world, from the **Main** menu, choose **File/Merge** and open "**Tutorials/ProjectFiles/Chapter 08/Tutorial-04/Stage-1/ Stage-1.c4d**." This Stage-1 project adds a glittering floor, a small round dance stage, two large arrays of volumetric spot lights, stage lights, and two cameras controlled by a Stage object.
12. To place Jessi on the stage, select the Poser object and in the Coordinates Manager, set its **Position** to **X** = 241, **Y** = 46.1, and **Z** = 1229.
13. In the **Main** menu, choose **Edit/Project Settings** and set the **Minimum** to 150 and **Maximum** to 730 to work with only those frames of Jessi's motion capture that contain the action.
14. Go to frame 730 and render to see that Jessi isn't well lit. This is because the light that is dedicated to lighting Jessi needs to be associated with Jessi. In the Objects Manager, select **Jessi Light**. In the Attributes Manager, **Scene** tab, drag the Poser Object from the Objects Manager into the **Objects** area (large empty space shown in Figure 8.58). Now the Jessi Light lights only Jessi. Render again to see a well-lit Jessi (shown in Figure 8.59).

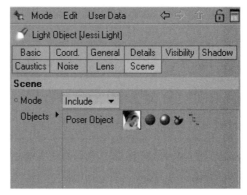

FIGURE 8.58   The Poser Object dragged into the Objects area of the Scene page of the Jessi Light.

FIGURE 8.59   A well-lit Jessi.

15. Now you can set your rendering parameters and render the finished animation. You can also view the rendered animation by going to "/html/dvideo.html" on the accompanying DVD-ROM.

Summary

By using motion capture data to animate characters in Poser, you introduce a level of realism to the character movement that your client and audience will easily and deeply identify with. This work flow of creating character animation with the powerful combination of Poser, BodyStudio, and Cinema 4D is streamlined and highly effective because you mainly animate the character with high-level control (Walk Designer and motion capture data). You spend no time modeling and rigging the character. This means you can deliver character animation in the most challenging of production deadlines and with high production value.

TUTORIAL 5   RPC

FIGURE 8.60   RPC content rendered in Cinema 4D 9.5.

The Commercial Cinema 4D plug-in is required from *http://www.archvision. com/*. No demo of this plug-in is available. Even though you may not already have this plug-in installed in your system, this tutorial is provided to empower you with the knowledge of just how easy the work flow to integrate RPC content into Cinema 4D is and just how visually effective such integration can be in digital media production. Even if you don't have this plug-in yet, when you read this tutorial and watch the video tutorial on the DVD-ROM, you will see a great solution for some of your challenges yet to come.

ON THE DVD

Covered in this tutorial:

- Archvision RPC objects
- Ambient Occlusion
- Align to Spline
- Stage Object

This tutorial is the "+" section of this "Character Animation +." This is because, unlike the previous tutorials where you animate a character, in this tutorial, the characters are a special class RPC object. RPC objects use the RPC plug-in from Archvision (*http://www.archvision.com*) to produce animation in which photo-quality people (and other content) are placed in the Cinema 4D scene based on a concept Archvision calls Smart Content. This smart content includes subclasses as follows:

TYPE	DEFINITION	PURPOSE	FEATURES	SHADOW
2D	RGB & alpha image	Static fixed content	Self-lit	Self-contained
2.5D	Video sequence of RGB and alpha	Fixed-perspective live people	Self-lit, variable start frame	Self-contained
3D	Photo image viewable 360 degrees around	Fixed-position content viewable from any location in the X and Z axes	Self-lit, variable start angle	Self-contained
3.5D	Video sequence viewable 360 degrees around	Moving content viewable from any location in the X and Z axes	Self-lit, variable start frame, variable start angle	Self-contained
Car	3D & image data	Automatically drives along a spline object including turning/steering the front wheel around corners	Self-lit, variable start frame, variable speed	None
Smart Object	3D objects with unique interactive properties	Example: laser printer that prints images sent to it in the 3D scene	Prints custom images in the 3D scene	None

RPC content is accessed in Cinema 4D via the RPC plug-in. The materials for RPC content are handled by the RPC plug-in rather than the Cinema 4D Materials Manager.

Though you will undoubtedly use RPC content in many animation projects, architectural previsualization is probably the area of animation production that receives the most use of this incredible content solution in Cinema 4D.

The Cinema 4D RPC plug-in taught in this tutorial is only available as a retail product. Demo RPC content and a viewer are available from the Launch Pad on the DVD-ROM accompanying this book. RPC content in this tutorial is taken from the Cinema 4D Starter Pack and the 2.5D Moving Business People Vol. 1. Two Cinema 4D files of this tutorial are included on the accompanying DVD-ROM in the tutorials folder. If you have the RPC plug-in but don't have a particular RPC file used in this tutorial, please substitute a file from your RPC folder on your hard drive or from the demo content provided by Archvision at *http://www.archvision.com/democontent.cfm*.

ON THE DVD

All of the images used in this tutorial are located in Tutorials/Project-Files/Chapter 08/Tutorial-05 on the Projects DVD-ROM.

1. Begin by opening "**Tutorials/ProjectFiles/Chapter 08/Tutorial 05/RPC-1/RPC-1.c4d**" from the DVD-ROM accompanying this book. This loads a project with a sky, floor, light, and two animated cameras in a 600-frame scene. This is the world in which your RPC content will be placed.

2. Several people and trees will be added as well as a car that will drive around the people. To add the first RPC person, in the **Main** menu, choose **Plugins/RPC Object**. An RPC object has now been added to the Objects Manager (shown in Figure 8.61).

FIGURE 8.61   RPC object added to the Objects Manager.

ON THE DVD

3. In the Attributes Manager, **Object** tab, in the **Object** field, browse to Open "**B1_Chuck.rpc**" from the RPC folder on your computer. Render the perspective view to see Chuck facing away from the camera with a **Start** angle of 0 (shown in Figure 8.62). Check the **Update** option as well so that traveling around the RPC object will cause it to update.

The Start angle in an RPC object determines where the object will face.

4. In addition to facing away, Chuck also seems to be casting a bit of an odd shadow. To adjust where Chuck is facing, in the Attributes Man-

ager, **Object** tab, set the **Start angle** to 30. This only adjusts Chuck's angle slightly. In the Objects Manager, select the **Compositing** tag for the RPC object. In the Attributes Manager, **Tag** tab, uncheck **Seen by AO** so that the Ambient Occlusion doesn't calculate a shadow for the RPC object.

FIGURE 8.62   Chuck's initial Start angle (0).

5. In the Objects Manager, select Chuck. In the perspective view, frame Chuck ("**o**"). Orbit the view and render a few times to see images similar to Figure 8.63.
6. Now that you have a basic idea of how RPC content works in Cinema 4D, add the following content and set the provided Start angle and X and Z positions (Y is set to 0):

RPC CONTENT	START ANGLE	X	Z
B1_Michelle.rpc	60	50.706	139.287
C1_Alex_10101.rpc	0	117.117	113.852
CHS1_Alvaro_10402.rpc	90	34.806	97.725
P1_Janai_21107.rpc	120	73.628	82.999
R_Linda_15110.rpc	80	11.671	196.078
C1_Jackie_10105.rpc	45	63.025	39.682
dogwood_50102.rpc	0	562.676	828.984

FIGURE 8.63   Chuck rendered from various viewing angles.

7. In the perspective view, local menu, choose **Cameras/Scene Cameras/Cam1**. Go to and render frames 40, 150, and 240 to see images similar to Figure 8.64. Notice that the characters are facing at different angles. This is due to the different start angles set in step 6.

Frame 40   Frame 150   Frame 240

FIGURE 8.64   Chuck rendered from various viewing angles.

8. Add the following content and set the provided Start angle and X and Z positions (Y is set to 0):

RPC CONTENT	START ANGLE	ANIMATION START FRAME	X	Z
M25_B1_Beth_Chris_25-11101.rpc		1	238.095	457.515
M25_B1_Flori_Chris_Shannon_ 25-11104.rpc		1	322.129	637.254
M25_B1_Jack_25-11106.rpc		1	459.85	487.861
M25_B1_Scott_Sothy_25-11112.rpc		1	522.876	672.268
S_AUTO2_BMW325ti_SC-10401.rpc		1	268.392	297.405
red_ash.rpc	0		129.119	965.575
T5_gray_birch_54105.rpc	0		202.096	993.644
Crocosmia_Lucifer_A.rpc	0		61.751	314.373
PennyDemo.rpc	180	500	438.433	681.188

9. In the **Main** menu, choose **File/Merge** and open "**Tutorials/Pro-jectFiles/Chapter 08/Tutorial-05/CarSpline-1.c4d**." In the Objects Manager, place the CarSpline into the Bmw 325ti (2002) Group as shown in Figure 8.65. Select the **Align To Spline** tag and drag the CarSpline into the Spline Path field in the Attributes Manager, **Tag** tab. Now the BMW will drive along the CarSpline.

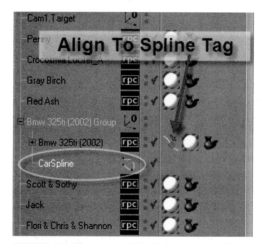

FIGURE 8.65   The merged CarSpline is placed in the Bmw 325ti (2002) Group hierarchy.

10. To control how fast the BWM drives, in the Objects Manager, select the Bmw 325ti (2002). In the Attributes Manager, **Object** tab, click the **Special Settings** button and set the **Speed** to 2.

11. The Stage object is currently switching between Cam1 and Cam2. Add a new **Camera With target** and rename the camera "**CarCam**" and the target "CarCam.Target." In the Coordinates Manager, set the CarCam **Position** to **X** = 560, **Y** = 220, and **Z** = 367. Set the Car-Cam.Target **Position** to **X** = –4.5, **Y** –75, and **Z** = 117. Place the Car-Cam and CarCam.Target into the Bmw 325ti (2002) hierarchy as shown in Figure 8.66.

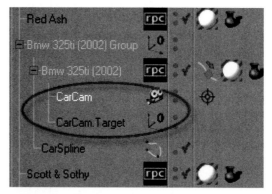

FIGURE 8.66 The new camera and target are positioned to always look at the car and are now children of the car.

12. Go to frame 91. In the Objects Manager, select the Stage object. In the Attributes Manager, drag the CarCam into the Camera field and **Ctrl-click** the Camera Key Frame Dot to switch to the CarCam at frame 91.

13. Finally, check to make sure that all the RPC objects (except for the BMW) have **Seen by AO** unchecked in the Compositing tags.

 Seen by AO must be checked for the BWM so that the floor's Ambient Occlusion will create quick cool shadows for the BMW.

14. Now you can set your rendering parameters and render the finished animation. You can also view the rendered animation by going to "/html/dvideo.html" on the accompanying DVD-ROM.

ON THE DVD

SUMMARY

RPC content is not only a very fast solution to adding people and other real-world content to a scene, but it brings features otherwise unavailable such as being able to see photo-quality images of people from any eye level angle, driving cars by simply adding a spline object, and having believable foliage that won't fail you. Used as a magical finishing touch, RPC can help you put your animation productions over the top, keep your competition wondering, and bring your client's dreams to life.

9

BROADCAST APPLICATIONS

In This Chapter

- Tutorial 1: Virtual Set Design
- Tutorial 2: Characters on Virtual Sets (HD)
- Tutorial 3: Cell Phone Ad
- Tutorial 4: James Escapes to Reality

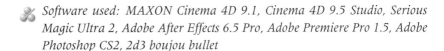 *Software used: MAXON Cinema 4D 9.1, Cinema 4D 9.5 Studio, Serious Magic Ultra 2, Adobe After Effects 6.5 Pro, Adobe Premiere Pro 1.5, Adobe Photoshop CS2, 2d3 boujou bullet*

In this chapter, we'll see some ways that Cinema 4D ties into the broadcast video industry by first creating a 3D world in Cinema 4D in which live actors and TV personalities can be presented to the viewing audience in Ultra 2, then use an Ultra 2 virtual set as a stage for a Cinema 4D animated character, then by create a TV commercial for the cell phone made in Chapter 3, and finally take a Poser 3D animated character and some live video footage motion tracked in boujou bullet 2 and bring them together in Cinema 4D so that the 3D character is walking around in the real world. Wow!

Having a working knowledge of key broadcast media factors of the broadcast world and how 3D animation will ultimately be used in broadcast applications is key to choosing the appropriate development path when planning a 3D animation project. Here are some key broadcast media factors you should know in the planning phase of a 3D animation project to be delivered for use in broadcast video:

Standards: From the perspective of producing animation for television, standards define video properties such as horizontal and vertical resolution and frame rate. In the Cinema 4D Render Settings, Output page, you can choose presents for the standards such as NTSC, PAL, and HDTV and it even provides for film formats as well (Figure 9.1). A recent format bringing HD (High Definition) production to the consumer market is HDV. This format supports High Definition video up to 1440 × 1080i (60 fields per second) resolution.

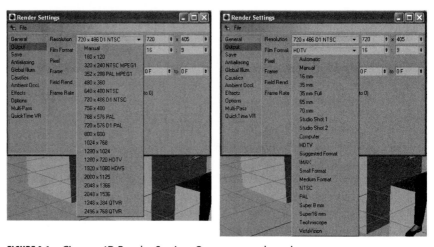

FIGURE 9.1   Cinema 4D Render Setting, Output page drop down presets.

Aspect Ratio: As we experience the surge of wide-screen TVs into the consumer market, it becomes even more important to be aware of the production issues to consider when supporting both standard and wide-screen aspect ratios. Aspect ratio is the ratio between the horizontal and vertical resolution. Aspect ratio can be expressed in numerical values (16:9) and in name (HDTV). In Cinema 4D, the aspect ratio is set in the Render Settings, Output page, Film Format (Figure 9.2). Setting the film format automatically sets the resolution as well. When setting the film format, take close note of the thin lines at the top and bottom of the viewport that indicate the area of the scene that will be rendered. Any objects outside of these lines will not be rendered. Aspect ratio is also known as display aspect ratio.

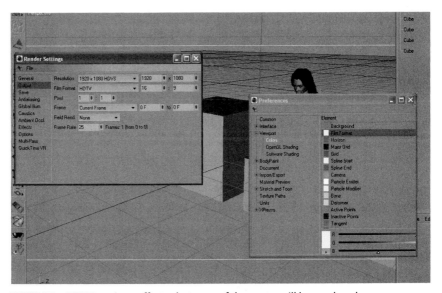

FIGURE 9.2   HDTV settings affect what area of the scene will be rendered.

Pixel Aspect Ratio: As you take your rendered animation (video clip or image sequence) into other broadcast video software applications, you may encounter a unique problem. Even though you may have rendered at the correct resolution, your animation may be too large or too small for the workspace. This is because if the broadcast video application is specifically set up for a certain format (such as DV), in addition to having the correct aspect ratio and resolution, the shape of the pixels (pixel aspect ratio) must also be set. Creating animation for the Web or other nonbroadcast applications can be done with the default aspect ratio of 1:1. Two common aspect ratios to be aware of are DV (1:0.909) and PAL (1:1.0925). Usually, the DV pixel aspect ratio is set to a simplified 1:0.9. HD uses a 1:1 (square pixels) pixel aspect ratio.

Interlacing: As a solution to producing smooth motion for television images, interlacing was developed in the early days of television as a method of alternating the display between the odd and even horizontal lines of video. In interlaced video, each frame of video is composed of two fields of video. One field contains all the even-numbered lines, and the other field contains all the odd-numbered lines. Because the inner surface of a picture tube contains phosphorous (with the property to briefly retain illumination), as each field of video is drawn, the screen continues to briefly retain the illumination of that field, so by the time the field begins to fade, the next field is displayed. While animation rendered for television, at the correct resolution but without interlacing, will play on a television, fast motion will not appear to be smooth. In addition to rendering interlaced video (known in animation as field rendering), you must also choose to make either the even (upper) or odd (lower) first (Figure 9.3). You determine which to choose based on which application your animation is being rendered for. If in doubt, choose odd (lower), as it is most common.

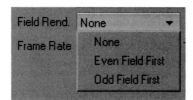

FIGURE 9.3   Field rendering options.

Title Safe, Action Safe, Render Safe: Title safe, action safe, and render safe are simply guides that define where certain things should occur visually in the viewport and the output file. These three safe guides are checked on and off when working in the perspective view, by starting at the local menu Edit/Configure, and then going to the View tab (Figure 9.4).

Title safe identifies the area of the output video where it is safe to place credits, titles, and other text. This ensures that such text will not get cut off when viewed on a TV or monitor of the same output format (4:3, 16:9). Action safe identifies a larger area than title safe. This is the area in which the important visuals (or action) should occur. Both title safe and action safe stem from the earlier designs of television sets with curved picture tubes and inconsistent calibration and designs among television manufacturers. What could be seen on the edge of the screen on one television could easily be totally lost on another television screen. Render safe simply defines the top and bottom border limits of what will be rendered. If, for example, your perspective viewport is set up with a 4:3 ratio and you are about to render 16:9 output, the render safe lines at the top and bottom of the viewport show the limits of the area that will be rendered. So even though you can see (or even test render) objects beyond the render safe guidelines, in the final render, only what is within the render safe area will be output.

FIGURE 9.4   Title safe, action safe, render safe.

ON THE DVD   These tutorials are also on the accompanying DVD-ROM as video tutorials, along with the tutorial project files.

Remember, as you make progress in each tutorial, to save your Cinema 4D projects.

TUTORIAL 1   VIRTUAL SET DESIGN

FIGURE 9.5   Suzy stands talking in a virtual set created in Cinema 4D.

Covered in this tutorial:

- Ultra 2
- Rendering with alpha channel
- Rendering for DV output including field rendering
- Ultra 2 background and overlay layers from Cinema 4D
- Adding the Ultra 2 input layer
- Keying the subject
- Casting shadows from the input layer
- Outputting the final render

Virtual sets are commonly used in the broadcast world today for news sets, talk shows, kid's shows, and more. The power of virtual sets is that they empower the production team to deliver a dynamic and expressive on-screen experience that effectively sets the mood and tells a story while saving both money and time. And if that wasn't great enough, they dramatically reduce the amount of storage space required for studios that must store recurring sets. Virtual sets are made to accommodate a certain range of subject matter use. For example, developing a close-up version and a wide-view version of a virtual set allows you to choose the appropriate set based on whether the person on camera is in a close-up or not.

Rather than simply replacing conventional sets, virtual sets raise the bar by offering new functionality that would be otherwise impractical or impossible with physical conventional sets. Some of this functionality includes features such as inserting multiple video sources into virtual TV monitors of any size, variable shadow control, and variable reflection control, to name a few.

There are two basic types of virtual sets, and they are in two entirely different price brackets. Hardware virtual sets (systems) are primarily used by large television networks and average in the low to mid hundred thousand dollar range. Software virtual systems are financially affordable by the rest of us. That's very important, as it means there are potentially more people with low-cost software-based virtual set applications who could benefit from your virtual set design services.

The main difference between hardware-based virtual systems and software-based systems is that hardware-based virtual set systems integrate with the video cameras to synchronize the camera panning and zooming with the virtual set. Additionally, the hardware systems perform all of this live. The software solutions simulate the camera motion amazingly well by allowing the user to specify zoom and pan values at key frames. This is done while maintaining the scale and position of the person (being brought into the virtual set) so that the final illusion is that the virtual set is real and the camera really did pan and zoom. One current disadvantage of software virtual sets is that you must render the final output, so you can't use them for live television and probably would make short clips with them rather than a 2-hour movie (but you could if you really, really wanted to).

Ultra 2 (from Serious magic: *http://www.seriousmagic.com/*) is a virtual-set broadcast application that allows you to build your own virtual sets for the background, overlay, and insert layers. In Ultra 2, video clips of the subject (person) shot against a keying (green or blue screen) or non-keying background are first chroma-keyed (the background is removed) and then composited with background and overlay layers. Additionally, this process is made even more effective by the use of proprietary true 3D virtual sets complete with motion tracking and animated elements.

Non-keying backgrounds refer to static (nonmoving) backgrounds such as an office, a wallpapered wall, a building, or some other static multicolored background. Ultra 2 is able to key (remove) such backgrounds by first starting the video clip with just the background and establishing that the background image is not to be used. Then, when the person comes on screen, since he is different than the background, only the person is seen.

By simply using what you've already learned about modeling and animating in Cinema 4D so far along with addressing some of the broadcast media factors, you will be making virtual sets in no time at all. As this tutorial will focus on outputting from Cinema 4D and setting up in Ultra 2, Cinema 4D projects will be loaded, discussed, and rendered.

The virtual set you will create in this tutorial will include rendering animation from Cinema 4D as a QuickTime video file, so you will create the illusion of 3D by design alone. This virtual set will be designed for use with a live-action (TV show host, interview, special topics presenter) person.

ON THE DVD Finished project files for two sections of this tutorial are included on the accompanying DVD-ROM in the tutorials folder. All of the images used in this tutorial are located in Tutorials/ProjectFiles/Chapter 09/Tutorial-01 on the Projects DVD-ROM.

To render the QuickTime files from Cinema 4D, you must install the authoring version of QuickTime (http://www.apple.com/quicktime/home/win.html). The prerendered files are also available on the DVD-ROM accompanying this book.

1. To build the background layer of your virtual set, load "**Tutorials/ProjectFiles/Chapter 09/Tutorial-01/BurnBack-01/BurnBack-01.c4d**." This is the wall and sidewalk you built in a previous chapter. The wall has been widened (by duplicating the plane called Wall) a bit to accommodate the format of the set you will assemble in Ultra 2. This will be the background layer that will be output as a still image. The following render settings are recommended:

Anti-aliasing	Best	Prevents video artifacts
Resolution	720 × 480	DV video resolution
Pixel aspect ratio	1:0.9	DV video pixel aspect ratio
Filed rendering	None	This is a still image
Frame	Current frame	This is a still image
Saving file format	BMP	This format is lossless; prevents video artifacts.

2. To build the background layer of your virtual set, load "**Tutorials/ProjectFiles/Chapter 09/Tutorial-01/BurnBack-01/Burn-Smoke-01.c4d**." This is the smoke, fire, and exhaust port you built in a previous chapter. The smoke, fire, and exhaust port have been moved over to the left to leave most of the screen free for an actor or other subject to take center stage. This will be the overlay layer and will be output as a video clip with the alpha channel enabled. The following render settings are recommended:

Anti-aliasing	Geometry	This animation has soft transparent edges
Resolution	720 × 480	DV video resolution
Pixel aspect ratio	1:0.9	DV video pixel aspect ratio
Filed rendering	None	This is a low-detail video clip
Frame	All frames	So the virtual set can accommodate 15 seconds of non-looped overlay
Saving file format	QuickTime (animation codec: millions of colors+, quality high)	Required to save the video clip with an alpha channel in the video clip
Alpha channel	Checked	Required to save the video clip with an alpha channel in the video clip

This animation will take some time to render. The finished video clip is available in "Tutorials/ProjectFiles/Chapter 09/Tutorial-01/Burn-01.mov" on the DVD-ROM accompanying this book in the tutorials folder.

ON THE DVD

3. With the background and overlay video files created in Cinema 4D, it's time to launch Ultra 2 (shown in Figure 9.6).

FIGURE 9.6   The Ultra 2 interface.

4. To very quickly learn how Ultra 2 works, click the Input Clip **Browse** button (Figure 9.7) and browse to "**Program Files/Serious Magic/ ULTRA/Content/Sample Clips**" and open "**Suzy – Tight – In Wind.avi.**" This opens the video clip of a tight shot of Suzy in front of a green screen with her hair blowing in the wind.

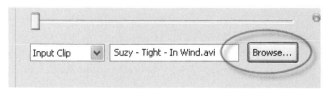

FIGURE 9.7   Browse for the input clip Suzy – Tight – In Wind.avi.

5. To turn off the video interlacing in the clip, in the **Input** page, set **Field Order** to No Fields.

6. To key out (remove) the green screen background from the input clip, click the **Keyer** page, then click to make several points on the green screen in the **Inputs** window (shown in Figure 9.8); then, in the **Keyer** page, click **Apply Points** to get rid of the green screen. To further improve the key, in the **Keyer** page, **Matte Generation**, set the **Start Threshhold** to 0.8. In the **Post-Processing** area of the **Keyer** page, set the **Soften Matte** to 0.5, **Sharpen Matte** to 0.4, and **Sharpen Range** to 0.7.

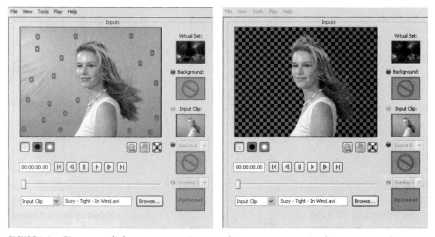

FIGURE 9.8   First you click to create points on the green screen in the Input window. Then you click Apply Points to remove the green screen background.

7. In the **Virtual Sets** page, double-click the **Outdoors** virtual set folder. Drag **Outdoors Cam 1 (Tight)** to the virtual set thumbnail (the top thumbnail). Click the **Play** button on the Transport Control to see the virtual set composite (Figure 9.9).

You can also double-click the virtual set Outdoors Cam 1 (Tight) icon to apply it to the Virtual Set channel.

FIGURE 9.9   Suzy is now keyed over the Outdoors virtual set.

8. To assemble the virtual set elements rendered in Cinema 4D, first start a new Ultra 2 session by using the **Main** menu to choose **File/New 4:3 Session**. Click **No** at the Unsaved session requester.

9. Click the **Background** thumbnail (shown in Figure 9.6) and browse to open "**Tutorials/ProjectFiles/Chapter 09/Tutorial-01/Back-01_0143.BMP**." The background of the ground and walls are now displayed in the Ultra 2 Preview window.

10. In the Input page, set the **Aspect Ratio** to 4:3 to fit the background image to the full Preview window.

ON THE DVD

11. To add the smoke and fire video clip to the virtual set, in Windows Explorer, navigate to the **"Tutorials/ProjectFiles/Chapter 09/Tutorial-01"** folder in the DVD-ROM accompanying this book and drag the **"Burn-01.mov"** file to the Ultra 2 **Overlay** thumbnail. Press **Play** on the Transport Control to see the smoke, fire, and exhaust port video clip play over the background. This virtual set is now ready for a person to be added.

Because the Burn-1.mov video clip was rendered in Cinema 4D with an alpha channel, keying is not required to composite it and see the layers beneath it.

12. To add the subject (person) to the virtual set, click the Input Clip thumbnail and browse to open **"C:/Program Files/Serious Magic/ULTRA/Content/Sample Clips"** and open **"Suzy–Wide–Walk in Left.avi."**

13. The Inputs window now displays with a light and stand on the right of the screen (shown in Figure 9.10). **Play** the Preview window to see Suzy walking in behind the smoke, then coming to a stop and expressively talking. In the **Input** page, set the **Field Order** to No Fields.

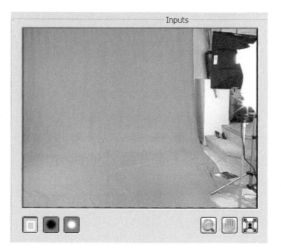

FIGURE 9.10   The unkeyed Suzy – Wide – Walk in Left.avi video clip when first loaded as the Input Clip.

14. With the Transport Control set to 00:00:00:00, to key the input clip, in the **Keyer** page, click **Set Key** to key out the green screen and all the stuff to the right of the screen. In the Preview window, go to **00:00:04:00** to see Suzy standing with a very slight green glow around her. To improve the key, in the **Keyer** page, **Matte genera-**

tion, set the **Start Threshold** to 0.6. In **Color Control**, set the **Spill Suppression** to 1. In **Post-Processing**, set the **Sharpen Matte** to 0.883 and **Sharpen Range** to 1. The Preview window should now look similar to Figure 9.11.

FIGURE 9.11   The key of the input clip is now tuned.

15. To further integrate Suzy with the virtual set originally created in Cinema 4D, in the **Shadows** page, check **Shadow 1 – Floor Left**. Now Suzy is casting a shadow on the ground. Set the **Opacity** to 0.5 and the **Baseline** to 0.3 to make the shadow more visible and closer to Suzy's feet.

16. **Play** the Preview window again to see that Suzy stops moving at 00:00:10:05. Since you will be rendering the final output as a video clip, you will need to set the smoke to end when Suzy stops moving. Select the **Overlay** thumbnail. Drag the playback head to 00:00:10:05. In the **Input** page, the **Out Point** is 00:00:14:14. Click **Set** to make it 00:00:10:02. **Play** the Preview window to see everything starting and stopping together.

17. It's time to output the final video clip. Click the **Output** page. Set the **Format** (file format) to QuickTime 4:3, **Codec** to Sorensen Video 3 Compressor, **Resolution** to 720 × 480, **Frame Rate** to 29.97, and

Field Order to Lower Field First. Choose the output path and file-name and click the **Start** button to render/output the final file.

Summary

In building this basic virtual set you have been exposed to a powerful broadcast application of Cinema 4D. What makes this application of Cinema 4D so useful is that the virtual set can now be used for any video clip captured in a wide shot. Although the background in this tutorial was a still image, an animation could have been used just as easily, and the smoke could have been a desk or a tree.

| **TUTORIAL 2** | **CHARACTERS ON VIRTUAL SETS (HD)** |

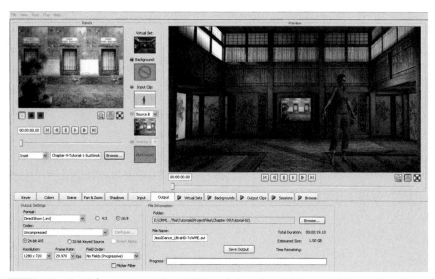

FIGURE 9.12   Jessi dances in an Ultra 2 Oriental virtual set. This tutorial is produced in HD.

Covered in this tutorial:

- Ultra 2
- Rendering a green screen
- Rendering for HD output
- Keying the animation in Ultra 2
- Casting shadows from the input layer
- Outputting the final render for HD
- Windows Media 9 Encoder: WMV HD

While virtual sets are usually used to insert people into virtual environments, another really cool use for virtual sets is to insert 3D animated characters into virtual sets for storytelling.

Each of the virtual sets in Ultra 2 (from Serious magic: *http://www. seriousmagic.com/*) include shots for several angles. Some of the virtual sets even include a camera "trak" so that you can travel through the virtual set. So placing your 3D characters from Cinema 4D in the virtual sets means that you can produce some high-quality storytelling, putting all of your real effort into the character animation and storytelling part of the production. Developing a production team with one person dedicated to virtual set design while others focus on character animation and props is a very effective strategy.

As this tutorial will focus on outputting from Cinema 4D and setting up in Ultra 2, Cinema 4D projects will be loaded, discussed, and rendered. The character animation you will create in this tutorial will include rendering animation from Cinema 4D as a QuickTime file sequence at HD resolution. This project will be produced for final output to HD at 1280 × 720 resolution and 30 frames per second progressive (non-interlaced).

Some specifications used in this tutorial are chosen based on playing the final HD video on the Link Theater (or Link Station) from Buffalo Tech (*http://www.buffalotech.com/buffalo-home.php*).

- In order to see true HD output at a certain HD specification (720p, 1080i, 1080p, etc.), three things must support that HD specification: (1) acquisition/render, (2) playback, (3) display. Aqusition/Render: While it is possible to up-convert (through scaling and cropping) DV video (720 × 480 × 60 FPS) up to HD, that would at best simply look like DV video. The HD production process starts with camera acquisition in HD, 2D or 3D rendering at HD specifications. For camera acquisition for 1080i output, the entry level approach is to use an HDV camera such as the Sony HVR-A1J. Rendering for 1080i is as simple as setting the Cinema 4D render settings resolution at 1920 × 1080.
- Playback: To play back HD video, you can either use an HD or HDV deck such as the Sony HVR-M10U HDV VTR Recorder Deck, you can export your HDV content back to an HDV camcorder, or you can render your HD video file as a Windows Media 9 HD file, burn it to a CD or DVD and play it back on the PC-P3LWG/DVD Link Theater from Buffalo (*http://www.buffalotech.com*). I highly recommend the Link Theater option whether or not you have other ways to output. Its versatility can put you in the HD content delivery game immediately. The keys to HD playback are that the device must have HD video output connectors (RGB Component, DVI, or HDMI), be able to provide true HD or HDV resolution output (1280 × 720p, 1440 × 1080i, 1920 × 1080i, or 1920 × 1080p), and be able to sustain the required video bandwidth. This bandwidth could range from 3 Mbits/second to 2 Mbits/second depending on the encoding or source of the HD video.

Some video playback devices have RGB component outputs but do not really output HD resolution. These component outputs are meant to be used for convenient connection and may in fact simply provide you with regular good old NTSC video up-converted (scaled and cropped) to be acceptable to an HD input, so when you see a $39 DVD player with component outputs, put that smile in perspective.

- Display: In order to see true HD video, the display must have HD video inputs (RGB Component, DVI, or HDMI) and it should have a native pixel resolution capable of displaying the particular HD specification of video you wish to display.

ON THE DVD

A finished project file for one section of this tutorial is included on the accompanying DVD-ROM in the tutorials folder. All of the images used in this tutorial are located in Tutorials/ProjectFiles/Chapter 09/Tutorial-02 on the Projects DVD-ROM.

This tutorial requires Cinema 4D 9.1. At this time, BodyStudio works with Cinema 4D 7 through Cinema 4D 9.1. Check the Reiss Studio Web site (http://www.reiss-studio.com/) for info on their release of a BodyStudio version for Cinema 4D 9.5.

1. Start in Cinema 4D. Open "**Tutorials/ProjectFiles/Chapter 09/Tutorial-02/JessiDance-Only-1/JessiDance-Only-1.c4d**." This is the animation of the Poser character Jessi from Chapter 8. This time, the animation is of only Jessi and no other visible scene objects. The camera and target have been positioned to zoom in on Jessi for maximum resolution benefit (shown in Figure 9.13).

The gray render safe lines can be a bit difficult to see among the gray grid lines. To adjust this, in the Main menu, choose Edit/Preferences. In Viewport/Colors, choose Film Format and adjust the color to something you can more easily see (such as red).

For fluid playback, the Poser object, Display Tracking is set to Box. Setting this to full will display the full geometry of the character and cause the interface to respond very slowly.

2. The Background has a simple green material applied. In this green material, the **Color** channel **Color** is set to 0, 255, 0 and the **Brightness** is set to 100. The **Luminance** channel **Color** is set to 0, 255, 0 and the **Brightness** is set to 100. This green background will be used later in Ultra 2 in the Keyer page.
3. Go to the **Render Settings** to see that the **Resolution** has been set to 1280 × 720 HDTV, **Pixel Aspect Ratio** to 1:1, and the **Frames** to be

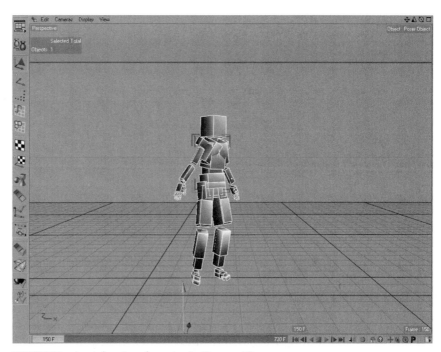

FIGURE 9.13   Jessi dancing character in Cinema 4D.

rendered are 150 to 730. **Field Rendering** is None, and the **Frame Rate** is set to 30. From the **Main** menu, choose **Render/Render In Picture Viewer** to output this sequence:

Anti-aliasing	Best	Prevents video artifacts
Resolution	1280 × 720	HDTV video resolution
Film Format	16:9	HDTV aspect ratio
Pixel aspect ratio	1:1	HD video pixel aspect ratio
Filed rendering	None	For progressive HD
Frame	150–730	Jessi's action frames
Frame Rate	30	
Saving file format	QuickTime (Sorensen 3, Quality: Best)	This is a practical file format to balance between high quality and reasonable file size.

ON THE DVD

This animation will take some time to render. Once rendered, it will be loaded into the input layer in Ultra 2. The finished video clip is available on the DVD-ROM accompanying this book in the tutorials folder.

4. Launch Ultra 2. Continuing the process of producing an HD video clip of the animated character placed in a virtual set, in Ultra 2, in the **Main** menu, choose **File/New/New/16:9 Session**.

ON THE DVD

5. **Browse** the Input Clip (shown in Figure 9.14) to open "**Tutorials/ ProjectFiles/Chapter 09/Tutorial-02/JessiDance-UltraHD-src. mov**."

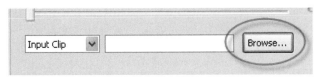

FIGURE 9.14   Browse the Input Clip.

6. Click the **Keyer** page and click once on the green area of the Inputs window. Then click **Apply Points** in the Keyer to see Jessie without the green background.

7. In the Preview window, go to **00:00:01:13** to see some green background pixels still around Jessi's arms and legs. To further clean up the key, in the Keyer window, set **Start Threshold** to 1, **Start Level** to 1, **Desaturation** to 0.770, **Spill Suppression** to 1, **Soften Matte** to 0.390, **Sharpen Matte** to 0.6, and **Sharpen Range** to 0.6.

It's very important to make sure that you have the correct layer (Input Clip, Inset, Live Preview) selected before making any adjustments to that layer.

8. In the **Virtual Sets** page, **Orient** folder, double-click **Orient Cam 2 (Wide)** to use this virtual set. Jessi is instantly placed in a beautiful large, open Oriental room. Don't be alarmed that the Preview window switched to a 4:3 view. In the **Output** page, **Output Settings**, click **16:9** to display the correct aspect ratio again.

9. The virtual set is originally a 4:3 design. Setting the output to 16:9 has added a black band on the left and right of the Preview window (Figure 9.15). To get rid of this and see true 16:9 content in the Preview window, click the **Pan & Zoom** page, check **Enable,** and select the first **Point Time (00:00:00:00)**. In the **Settings for Current Point**, set **Z** to −0.333. Select the second **Point Time (00:00:19:09)**. In the **Settings for Current Point**, set **Z** to −0.333. Now the Preview window shows true 16:9 content, and this is what will be rendered (Figure 9.16).

FIGURE 9.15   A black band appears on the left and right on the 4:3 virtual set in the 16:9 project preview window.

FIGURE 9.16   The virtual set now provides true 16:9 content.

10. In the **Scene** page, set the **Size in Scene** to 1.250 and the **Position in Scene X** to −0.190, **Y** to 0.160, and **Z** to −2.0 to move Jessi over to the right.

11. To better immerse Jessi into the Oriental room, you can have her cast a shadow on the floor. To do this, click the **Shadows** page and check **Shadow 1 – Floor left**. The shadow isn't immediately visible yet.

Unlike a Cinema 4D shadow, this shadow is a modified copy of the Jessi video clip. For the moment, set the **Opacity** to 0.880, and the shadow appears on the floor. Set the **Baseline** to 0.266 so that the shadow starts at Jessi's feet. To soften the shadow, set the **Blur** to 0.750. Finally, with all the other parameters set, set the **Opacity** back down to 0.500 so that the shadow isn't too pronounced.

12. Click the **Source B** thumbnail and Browse to open "**Tutorials/ProjectFiles/Chapter 09/Tutorial-01/Chapter-9-Tutorial-1-SuziSmoke.avi**." The SuzySmoke video clip is placed in the large wall monitor at the far end of the room. **Play** the Preview window to see the action all composited together.

If your video card is a high-performance model (such as the NVidia Quadro FX 3000) and supports Pixel Shading 2.0, then you can increase preview playback and output rendering by checking GPU Boost in the Keyer page. This offloads processor-intense functions from your CPU to the GPU on your graphics card.

13. To output the HD file, in the **Output** page, **Output Settings**, set the **Format** to DirectShow (.avi) 16:9, **Codec** to Uncompressed (for the cleanest looking HD video), Resolution to 1280 × 720, **Frame Rate** to 29.970, and **Field Order** to No Fields (Progressive). In File Information, click the **Browse** button to set the file path and file name ("**JessiDance_UltraHD-1.avi**") in a folder on your hard drive. Then click the **Save Output** button to render the HD .avi video clip.

Outputing an uncopressed AVI in this tutorial produces a 1.47-GB video file for a 19-second (and 10 frames) video clip. This file is not available on the DVD-ROM because of available space on the disc. Amazingly, the final Windows Media HD file (available on the DVD-ROM) will be only 6 MB.

It is possible to create smaller, more easily managed video files by choosing a traditional AVI codec. Certain video scenes, however, will show compression artifacts in HD playback, so if you really want to use a particular codec, perform some sample tests before committing an entire project to such a work flow decision.

14. In Windows Media 9 Encoder, in the New Session window, choose **Custom Session** (Figure 9.17) to set up the final HD encode.

15. In the Session properties window, set **Source** to File. Since there is no audio in this file, uncheck **Audio**. Browse to open the "**Jessi-Dance_UltraHD-ToWME.avi**" file output (rendered) to your hard drive from Ultra 2.

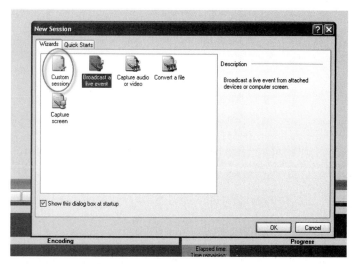

FIGURE 9.17   Windows Media 9 Encoder–New Session

If Audio is checked more than once in the Session properties window, be sure it is unchecked before you move to the next step to make an efficient HD file. In projects containing audio, you would (of course) have audio checked.

16. In the **Output** page, uncheck **Push to Server** and check **Archive to File** to render the final WMV HD file to your hard drive. Browse to set the file name and file path of the WMV file to be output.

17. In the **Compression** page, set **Destination** to Hardware devices. Then click the **Edit** button and in the **5009 Kbps** page, set the **Video peak bit rate** to 6000 Kbps so that when this file is played on the Buffalo Tech Link Theater DVD player as a Windows Media HD file, the bandwidth will not exceed the 7 Mbps specification of that device. Set the **Key Frame Interval** to 2 sec and then click **OK**. Click **Apply**. This will take a few minutes.

The value set in Key Frame Interval determines how frequently key frames (frames of video containing all data needed to render a frame) are rendered. All frames between key frames are delta frames. Delta frames contain only the information needed to represent the visual changes since the previous frame and therefore are smaller in size than key frames. Thus, for cartoon animation, you could use a high key frame interval. For an action fight scene, you would use a low key frame interval.

Always be sure to know the HD media bandwidth specifications of the device on which you will play back the HD media file. Getting this wrong will result in failure to maintain smooth uninterrupted playback.

18. Click the **Start Encoding** button to encode and output the Windows Media HD file to hard disk.
19. Once encoded, to play the Windows Media HD file on the Buffalo Tech Link Theater, use any CD or DVD writer (e.g., Easy Media Creator–Roxio, Nero Burning ROM–Nero) to burn the Windows Media HD file to disc. Play the disc in the Link Theater and view the full HD playback (using HD component output) on an HD monitor or television at true HD resolution.

Summary

This tutorial gives a little peek into how Cinema 4D can be integrated into an HD (High Definition) broadcast application that can streamline your animation production process. It also provides a good way to divide tasks and job functions between animation, video file prep, virtual sets and media encoding. With proper preparation, multiple 3D characters and live-action (real people) can be combined with this process to make some really impressive high-quality media.

Arming yourself or your studio with the ability to deliver HD animation integration can mean the difference between playing on a production team or leading it.

TUTORIAL 3   **CELL PHONE AD**

FIGURE 9.18   Final Adobe After Effects composite of a TV ad using Cinema 4D animation.

Covered in this tutorial:

- Lighting a scene without using lights (Ambient Occlusion)
- Sky
- Rendering for DV output including field rendering
- Ultra 2 background and overlay layers from Cinema 4D
- Material Gradient
- After Effects text animation presets

In this tutorial, you will build a TV ad for the cell phone you modeled in Chapter 3. Your job function will be digital media producer. Your animator has set up the Cinema 4D project file. You'll look it over before the final Cinema 4D render. Your sound producer has delivered a sound track for the ad, and in Adobe After Effects, you'll be synchronizing some of the visual effects to specific beats in the music. You will also introduce the message text sequences using the text animation presets found in Adobe After Effects Pro 6.5. The final title for the ad was done by your graphic artist in Adobe Photoshop and will be animated on its own layer in After Effects. When it all comes together, it will be sweet.

ON THE DVD

A finished Cinema 4D project file and Adobe After Effects file for this tutorial are included on the accompanying DVD-ROM in the tutorials folder. All of the images used in this tutorial are located in Tutorials/ProjectFiles/Chapter 09/Tutorial-03 on the Projects DVD-ROM.

ON THE DVD

To render the QuickTime files from Cinema 4D, you must install the authoring version of QuickTime (http://www.apple.com/quicktime/home/win.html). *The prerendered files are also available on the DVD-ROM accompanying this book.*

1. Start by loading the Cinema 4D project from "**Tutorials/Project-Files/Chapter   09/Tutorial-03/CellPhoneAd-01/CellPhoneAd-01.c4d**." This 600-frame (20-second) project includes the cell phone modeled in Chapter 3 on a white floor (shown in Figure 9.19). At frame 320, a particle emitter will send balls out of the floor into the air. Gravity will bring them back down to the floor. A metaball system will form the balls into water, while a Banji shader will give the water surface some further appearance of fluidity. The Sky above is made of layers of clouds that are set to animate to add an element organic of life to the scene. Way in the distance, a very wide white plane object has a gradient in its luminance and alpha channels to cause a smooth transition from the white floor to the sky and clouds (shown in Figure 9.20).

In the Floor material Color and Diffusion channels, the Texture is set to Ambient Occlusion. The ambient occlusion is calculating the shadows of the cell phone on the floor without the aid of lights. The floor's Compositing tag has the Compositing Background checked. During the first 10 seconds, the cell phone turns around and flips open to reveal a video of a

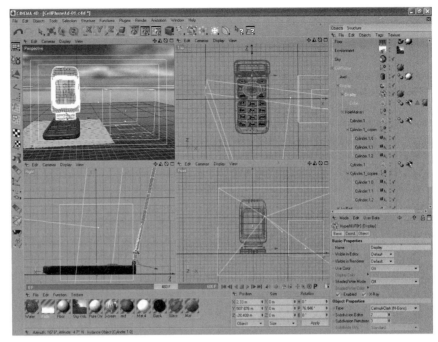

FIGURE 9.19   The cell phone project in Cinema 4D.

lady speaking in the cell phone display. Render the animation, then close
Cinema 4D and open Adobe After Effects 6.5 pro.

The following render settings are recommended:

Anti-aliasing	Best	Prevents video artifacts
Resolution	720 × 480	DV video resolution
Pixel aspect ratio	1:0.9	DV video pixel aspect ratio
File rendering	Off Field First	Smooth video motion
Frame	All Frames	The whole animation
Saving file format	QuickTime (Sorensen 3)	High-quality video output

2. In Adobe After Effects, in the **Main** menu, choose **File/Import/File**
   and navigate to "**Tutorials/ProjectFiles/Chapter 09/Tutorial-03**"
   and open "**CellAd-1.mov**" to import the video clip output from Cinema 4D. In the **Main** menu, choose **File/Save As** and save the project as "**CellSource-01**." After Effects will add the .aep After Effects
   Project extension to this project file.

FIGURE 9.20   Gradient fade on distant plane object used to fade between the floor and the sky.

3. In the Project window, drag CellAd-1.mov to the **Create a new Composition** icon at the bottom of the project window (shown in Figure 9.21). This creates a Composition window and a Timeline window and places the CellAd-1 video clip on the first layer of the Timeline. The Composition window is set to the rendered resolution of the CellAd-1 video clip. The Timeline is set to the rendered frame length 0:00:20:00 (20 seconds) of the CellAd-1 video clip. All future elements of the production of this TV ad will be within these parameters.

4. Click the **Make RAM Preview** on the Time Controls (shown in Figure 9.22) to see the video playback.

If your system is running low on memory, reduce the quality of the Composition window from full to half, third, or quarter preview quality.

5. Double-click in an empty area of the Project window to import another file. Import "**Tutorials/ProjectFiles/Chapter 09/Tutorial-03/MakeItAll-080805d.wav**." This is the sound track for the ad. First, click the **Go To First Frame** button (shown in Figure 9.23) on the Time Controls. Drag the sound track to the Timeline. This creates a second layer on the Timeline.

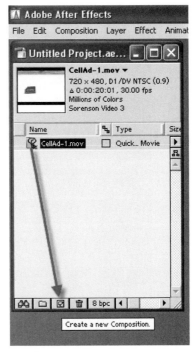

FIGURE 9.21   The cell phone project in Cinema 4D.

FIGURE 9.22   The Make RAM Preview button.

FIGURE 9.23   The Go To First Frame button.

6. You will add four animated text messages to the ad. These text messages will be visually synchronized with the sound track. To add the first text message, in the Timeline, drag the Current Time Indicator to **0:00:01:00** (1 second). Then click the **Horizontal Type** tool (Figure 9.24) and click in the **Composition** window to add the text. This adds a text layer to the Timeline.

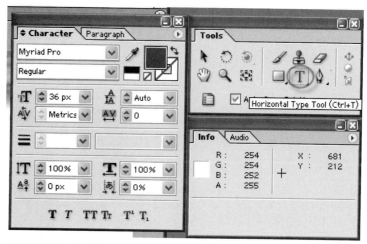

FIGURE 9.24   Click the triangles indicated above to reveal the sound track's waveform.

7. Type "**Make It All Sound**" and then press **Enter** and type "**Clear**." Highlight **Make It All Sound**, and in the Character window, set the **Font** to Myriad Pro and the **Size** to 24 px (shown in Figure 9.25).

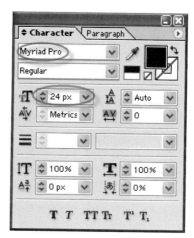

FIGURE 9.25   Setting the font and size for the first line of text.

8. Highlight **Clear** and set the **Font** to Myriad Pro and **Size** to 60 px.
9. With the Current Time Indicator still at 1 second and the text layer still selected, to the right of Time Controls, click **Effects & Presets**.

Click the **Animation Presets** triangle, then the **Text** triangle, then the **Animate In** triangle and then double-click the **Decoder Fade In** preset (shown in Figure 9.26) to animate the text layer currently selected. Press the **Space Bar** to see the text animate in.

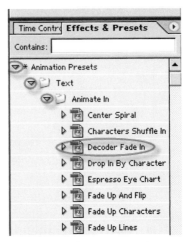

FIGURE 9.26   The text animation preset is selected.

10. To open the text layer hierarchy, in the text layer, just left of the pink box, click the **triangle** that is pointing to the right. This reveals the Text and Transform hierarchies. Open the **Transform** as indicated in Figure 9.27 and set the **Position** to 480.0, 153.0. With the Current Time Indicator at **0:00:03:14**, click the **Opacity** Stop Watch to create an opacity key frame at 3 seconds and 14 frames with a value of 100 percent opacity. Move the Current Time Indicator to **0:00:04:22** and set the **Opacity** value to 0. This creates an opacity key frame at 4 seconds 22 frames with a value of 0 so the text fades out.

FIGURE 9.27   The text layer Transform hierarchy.

11. With the text layer selected, in the **Main** menu, choose **Edit/Dupli-cate** to create the second text layer with all the font, size, and anima-tion preset information already defined. Drag this new text layer so it starts at 0:00:05:21. With the Current Time Indicator at **0:00:08:05**, select the **Horizontal Text** tool and click once in the word **Clear**. Highlight Clear and change it to **Bright**.

12. With the second text layer selected, in the **Main** menu, choose **Edit/Duplicate** to create the third text layer. Drag this new text layer so it starts at 0:00:10:12. With the Current Time Indicator at **0:00:12:26**, select the **Horizontal Text** tool and click once in the word **Bright**. Highlight Bright and change it to **Live**.

13. With the third text layer selected, in the **Main** menu, choose **Edit/Duplicate** to create the fourth text layer. Drag this new text layer so it starts at 0:00:14:22. With the Current Time Indicator at **0:00:17:06**, select the **Horizontal Text** tool and click once in the word **Live**. Highlight Live and change it to **Tonight**. Select the word **Sound** and change it to **LIQUID**. Highlight **LIQUID** and change the **Font** to Myriad Pro Bold. Click the **Fill Color sample** (shown in Figure 9.28) to change the color to Blue (0, 11, 144).

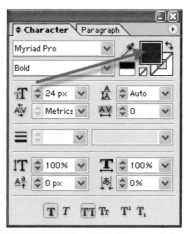

FIGURE 9.28   The Fill Color sample is indicated.

14. Move the Current Time Indicator to **0:00:16:29**. Import "**Tutorials/ProjectFiles/Chapter 09/Tutorial-03/LiDfone1-1.png**." This is the title logo art prepared in Adobe Photoshop CS2.

15. In the **Main** menu, choose **Effect/Blur & Sharpen/Fast Blur**. In the **Main** menu, choose **Effect/Distort/Wave Warp**. Arrange the LiDfone1-1 hierarchy to be like Figure 9.29.

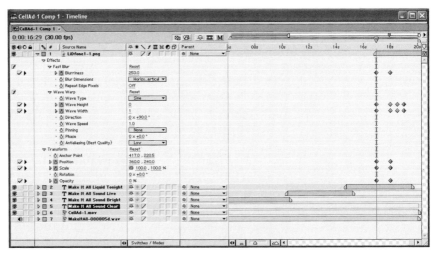

FIGURE 9.29 LiDfone1-1 hierarchy of effects and transforms.

16. In the LiDfone1-1 hierarchy, in **Transform**, click the stop watches for **Position**, **Scale**, and **Opacity**. Set the **Position** to 360.0, 240.0. Set the **Opacity** to 0. Click the **Fast blur** stopwatch for **Blurriness**. Click the **Wave Warp** stopwatch for **Wave height** and **Wave Width**.

17. At **0:00:17:21** set the **Blurriness** to 0, **Wave Height** to 0, **Wave Width** to 1, **Position** to 480.0, 189.0, **Scale** to 34.0, 34.0, and **Opacity** to 100 to fully reveal the logo art (shown in Figure 9.30).

FIGURE 9.30 Logo art is now revealed.

18. At **0:00:18:26**, set the **Wave Height** to 10 and **Wave Width** to 40.
19. At **0:00:19:22**, set the **Wave Height** to 0 and **Wave Width** to 0.

Step 18 and 19 send a wave warp through the logo.

20. In the **Main** menu, choose **Composition/Add To Render Queue**. This opens the Render Queue window shown in Figure 9.31.

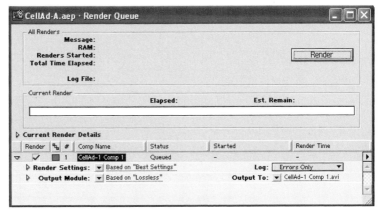

FIGURE 9.31   The Render Queue window.

21. In the Render Queue window, **Render Settings**, click **Based on "Best Settings"** and set **Field Rendering** to Lower Field First. Then click **OK** so the video will be interlaced.
22. In the Output module, click **Based on "Lossless."** The Format defaults to Video For Windows. That's what you want for the production. In the **Format Options**, choose Microsoft DV and click **OK**. Be sure that **Audio Output** is checked with the settings of 44.100 kHz, 16 Bit, Stereo. Click **OK**.
23. In **Output To**, click **Comp 1.avi** to set the path and file name.
24. In the **Main** menu, choose **File/Save**.

If you don't save your project before rendering and then make changes after rendering and wish to render again, you will have to make all settings to the Render Queue again.

25. Click the **Render** button to output the final DV video file. Once rendering is complete, this DV video file can be recorded to a DV video deck, camcorder with editing software like Adobe Premiere. Alternatively, you can save this file to a folder on your computer and wirelessly play it

on the Buffalo Tech Link Theater. You can also simply double-click the file to play it in your computer.

Summary

It is incredibly important to fully appreciate that when working in broadcast video, though Cinema 4D is captivatingly powerful, it is the integration of Cinema 4D with applications such as Adobe After Effects that can truly empower you to deliver media content in a broadcast world. While ultimately you can do virtually everything accomplished in this tutorial working exclusively in Cinema 4D, integrating Cinema 4D with After Effects makes a much more efficient and effective work flow.

This tutorial made use of only one Cinema 4D rendered layer. The limit to the layers you can bring to a real-world broadcast application is limited only by your system memory and your imagination.

TUTORIAL 4   **JAMES ESCAPES TO REALITY**

FIGURE 9.32 Warning! James has escaped the Cinema 4D world and is now walking in the real world.

Covered in this tutorial:

- Virtual camera live action match moving in boujou bullet 2
- Virtual camera integration with live action footage in Cinema 4D
- Camera mapping
- Integrating Poser character animation with live action footage

Now it's time for something revolutionary, fresh, and completely different. This tutorial will teach you how to truly integrate video with 3D animation by using boujou bullet (by 2d3 *http://www.2d3.com*) and Cinema 4D. Boujou bullet imports an image sequence or video clip and tracks features such as the corners of a window or edges of a car or furniture in a room and produces 3D markers that form a point cloud and extrapolates a virtual camera that represents the original motion path of the real video camera that captured the video footage. This point cloud, virtual camera, and video footage are then imported into Cinema 4D. Cinema 4D models and camera mapping combine with the video footage and boujou bullet data to produce the master illusion that 3D objects have indeed entered the real world.

Because match moving is something a bit different than most other applications in 3D animation work flow, 2d3 offers a highly effective wizard-driven, guided production process to aid you in very quickly learning match moving and producing output for your projects, so although this really is something completely different, you will learn it in record time and be incredibly empowered to take on challenges that would make most animation double talk and run for the hills.

The applications for this kind of high-end media include TV commercials, video architectural previzualization, and motion picture visual effects.

This tutorial could well be called "Producing for Hollywood from Your Bedroom."

ON THE DVD A finished Cinema 4D project file and boujou bullet file for this tutorial are included on the accompanying DVD-ROM in the tutorials folder. All of the images used in this tutorial are located in Tutorials/Project-Files/Chapter 09/Tutorial-04 on the Projects DVD-ROM.

1. To motion match some hand-held camcorder video footage, start by launching boujou bullet. At the bottom of the interface, in the wizard **New Project** page, click the **Browse** button to set the file path and file name of the project "**MT-1.**" Click **Next**.

2. In the wizard **Importing Footage** page, to import the footage that is to be motion matched, click the **Browse** button to open "**Tutorials/ProjectFiles/Chapter 09/Tutorial-04/tutorial_1_source_images/tutorial1_cottage.001.jpg.**" This is the first frame of a 100-frame sequence. Click **Next**.

3. The footage is now imported into boujou bullet (Figure 9.33). In the Transport Control and the top of the interface, click the **Play** button

to see the original motion of the footage. Now imagine where the camera must have been held as the camera operator walked through the scene. This virtual camera location will be extrapolated during this boujou bullet session. Click the **Stop** button. In the wizard **Choose Sequence Length** page, accept the defaults of **Start Frame** set to 1, **Step** set to 1, and **End Frame** set to 100. Click **Next**.

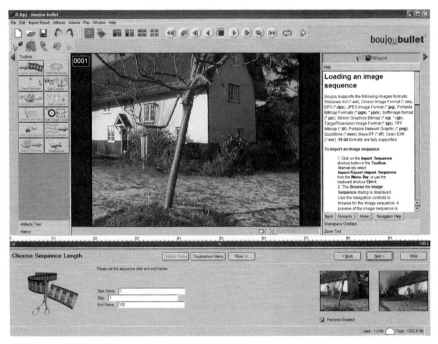

FIGURE 9.33 Footage imported into boujou bullet.

4. In the wizard **Edit Camera** page, accept the defaults and click **Next**.
5. In the wizard **Shot Type** page, accept the default of Free Move since the camera is moving through the scene. Click **Next**.
6. In the wizard **Masking Moving Objects** page, accept the default of No since there are no moving objects in the footage that need to be tracked. Click **Next**.
7. In the wizard **Setting Interlaced Type** page, accept the default of No since footage is not interlaced. Click **Next**.
8. In the wizard **Focal Length** page, accept the default to allow boujou bullet to determine the focal length of the virtual camera. Click **Next**.
9. In the wizard **Advanced Project Setup** page, accept the default of No just track it. Click **Next**.

10. In the wizard **Feature Tracking** page, accept the default. Click
    Next. The feature tracking process begins and you see a few hundred
    motion vectors tracking prominent features in the footage (Figure
    9.34). When the feature track is complete, boujou bullet solves the
    free move to extrapolate the virtual camera. This is an automated
    feature and is processed so quickly that you might miss seeing it
    done. No problem.

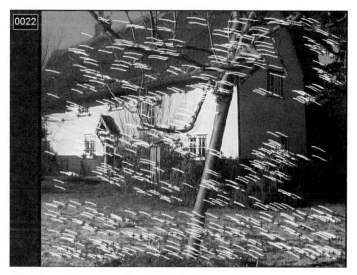

FIGURE 9.34   Feature tracking has begun.

11. Boujou bullet has determined which of the feature tracks are valid
    and has built the 3D point cloud (Figure 9.35). Click the **Play** button
    to see the 3D point cloud staying attached to the feature elements of
    the video footage. Click the **Stop** button. In the very top row of
    icons, click the **3D** icon to see just the point cloud in 3D (Figure
    9.36).
12. In the wizard **Tracking Successful** page, accept the default of This
    looks good. Click **Next**.
13. The virtual camera and point cloud are saved in the native boujou
    (.ban) format. The Cinema 4D plug-in must be installed in order for
    Cinema 4D to open a .ban file. In preparation for outputting such a
    file for Cinema 4D animation, in the **Main** menu, choose **Edit/Pref-
    erences**. In the Preferences window, set **Camera Export/boujou
    Animation/Camera Format** to **Both Formats for Each Key** (Fig-
    ure 9.37), then click **OK**. Click **Next**.

FIGURE 9.35   3D point cloud now added to the project.

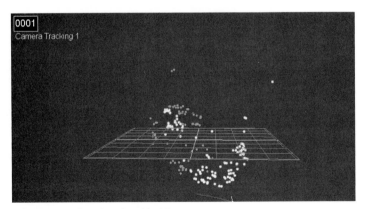

FIGURE 9.36   3D point cloud in 3D.

14. In the wizard **Add Scene Geometry** page, accept the default of No. Click **Next**.
15. In the wizard **Export Camera** page, set **Export Format** to boujou Animation, **Filename** to MT-1, and **Scale Scene by** to 1. Click **Next**.
16. In the wizard **Tracking Completed** page, click **Finish**. You are now finished with the boujou bullet portion of this project.
17. Continuing in Cinema 4D 9, open "**Tutorials/ProjectFiles/Chapter 09/Tutorial-04/MT-1.ban**" from the DVD-ROM. This loads the virtual camera as "**Camera_1**" and point cloud as "**Reference_ points**" in the Objects Manager (Figure 9.38).

ON THE DVD

FIGURE 9.37   Setting the boujou bullet camera format for Cinema 4D use.

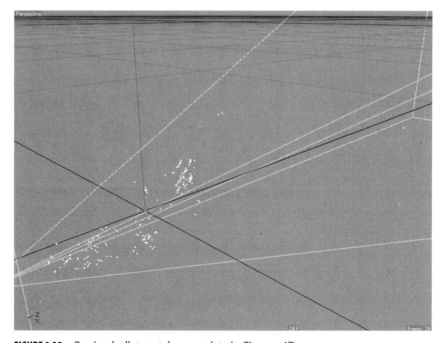

FIGURE 9.38   Boujou bullet match move data in Cinema 4D.

18. In the perspective view local menu, choose **Cameras/Scene Scam-eras/"Camera_1"** to make the virtual camera extrapolated in bou-jou bullet become the active Cinema 4D camera. **Play** the animation to see the perspective view camera traveling through the point cloud.

19. In the **Main** menu, choose **Edit/Project** Settings. Set **Frame Rate** to 25, **Minimum** to 1, and **Maximum** to 100. These settings are made to match the video footage.

20. In preparation for adding the video footage to the scene, add a **Back-ground** object (**Objects/Scene/Background**).

21. In the Materials Manager, create a new material named "**Video.**" In the **Color** channel **Texture**, browse to open "**Tutorials/Project-Files/Chapter 09/Tutorial-04/tutorial_1_source_images/tutor-iall_cottage.001.jpg**" on the DVD-ROM, which is the same footage imported into boujou bullet earlier. At the pop-up (this image is not in the document search path) click **No**.

Clicking Yes in the pop-up will result in loading the selected first image (tutorial_ cottage.001.jpg) only.

22. In the **Color** channel **Texture**, click the file path (Tutorials/Project-Files/Chapter 09/Tutorial-04/tutorial_1_source_images/tutoriall_cottage.001.jpg) to the left of the browse button. In the **Animation** tab, set **Timing** to Range, **Range Start** to 1, and **Range End** to 100. Click **Calculate**. Now apply this video material to the background object in the Objects Manager.

This is a crucial point. Because the video footage is from "1 to 100" frames, both the project settings and the material range must also be set to go from "1 to 100" and NOT "0 to 99." Getting this wrong will result in causing the 3D objects to wobble around the video scene and seem like they are not part of the real world. In other words, it will kill the illusion.

23. James, the animated Poser character, will walk on the ground in the video footage. Because the video footage has no 3D ground on which James can cast a shadow to complete the illusion that he is in the real world, you need to add a primitive **Plane**. In the Attributes Manager, set the **Width Segments** and **Height Segments** to 1. Check the **X-Ray** option to see the video footage ground through the plane.

24. To orient, position, and shape the plane to match the ground in the video footage, in the Coordinates Manager, set the **Position** to **X** = –6, **Y** = –1.629, and **Z** = –6. Switch to **Object** mode and set the **Size** to **X** = 60 and **Z** = 25. Set the **Rotation** to **H** = –50.

25. Render the perspective view to see that the plane is not blending with the video footage yet (Figure 9.39).

FIGURE 9.39   The plane is not blending with the footage yet.

26. Apply the video material plane object and in the Objects Manager, right-click on the plane and choose **CINEMA 4D Tags/Compositing** to add a compositing tag to the plane. With the compositing tag selected, in the Attributes Manager, in the **Tag** tab, check **Compositing Background**.

27. On the plane object, select the video material. In the Attributes Manager, change the **Projection Type** to Camera Mapping. Drag the **"Camera_1"** from the Objects Manager to the **Camera** field in the Attributes Manager, **Tag** tab of the selected video material. Render the perspective view to see the plane object totally blended with the video footage (Figure 9.40).

Because of adding the plane this way, an object placed on the plane object can appear to cast a shadow on the ground outside the house in the video footage.

FIGURE 9.40   The plane is completely blended with the video footage now.

ON THE DVD

28. To add James to the scene, in the **Main** menu, choose **Plugins/Poser Object**. In the Attributes Manager, **Object** tab, browse to open "**Tutorials/ProjectFiles/Chapter 08/Tutorial-03/JamesWalk-1B.pz3**" on the DVD-ROM.

29. James is a bit too large for this scene when first loaded (Figure 9.41). In **Object** mode, with the Poser object selected, in the Coordinates Manager, set the **Position** to **X** = 1.145, **Y** = −1.668, and **Z** = −4.435; **Size** to **X** = 0.168, **Y** = 0.22, and **Z** = 0.412; and **Rotation** to **H** = −90, **P** = 0, and **B** = 0. James now appears to fit into the real world (Figure 9.42).

30. To get very fluid playback of the Poser character in the animation while in the editor, with the Poser object selected, in the Attributes Manager, **Object** tab, set **Display Tracking** to Box. James becomes a group of bounding boxes and the animation plays back smoothly.

31. Render the perspective view to see that James has no materials and doesn't cast a shadow on the ground. To correct James' materials issue, with the Poser object selected, in the Attributes Manager, **Object** tab, click **Create Materials** for the BodyStudio plug-in to build the appropriate Cinema 4D materials for James to look as he did in Poser. Once the materials have loaded completely, render the perspective view to see that James looks normal now.

FIGURE 9.41   James is at first too big for the real world.

FIGURE 9.42   James fits perfectly now.

Even though you see James' materials added in the Materials Manager, be sure to wait for the materials to be added to the Poser object in the Objects Manager as well before moving on. Failure to wait could result in a malfunction or software crash.

32. For James to appear to cast a shadow on the ground, add a Light (Point light). In the Coordinates Manager, set the **Position** of the light to **X** = 0, **Y** = 7, and **Z** = -4. In the Attributes Manager, **General** tab, set the **Shadow** to Soft. In the **Shadow** tab, set the **Shadow Map** to 500 × 500, **Sample Radius** to 8, and **Bias** to 0. Render the perspective view to see James casting a shadow on the ground. James is not well lit yet.

33. Add an Instance of the Light. In the Coordinates Manager, set the **Position** of the light instance to **X** = 2.7, **Y** = 2, and **Z** = −6. Render the perspective view to see that James' features can now be seen. To render the final animation, click the **Render Settings** icon. Use the following settings or choose your own:

Anti-aliasing	Geometry
Resolution	800 × 600
Film Format	Automatic
Pixel aspect ratio	1:1
Filed rendering	None
Frame	All Frames
Frame Rate	30
Saving file format	QuickTime (Sorensen 3, Quality: Best)

You then set the file path and file name and click the Render In Picture Viewer icon.

SUMMARY

This tutorial presents a powerfully effective solution to what is arguably one of the greatest challenges in visual effect compositing. Mastery of the integrated work flow between boujou bullet and Cinema 4D will make you a prime candidate for real-word 3D animation production.

10

VIDEO GAMES AND SIMULATION

In This Chapter

- Tutorial 1: iDrive—Video Game Development
- Tutorial 2: Interactive 3D Objects in a PDF Document

 Software used: MAXON Cinema 4D 9.1, Cinema 4D 9.5, Right Hemisphere Deep Creator 2, Code Gardeners XPort 1.3, Microsoft Office Word, Adobe Acrobat Professional 7

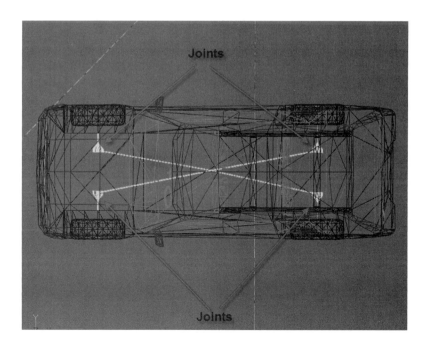

One of the most rapidly growing areas of computer graphics application today is video games. Video games captivate, challenge, liberate, inspire, frustrate, teach, and fill our hearts with wonder: wonder at how humans have evolved to create amazing things and wonder at the amazing format of interactive experiential storytelling. The explosive growth of the video game industry mesmerizes 3D animators as the promised land of great fortune and unleashed creative possibilities, but that's usually tucked away securely in fantasy land, because the link connecting being a 3D animator and being a video game designer is invisible to most.

This chapter connects the world of 3D modeling and animation in Cinema 4D 9 with the world of video game and simulation design in Deep Creator 2. Deep Creator is a drag-and-drop, WYSIWYG (what you see is what you get) video game and simulation authoring environment and real-time engine.

> **Architectural Previsualization**:   Imagine that you've just modeled an excellent architectural previsualization for a client who must now distribute it to 250 people around the world with different cultural and professional interests and backgrounds. How will you know what perspective angle shot of the building or what area of the building would be the most effective to present? While there is no silver bullet solution for such a challenge, you can improve your probability of acceptance and success by providing delivery of the architectural previsualization as an interactive fly-through experienced in the viewer's Web browser. Then, 250 people could view the building from the perspective angles and areas of interest that are of the greatest value to them. This is just one sample of the benefit of integrating Cinema 4D and Deep Creator.

> **Simulation:**   The application of Cinema 4D and Deep Creator to producing rich interactive simulations is a product type in growing demand by the military and commercial clients. Such simulation is able to connect to the real world via solution providers such as "P.I. Engineering" (*http://www.ymouse.com/*) by providing the hardware switches and physical touchable devices that control the simulations in the computer. Just imagine creating a fighter jet simulation and having the switches in a cockpit mockup actually control the on-screen 3D. It's not just imagination anymore.

> **Video Games:**   Video game development in this symbiotic environment is not just powerful; it's lots of fun. Being an animator, it's a real rush to see an audience appreciate your work, but it's a whole other ball of wax to see someone really get into a game you personally worked on. That's what Cinema 4D and Deep Creator combine to give you the power to do.

Objects modeled, textured, and animated in Cinema 4D are exported via the XPort plug-in from Code Gardeners (*http://213.239.195.198/~philipp/index.php*). Deep Creator then imports these objects with the textures and animation.

These tutorials are also on the accompanying DVD-ROM as video tutorials, along with the tutorial project files.

Remember, as you make progress in each tutorial, to save your Cinema 4D projects.

TUTORIAL 1   iDRIVE—VIDEO GAME DEVELOPMENT

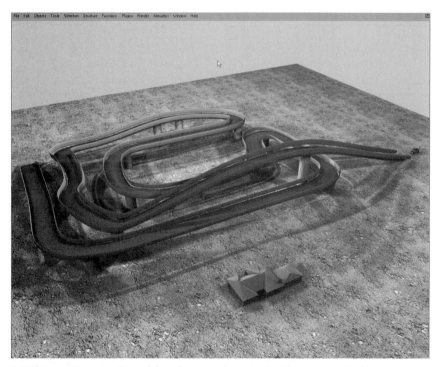

FIGURE 10.1 Cinema 4D models to be turned into a 3D video game in Right Hemisphere's Deep Creator's real-time authoring environment.

Covered in this tutorial:

- Modeling for exporting to Deep Creator
- Cinema 4D object baking
- Exporting to .x file with XPort
- The Deep Creator interface

- Baking Cinema 4D object textures for video games
- Importing a .x file
- Managing materials and stages
- Real-Time fly-through
- Building a physics-based car and driving it in real-time
- Real-time lights and shadows
- Publishing the video game to the Web

In this tutorial, you will author a simple introductory 3D driving video game. This game will be made primarily from Cinema 4D modeled objects, exported as a single .x file, imported into Deep Creator, and authored into a real-time 3D environment. You will look at how very differently light and shadows work in this real-time environment and how materials and stages are similar to Cinema 4D's materials and channels. Your finished project will be a playable game that you will learn how to publish online. You will also learn how to take 3D content and embed it into a PDF document for interactive viewing.

When modeling for real-time 3D animation, some additional considerations are very important in order to make efficient use of the real-time engine. For example, modeling with fewer polygons and smaller well-detailed textures can have a dramatic impact on the real-time frames per second performance.

Because collision detection is computationally expensive, in the real-time authoring environment, it is wise to think clearly and choose the most efficient collision shape that still allows for a believable experience. When working with your Cinema 4D exported models in Deep Creator, this means using the collision type of "Mesh" very sparingly.

It's also important to be mindful of the video performance capabilities of your end user. For some corporate client applications where there is a fixed known specification, the real-time experience can be authored to that spec using the level of polygonal and texture detail necessary to satisfy that client. However, when looking at a broader distribution of the real-time game or simulation, care should be taken to author the experience so as not to result in degraded performance on the less capable systems among your audience. In such cases, efficient modeling, texturing, and collision shape choices (as well as other efficiency tuning methods in Deep Creator) are crucial to defining how your audience rates the success of your real-time experience.

ON THE DVD

Finished project files for two sections of this tutorial are included on the accompanying DVD-ROM in the tutorials folder. All of the images used in this tutorial are located in Tutorials/Chapter 10/Tutorial-01 on the Projects DVD-ROM.

1. In Cinema 4D, start by loading Tutorials/ProjectFiles/Chapter 10/Tutorial-01/iDrive-A/iDrive-A.c4d. This scene contains a driving cone, a

polygon ground, 1 road, 17 road support columns, the SUV body and 4 tires, and a house polygon object. (shown in Figure 10.2).

Since this Cinema 4D scene is intended to be exported for use in the real-time environment of Deep Creator, the 17 road support objects are separate polygon objects rather than one big object. This will allow much more efficient collision detection and therefore a higher frame rate for smoother playback. These kinds of decisions in the modeling stage of game and simulation development have a real impact on the end-user experience.

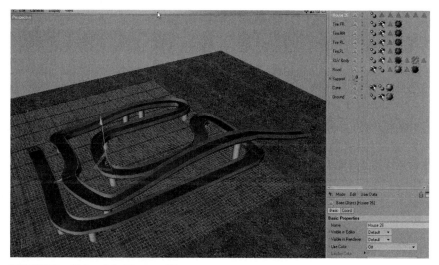

FIGURE 10.2   iDrive-A in Cinema 4D.

(Optional) In the top view, you can see that the Tutorials/ProjectFiles/Chapter 10/Tutorial-01/RoadTraceSource-1.jpg is displayed in the viewport. This image was used in the modeling of the road object. If you wish to build your own road, load Tutorials/ProjectFiles/Chapter 10/Tutorial-01/Build-A-Road/Build-A-Road. c4d, select Spline1 and Spline2 together and move pairs of points (one point from Spline1 and one point from Spline2). Then select the Sweep NURBS object and click the Make Editable icon. Select Sweep NURBS, Cap 1 and Cap 2 and in the Main menu, choose Functions/Connect. This creates a new polygon object named Sweep NURBS.1. Delete the two polygon selections (C1 and C2). Rename Sweep NURBS.1 "Road." In Polygon mode, select a polygon from both sides of the guard rails and in the Main menu, choose Selection/Select Connected to select all polygons in the guard rails. Then in the Main menu, choose Selection/Set Selection. Name this selection "Guard Rails." In the Objects Manager, be sure to deselect the polygon selection. In the Main menu, choose Selection/Invert and make another polygon

selection and name it "Road2." Drag the materials from Road to Road2 and copy Road2 into the iDrive-A document. Be sure to delete the original road object before exporting or you'll have two road objects overlapping. Once completed, copy your new road and paste it into the iDrive-A.cad project. Scale your new road to match the other objects in the project and delete the original road object.

2. Looking at all four viewports, in the Objects Manager, select the SUV body and all four tires, then frame the selected objects with **Alt-o**. As you can see, this is the same Marlin Studios SUV model used in previous tutorials except that the four tires are separate polygon objects now. Notice the name of each of the five selected objects.

3. The "House 26" object has 26 materials.

4. Importing this house into Deep Creator would require managing these 26 materials (for just this house) in Deep Creator. This is further compounded because the names of the materials will be lost and replaced with numerical naming (material 1, material 2, material 3 …). All materials in the Materials Manager beginning with "surface" are assigned to the house. Double-click surface9 and look at the Diffusion channel Texture. It is set to Ambient Occlusion. Click the Ambient Occlusion to see that the Contrast is set to 10. The Ambient Occlusion causes the surface9 material to receive shadows without the aid of a light source. All of the house materials have the ambient occlusion set in their diffusion channel texture.

5. The ambient occlusion in the previous step was set in preparation for you to bake all 26 of the house materials into one texture, complete with shadows. In the Objects Manager, select the House 26 object. In the **Main** menu, choose **Render/Bake Object** (shown in Figure 10.3). Check **Single Texture**. Set **Supersampling** to 2, **Pixel Border** to 1, **Width** and **Height** to 1024, and **Format** to JPEG and choose the **Path Name** for the baked texture to be saved. Then click the **Bake** button to bake the house texture.

When preparing a Cinema 4D project for use in Deep Creator, it's important to save the project using File/Save Project because this gathers all the required textures and places them in a folder called "Tex." The baked texture path should be this Tex folder so that Deep Creator will import the textures along with the objects.

Before Cinema 4D bakes the texture, a new and highly optimized UVW tag will be generated for the most efficient application of the texture that will be baked. When the materials are being baked into the texture, the new UVW mapped texture will be seen in the Bake Object window.

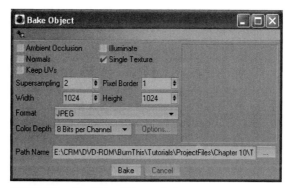

FIGURE 10.3   The Bake Object window.

6. Once the baking is finished, a new object (House 26.1) is added to the Objects Manager. This is the baked object that now uses only one material. Delete the original **House 26** object. In the Materials Manager, clean up the unused materials by choosing **Function/Delete Unused Materials**. Rename House 26.1 "**House 26**."

7. To compare your work so far, load Tutorials/ProjectFiles/Chapter 10/Tutorial-01/iDrive-A/iDrive-B.c4d.

8. To save the models for use in Deep Creator, in the **Main** menu, choose **File/Export/X-File Export**. Navigate to the folder where the project textures are located and the house texture was baked and save the "**iDrive-B.x**" file. This opens the XPort window.

9. Click on the **Textures Settings** button and set **Convert textures into** to JPEG and then click **OK**. Uncheck **Add Unique Number to each entity name** since all objects in the Cinema 4D project already have unique names. Check **Scale Scene** and set **X**, **Y,** and **Z** to 1. Then click **OK** (shown in Figure 10.4).

10. Icons are available on all four sides of the Deep Creator interface. Items that will be used in this tutorial are identified in Figure 10.5. Click the Toggle Viewports icon to switch between one and four views. When in the four view mode, left-clicking in a viewport and then clicking the Toggle Viewports icon makes the selected viewport a single large viewport. Right-clicking a viewport's label (Perspective, Top, Right, Front) accesses a menu where you can set the viewport display mode (Solid, Wireframe...). The Zoom, Pan, and Orbit viewport controls work similarly to the viewport controls in Cinema 4D. The Objects and Materials pages are similar to Cinema 4D's Objects and Materials managers. The Settings page is similar to Cinema 4D preferences. With an object in the Objects page selected, clicking the Zoom Extents Selected icon frames the object in the current view

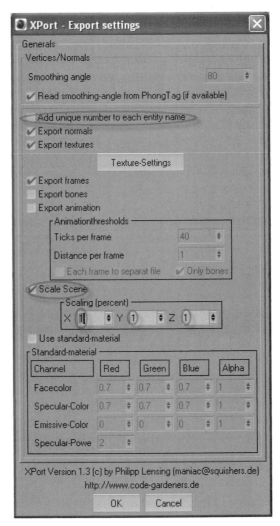

FIGURE 10.4   XPort window settings.

(just like pressing "o" in Cinema 4D). With an object in the Objects page selected in four-view mode, clicking the Zoom 3D Extents Selected All icon frames the object in all views (just like pressing Alt-o in Cinema 4D).

11. To work with the models exported from Cinema 4D, in the **Main** menu, choose **File/Import Objects** and open the "**iDrive-B.x**" file. This loads the models into Deep Creator. They look pretty much the way they did in Cinema 4D.

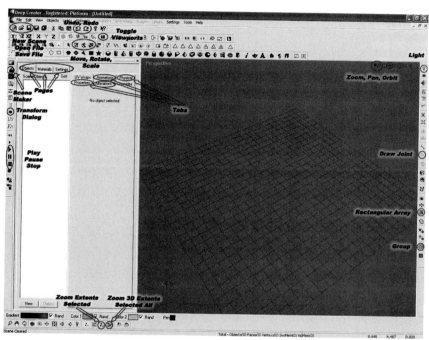

FIGURE 10.5   Deep Creator interface items used in this tutorial.

12. All work in Deep Creator is done in a real-time environment. To see this, press the F2 key to see a display including the FPS (frames per second) performance of your video card with the loaded objects.
13. In the Objects page, in the XPORT_ROOT/Ground hierarchy, select the **M_Ground** object. So that rigid body dynamics objects don't fall through the ground, in the **Physical** tab, check **Object is Floor or Ground** and set the **Collision Shape** to Plane. Set **Bounce** to 0 and **Friction** to 2000.

"M_" before an object name indicates it is a polygon Mesh object.

14. In the Objects page, in the XPORT_ROOT/Road hierarchy, select the **M_Road** object. So that the SUV doesn't fall through the road, in the **Physical** tab, check **Object is Floor or Ground** and set the **Collision Shape** to Mesh (since the road is an irregularly shaped object and must collide accurately). Set **Bounce** to 0 and **Friction** to 2000.
15. In the Objects page, in the XPORT_ROOT/SUV_Body, select the **M_SUV_Body** object. In the **Physical** tab, set the **Collision Shape** to Box.

16. In the **Objects** page, clean up the hierarchy to look like Figure 10.6 by dragging and renaming the tire polygon mesh objects and deleting empty group objects.

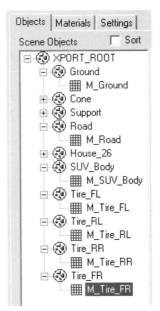

FIGURE 10.6   Deep Creator hierarchy cleaned up.

17. In the **Objects** page, select the **SUV_Body** group. Hold the **Shift** key and select the last tire group in the hierarchy (**Tire_FR**). Click the **Zoom Extents Selected** icon to frame the SUV and tires to see an image similar to Figure 10.7.
18. In the **Objects** page, select "**M_Tire_FL.**" In the **Physical** tab, set the **Collision Shape** to Sphere. Do this for the other three tires as well.

 It may seem that the correct collision shape for the tire would be a cylinder. A sphere produces better collision detection because it doesn't require as much calculation processing time. This affects the user game play experience because the stability of the simulation as well as the frame rate are improved by choosing a collision shape of sphere.

19. In the perspective view, using the viewport Orbit control, orbit around the SUV to observe that segments of the SUV body disappear.

FIGURE 10.7   The SUV and tires.

To correct this, in the **Objects** page, select the "**M_SUV_Body**" polygon object. In the **Properties** tab, **Material** is set to "Material1." In the **Materials** page, select **Material1** and right-click to rename it "**SUV.**" In the **Material Properties**, check **Two Sided Material**. Now, when you orbit the perspective view, the SUV body no longer disappears.

ON THE DVD

20. Save your work so far and open "**Tutorials/ProjectFiles/Chapter 10/Tutorial-01/DeepCreator/iDrive-2.rsn**" from the DVD-ROM. This loads what looks like the same project you've worked on so far, but with a few additional items set up.

21. Select the **M_SUV_Body** polygon object in the **Objects** page. In the **Animations** tab, you see three items: **Rigid Body** with the **Mass** set to 150 (similar to the rigid body in Cinema 4D; this causes the SUV body to respond to gravity and collisions), **4 Wheel Car Controls** (to make the SUV drivable), and **View Follow Object** (to make the camera follow the SUV as it drives around the scene. The

four tire polygon objects also have a rigid body added in the Animations tab. Note the difference in mass set for the front vs. the rear tires. This is done for driving stability.

Unlike in Cinema 4D dynamics, in Deep Creator, you don't add a gravity dynamics object. Gravity is a natural component of this real-time environment.

22. In the Objects page, at the bottom of the hierarchy, there are four joint objects (shown in Figure 10.8). These joints connect the tires to the SUV body.

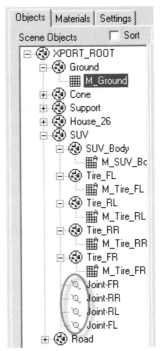

FIGURE 10.8 Four joints that connect the four tires to the SUV body.

23. Select the top view and click the **Toggle Viewports** icon to make the top view a single large view. Right-click on the viewport label ("**Top**") and change it from Solid to **Wireframe** to better see how the joints are positioned (shown in Figure 10.9). Notice how each joint points toward the tire it connects to the SUV body.

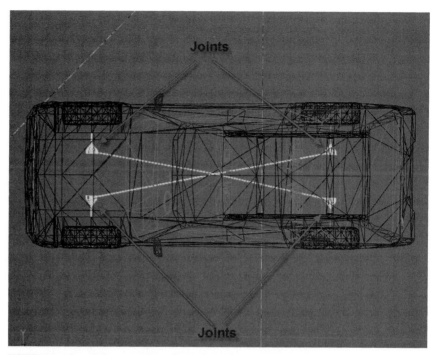

FIGURE 10.9   Four joints positioned to link the four tires to the SUV body.

24. In the **Objects** page, select the **M_SUV_Body** polygon object. In the **Physical** tab, click **Transform Collision Shape** to see the area of the SUV that can actually collide (shown in Figure 10.10). The collision shape of the front right tire is shown in Figure 10.11.

The collision shape is narrow because since the collision shape of the tires is set to sphere and since the tires are visibly within the bounding area of the SUV body, it is necessary to make the collision shape narrow so as not to intersect the SUV body collision shape with the tires collision shapes.

25. In the **Objects** page, select **Joint-FR**. In the **Properties** tab, **Body 1** is set to M_SUV_Body, **Body 2** is set to M_Tire_FR, and **Type** is set to Wheel Axle. The other three joints connect each tire to the SUV body in this way. This is the first way that the joint connects the SUV body to the tires.

Wheel Axle is only one type of joint in Deep Creator. Joints are used to simulate axles, ball sockets, and several other connecting movable parts.

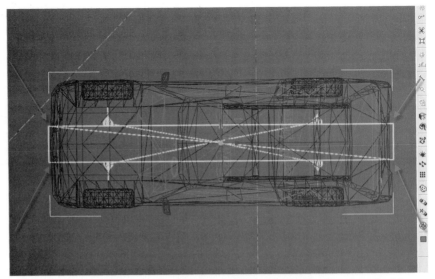

FIGURE 10.10   The collision shape of the SUV body is indicated by the arrows in this figure.

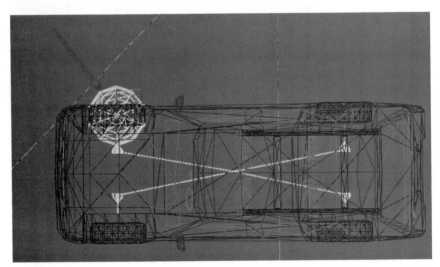

FIGURE 10.11   The collision shape of the front right tire is indicated by the arrows in this figure.

26. In the **Objects** page, select the **M_SUV_Body** polygon object. In the **Animations** tab, select **4 Wheel Car Control01**. Notice that the four joints are associated there with the SUV body as well. This is the second way joints connect the SUV body to the tires. The following setting for the four Wheel Car Controls are used in this tutorial:

Max forward velocity	100	Sets the top speed of the SUV. Setting this value too high can cause unstable behavior in your game. This is because very fast collisions may not be detected.
Max reverse velocity	50	Sets the top reverse speed of the SUV.
Max engine torque	500	Like horsepower. This value is set so the SUV can climb the ramps. Setting this value too high can make the SUV jump a lot and be very difficult to drive.
Braking torque	300	If this value is too low, the SUV will roll for a long time when trying to stop. If the value is too high, it may flip over when trying to stop.
Flip over torque	9000	If the vehicle turns over, this is the amount of torque that is applied to right it. Set this too low and the SUV stays like a helpless turtle. Set this too high and the SUV will flip forever.
Turbo multiplier	1.5	Turbo booster power factor.
Accel time sec	3	The time from stand still to max speed.
Max turn	40	How wide a corner the SUV can turn.
Turn speed	2	From a stand still, how quickly will the SUV turn? Set too high, the SUV will lose control when cornering.
Suspension softness	1	This is used to set how firm the suspension will handle. The current value is set to be stiff. Set this value higher for the suspension of a luxury car, or lower for the suspension of race car.
Drive	All wheels	All-wheel drive gives the best traction. Front-wheel drive gives the best stability.
Automatic upright	Un-Checked	Checked, the SUV will automatically right itself if flipped turned.

You can drive around now by clicking the Play button. Use the following keys to control the SUV (press the Stop button to resume game authoring):

Forward	Up arrow
Backup	Down arrow
Left turn	Left arrow
Right turn	Right arrow
Turbo	Tab
Brake	Spacebar
Parking brake	B
Flip over	Backspace

If you wish to place this game online, set Forward to **W**, Backward to **S**, Left to **A**, Right to **D** Flip Over to **Escape** and at the start of the game, left click in the game once to start. You cannot use the standard 4-arrow keyboard keys online in Deep Creator since the browser already uses these same keys.

27. In the perspective view, click the **Scene Maker** icon to have maximum use of the viewport. Click the **Play** icon and use the keys indicated above to drive the SUV.
28. You may take it for granted that the camera is following the SUV as you drive around, but that's not something that automatically happens. Click the **Stop** icon and then the **Scene Maker** icon. In the **Objects** page, select the **M_SUV_Body** polygon object. In the **Animations** tab, select **View Follow Object**. This is what makes the camera follow the SUV wherever it goes. Playing with its parameters will affect how the camera follows the SUV. The **Dist Above Target**, **Dist Above View**, **Distance from,** and **Angle of** parameters determine where the camera is in relation to the SUV. The **Dampening** parameter affects the soft lag as the camera follows the SUV.
29. Click the **Play** icon and look at the frame rate (press **F2** if the frame rate is not currently visible) as it fluctuates (averaging about 40 FPS in the tutorial video). In the **Objects** page, select the **M_Road** polygon object. Click the **Alterations** tab, to see the **Slice And Dice01** alteration. Its **X** and **Y Slices** are set to 3, while the **Z Slices** is set to 1. Temporarily disable the Slice And Dice01 by unchecking **Alteration** to see the frame rate drop (averaging about 30 FPS in the tutorial video). Remember, faster frame rates equal better user gaming experience.

*The Slice And Dice alteration divides the road into nine segments (3X Slices * 3Y Slices) so that collision detection between the SUV body and tires is not tested against the entire road polygon object, but rather, the collision testing is done only in the area where the SUV is driving.*

30. Save your work so far and open "**Tutorials/ProjectFiles/Chapter 10/Tutorial-01/DeepCreator/iDrive-3.rsn**" from the DVD-ROM. This loads what looks like the same project you've worked on so far, but with a few additional items set up.

31. Click the **Play** icon and drive under the road to see the shadows being cast on the ground. To accomplish a similar look in Cinema 4D, you would add a light and choose its shadow type. In Deep Creator, lights themselves don't directly cast shadows.

32. Click the **Toggle Viewports** icon to see all four viewports. The light object can be seen in the top, front, and right views (shown in Figure 10.12). Click the **Properties** tab to see that the light is a **Point** light. There is no shadow option in the light properties. Instead, that is handled on the road object.

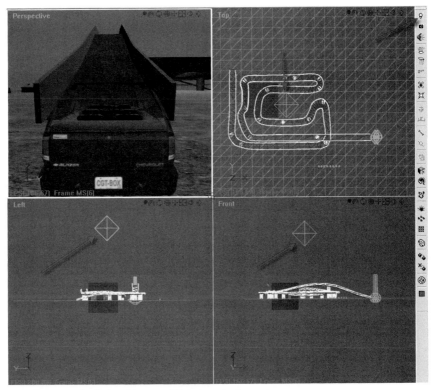

FIGURE 10.12   The light object and light icon indicated.

33. Select the **M_Road** polygon object in the **Objects** page and click the **Alterations** tab. Select the inserted **Shadow01** alteration and notice that its **Type** is set to Volume Stencil and **Light** is set01 (the only light in the scene).

Because this tutorial introduces real-time lighting at only the most basic level, review the Deep Creator documentation to better understand the underlying aspects of selecting, preparing for, and using lights in Deep Creator.

34. In the **Objects** page, in the **Support/Cylinder_1** hierarchy, select the **M_Cylinder_1** polygon object. In the **Physical** tab, notice that the **Object Is Wall** is checked and set the **Collision Shape** to Cylinder. This has been done for the remaining support columns.

35. Click **Play** and drive under the road to test the column collisions.

36. Save your work so far and open "**Tutorials/ProjectFiles/Chapter 10/Tutorial-01/DeepCreator/iDrive-4.rsn**" from the DVD-ROM. This loads what looks like the same project you've worked on so far. It's time to look at how the driving cones are set up.

37. As shown in Figure 10.13, the M_Cone polygon object now has a rigid body added with a Mass of 5 and has been copied seven times. These eight cones are placed in a straight line on the ground, to the left of the road object (shown in Figure 10.14). The mass of the cone's rigid body needs to be much smaller than that of the SUV body. Click the **Play** icon and drive through the cones to see how they interact with the SUV. Now set the cones' Rigid Body Mass to 2 and click **Play** and drive through them again to see how the interaction between the cones and the SUV has changed.

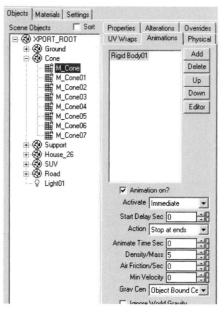

FIGURE 10.13   Objects page and Animations tab showing cones set up.

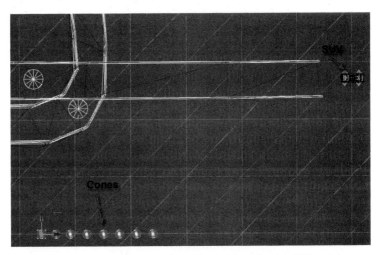

FIGURE 10.14 Top view showing starting positions for the SUV and the cones.

38. At this point, all the game elements for this very simple introductory driving game are ready. You could spend more time adding cool features like four walls around the perimeter to keep the car from falling off of your flat Earth, covers over the road to create tunnels, interesting textured objects, and identification text navigation objects (to name just a few). At this point, to publish the game so that it can be distributed to end users, in the **Main** menu, choose **File/Publish User File**. Click **Yes** at the prompt to **Save Changes**. In the **Input**, browse to open "**Tutorials/ProjectFiles/Chapter 10/Tutorial-01/ DeepCreator/iDrive-4.rsn**" from the DVD-ROM. In the **Output**, browse to set the file path (to a folder on your hard drive where the project textures have been copied) and file name for the file to be generated. Choose the **Type** (RHI is OK for now) and click **Create User File**. At the **Possible Missing Asset** Prompt, click **Yes**.

ON THE DVD

To distribute to users who don't have the Deep Creator Viewer installed, choose Executable or Zipped. To create a screen saver from your game, choose Screen Saver.

39. To publish the game online, in the main menu, choose **Publish/Publish To HTML**. In the Output Path to set where the published files will be saved locally on your computer. Set the **Template** to simple.html and set the **Viewport Height** and **Width** to an appropriate presentation size (eg. Height = 600 and Width = 800). Then click OK to publish the game. In the output path on your local computer's hard drive, you will find a folder named "**files**." Copy all contents of this folder to a

folder on your remote web server. Access that remote web server folder by it's web address (eg. *http://www.mydomain.com/idrive*) to play the game online.

Be sure to set the .rhi and .rn mime types (.rhi application/deepcreator and .rsn application/deepcreator) on your server so those files can be recognized. Depending on your Web hosting arrangement, you may have to request this.

Deep Creator 2.2 and above are required for use of keyboard controls in Web published Deep Creator authored interactive files.

Summary

Hopefully, this very cursory intro to integrating Cinema 4D with Deep Creator to create a 3D video game that can be published online has triggered some questions, offered some answers, and fueled some deep inspiration to view the application of Cinema 4D to video games and simulations as something very accessible that you can learn to do.

Further exploration of the Deep Creator documentation and sample projects can give you a sense of just how far you can take this integration between Cinema 4D and Deep Creator.

Although this tutorial focused on one simple real-time application (a simple video game), the same principles and methods are applied to produce architectural fly-throughs, medical and military simulations, and industrial interactive product prototyping.

| **TUTORIAL 2** | **INTERACTIVE 3D OBJECTS IN A PDF DOCUMENT** |

Covered in this tutorial:

- Importing a .x file
- Outputting Interactive 3D to a PDF document

In this tutorial, you will import a house object baked in Cinema 4D and then exported as a .x file into Deep Creator for export as a Universal 3D document for ultimate placement as a user interactive 3D element of a PDF document.

While Right Hemisphere provides tools more suited to this application, this short tutorial is meant to give you a behind the scenes look at just one more way I (as a full-service digital media producer) have integrated Deep Creator into my work flow.

ON THE DVD Finished project files for this tutorial are included on the accompanying DVD-ROM in the tutorials folder. All of the images used in this tutorial are located in Tutorials/ProjectFiles/Chapter 10/Tutorial-01 on the Projects DVD-ROM.

1. In the Deep Creator **Main** menu, choose **File/Import Objects** and open "**Tutorials/ProjectFiles/Chapter 10/Tutorial-01/House10/ Tex/House10.x.**" to load a fully textured house.

2. In the **Objects** page, expand the hierarchy and select M_House010 _1_0.

3. In the **Main** menu, choose **File/Export Objects**. Set the **Save as type** to Universal 3D. Choose the file path and file name. Then click **Save**.

4. In Microsoft Word, create and save a new document. A blank page is OK.

5. In Adobe Acrobat 7 Professional, in the **Main** menu, choose **File/ Create PDF/From File** and open the document saved from Microsoft Office.

6. In the main menu, choose **Tools/Advanced Editing/3D Tool** and draw a rectangle in the document where you wish to place the 3D object. Then click OK.

7. The red outline shows that the size and placement of the 3D object can still be adjusted.

8. Click the **Hand** icon in the upper right (shown in Figure 10.15) to activate the 3D object in the document.

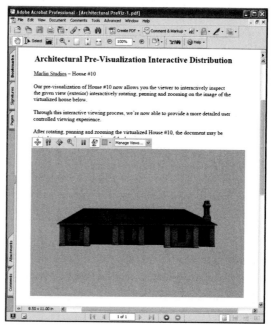

FIGURE 10.15   The hand icon.

9. Click the 3D object to interactively drag, zoom, and move it.

Summary

When servicing a digital media client, it is crucial to be able to take them as far as their imagination can go. And now you know how!

ABOUT THE DVD-ROM

The DVD-ROM included with this book contains the resources to perform all tutorials in this book. These resources compliment the experience gained in performing the written tutorials, and include the following components:

Demo Software: Demo versions of software used in the tutorials are provided on the DVD-ROM or are accessible on the web via the DVD-ROM. As all demo software is inherently limited in some functionality, please consult the software publisher's Web site for a description of the demo's limits. All demo software is zip compressed and must be un-compressed before installation.

Goodies: In addition to content used in the tutorials, supplementary content (image textures, 3D models, motion textures, Photo Objects, motion capture data) is provided in the Goodies folder for your further educational exploration. This content is provided for non-commercial use only.

Color Figures: All figures in the book are available on the DVD-ROM in their original color and at their original captured resolution to further provide instructional detail.

Tutorial Project Files: Project files for each tutorial are provided for comparison to your work as you progress through the tutorials. In addition to functioning as tutorial comparisons, the completed versions of these projects can serve as starting points for your future projects. While Cinema 4D project files are included for each tutorial, additional project files are also provided for software integrated with Cinema 4D in the tutorials.

Video Tutorials: Each written tutorial is also provided as an "over the shoulder" how-to guided tour that takes you step-by-step through each of the processes and concepts covered in this book. These video tutorials serve as a dynamic compliment to the written tutorials by showing the visual nuances in motion of each step, while further supported with commentary of not only the procedure, but relevance as it applies to real-world production.

Tutorial Movies: A demo reel of the finished movies for the tutorials is included on the DVD-ROM to give you a more complete sense of what the finished work should look and move like. To view this demo reel, double-click the "C9D95-LM-CRM-DemoVideo.mov" QuickTime video file. QuickTime 6.5 or higher is required to view this video file.

The DVD-ROM content is accessible on the Mac or PC as five folders and QuickTime video files. Some DVD-ROM content requires an Internet connection.

SYSTEM REQUIREMENTS

Minimum: Mac OS X 10.3 or Windows 2000 / XP, 512 MB RAM, CPU 1GHz.

Suggested: Mac OS X 10.3 or Windows 2000 / XP 1024 MB RAM, CPU 2 GHz, QuickTime, current OpenGL-capable graphics card, CD-ROM-drive, hard drive. Depending on license, Macintosh or Windows only.

Access of the HTML document on the DVD-ROM requires the free Macromedia Flash 7 (*http://www.macromedia.com/*) plugin be installed on your web browser.

INDEX